"Oates and Deaconu grapple [...] framework of human meaning. Once we [...] difficult to consider alternative views. T[...] to the complex community dynamics of [...] model of inquiry, re-evaluation, and re-integration that can be applied to other constructs of meaning that may be overdue for an overhaul."

N. Michel Landaiche III, *psychotherapist, consultant, and trainer*

"Oates and Deaconu deliver a critical reflection on the development of transactional analysis that offers a deep respect for its history. This book provides a philosophical overview, making it an essential read for students and advanced practitioners. By contextualizing the history and development of TA, it provides a go-to resource that readers have long been awaiting."

Helen Rowland *is a transactional analysis psychotherapist, trainer and supervisor in private practice and a co-editor of the* Transactional Analysis Journal

"I was enthralled by this book. I recommend it because I found it the most complete history of the evolution of Eric Berne's thought and of TA that I have seen, but also because it opens the doors to the future. TA encountered resistance for years because it was too far ahead of its time. This book highlights how revolutionary those ideas were, and how much they stimulate our creativity today."

Marco Mazzetti, *M.D., is a psychiatrist, a teaching and supervising transactional analyst (psychotherapy). He was the recipient of the Eric Berne Memorial Award in 2012 and is a co-founder of the Eric Berne Archive Project*

A Living History of Transactional Analysis Psychotherapy

This important book offers a comprehensive review of over 70 years of transactional analysis psychotherapy from within the field, considering its historical context and various applications, as well as how different aspects of the theory emerged and how they are applied.

The book examines the structure of transactional analysis, taking readers on a journey from the inception of the method to present-day applications of the theory. The authors raise questions around the way the theory may be taught as doctrine and ask readers to consider how new aspects of theory are fully integrated into the already existing schema. The authors also highlight the zeitgeist within which TA was developed and offer reflections as to how further developments are also part of a particular spirit and mood of the times in which they were developed.

A Living History of Transactional Analysis Psychotherapy offers coherence between different aspects of TA theory and when, where, and why they are used, making it important reading for TA scholars, students, and practitioners.

Steff Oates is a Teaching and Supervising Transactional Analyst in Psychotherapy, living and working in Wales. She is former Vice President of the International Transactional Analysis Association and is the author of many articles in the *Transactional Analysis Journal*.

Diana Deaconu is a Certified Transactional Analyst in Psychotherapy, living and working in Romania. She complemented her studies with a specialization in Anthropology and served as a co-editor of the *Transactional Analysis Journal* for many years.

Innovations in Transactional Analysis: Theory and Practice
Series Editor: William F. Cornell

This book series is founded on the principle of the importance of open discussion, debate, critique, experimentation, and the integration of other models in fostering innovation in all the arenas of transactional analytic theory and practice: psychotherapy, counseling, education, organizational development, health care, and coaching. It will be a home for the work of established authors and new voices.

Radical-Relational Perspectives in Transactional Analysis Psychotherapy
Oppression, Alienation, Reclamation
Karen Minikin

Revitalization Through Transactional Analysis Group Treatment
Human Nature and Its Deterioration
Giorgio Piccinino

Working with Dreams in Transactional Analysis
From Theory to Practice for Individuals and Groups
Anna Emanuela Tangolo and Francesca Vignozzi

Conceptualizing Ego States in Transactional Analysis
Three Systems in Interaction
José Grégoire

A Transactional Analysis of Motherhood and Disturbances in the Maternal
Emma Haynes

A Living History of Transactional Analysis Psychotherapy
Engaging Reflectively with Theory and Methodology
Steff Oates and Diana Deaconu

https://www.routledge.com/Innovations-in-Transactional-Analysis-Theory-and-Practice/book-series/INNTA

A Living History of Transactional Analysis Psychotherapy

Engaging Reflectively with Theory and Methodology

Steff Oates and Diana Deaconu

Routledge
Taylor & Francis Group
LONDON AND NEW YORK

Designed cover image: © Steff Oates, Diana Deaconu and Daniel Stanciu

First published 2025
by Routledge
4 Park Square, Milton Park, Abingdon, Oxon OX14 4RN

and by Routledge
605 Third Avenue, New York, NY 10158

Routledge is an imprint of the Taylor & Francis Group, an informa business

© 2025 Steff Oates and Diana Deaconu

The right of Steff Oates and Diana Deaconu to be identified as authors of this work has been asserted in accordance with sections 77 and 78 of the Copyright, Designs and Patents Act 1988.

All rights reserved. No part of this book may be reprinted or reproduced or utilised in any form or by any electronic, mechanical, or other means, now known or hereafter invented, including photocopying and recording, or in any information storage or retrieval system, without permission in writing from the publishers.

Trademark notice: Product or corporate names may be trademarks or registered trademarks, and are used only for identification and explanation without intent to infringe.

British Library Cataloguing-in-Publication Data
A catalogue record for this book is available from the British Library

ISBN: 978-1-032-18135-6 (hbk)
ISBN: 978-1-032-18134-9 (pbk)
ISBN: 978-1-003-25301-3 (ebk)

DOI: 10.4324/9781003253013

Typeset in Times New Roman
by KnowledgeWorks Global Ltd.

Contents

Preface by William F. Cornell   *viii*
Acknowledgments   *xiii*
Abbreviations   *xv*

1   A Historical Perspective on the Evolution of Transactional Analysis Theory   1

2   Growth, Challenge, and Expansion of the Theory   30

3   Bringing Transactional Analysis Theory into Practice: Complexities Generated by the Emergence of Special Fields of Application   43

4   Development of the Cathexis and Redecision Schools   55

5   Room for a Diversity of Thinking and Approach: The Development of Constructivist, Constructionist, and Co-Creative Approaches in Transactional Analysis   76

6   The Development of Relational Transactional Analysis   89

7   Evolutions at the Intersections of Transactional Analysis   111

8   An Appreciation of a Dynamic, Sustainable Robust Theory and Those Who Ensure It   125

9   Evolution and Innovation: Some Ways Forward: Honoring the Legacy and Welcoming Mutative Change   133

Index   *144*

Preface by William F. Cornell

Readers might wonder how it is that a book on transactional analysis history is being included in a series entitled "Innovations in Transactional Analysis." This history, deeply researched and passionately written by Steff Oates and Diana Deaconu, is, as the title denotes, a living history. It is a history that points to the future.

Theory building is a precarious enterprise. At their best, innovations in theory and methodology are manifestations of human aspirations for deeper understanding of our minds and relations. Theories often, on the one hand, offer new insights into the human psyche and the challenges of being human, while on the other, can ossify into rigid beliefs and methodologies that restrict new discoveries. Here, Oates and Deaconu tell the stories of that inevitable tension over the history of TA, but they make it clear that the spirit of creativity, challenge, and innovation carry transactional analysis forward. Most importantly, they place the diverse and evolving TA theories and models within the context of the human and developmental problems they were trying to address:

> We have looked for ways to "listen" to the clinical challenges that they were trying to conceptualize, the aspects that were overemphasized, underemphasized, or completely overlooked, as well as threads of the wider socio-historical contexts in which they emerged.

Their book provides an extraordinary exploration of the evolution of transactional analysis. I consider myself rather well read in the transactional analysis literature, but this coauthor team dug deep into garden and the weeds of TA history. They have not shied away from speaking directly to critique problematic areas of TA, while maintaining a balanced, nuanced discussion of its history.

The opening chapter of the book is the most comprehensive and balanced discussion of Berne as a man, a psychiatrist, and a psychotherapist that I have ever encountered. Oates and Deaconu thoroughly combed the Berne archives and his extensive published history before he began to develop transactional analysis to provide a rich accounting of the wide-ranging clinical and ethical interests that underlay his development of transactional analysis.

Berne's first book, *The Mind in Action*, was an effort to make psychoanalytic thinking comprehensible and usable to ordinary people. It was fundamental to Berne's vision and ethic that people should be able to use the insights offered in psychoanalysis to better understand themselves and gain more autonomy and intimacy in their lives. This was the intention that then later laid the foundation for transactional analysis.

The psychoanalysis of Berne's era was that of ego psychology, a model developed by the analytic refugees of the Nazi era, dominating psychoanalysis in the United States into the 1980s. It was a model focused on interpreting defenses managing/repressing intrapsychic conflict, with little regard to social forces. This was a theory that became dogmatic and evolved without interchange with the analytic approaches being developed in the UK and Europe. It was as though these European refugees, split off from their own traumatic flights to the United States turned their backs on their European roots to develop a "new" psychology of the ego and adaptation. Bergmann (2000) observed:

> ...the [Heinz] Hartmann group showed surprisingly little interest in the outside world. Hitler, World War II, and the Holocaust left no discernable impression on their thinking. This is all the more surprising because they were Hitler's refugees.
>
> (p. 66)

Oates and Deaconu offer a comprehensive overview of Berne's earliest publications, preceding transactional analysis, which were focused of the social, cultural, and group influences in the practice of psychiatry and psychotherapy—all published in psychiatric rather than psychoanalytic journals. For reasons never made clear, Berne was refused certification as a psychoanalyst by the San Francisco Psychoanalytic Society. I suspect it was Berne's abiding interest in social and political realities that made him a persona non gratis in the formal psychoanalytic circles of the 1950s.

Heinz Hartmann, the leading figure of psychoanalysis in the United States, chose to name this new model a psychology rather than psychoanalysis (Hartmann, 1958). Berne, too, was a refugee, leaving the antisemitism of Catholic Montreal, in search of a more welcoming environment in the United States. We can see the appeal of this newly emerging, post-war model of psychoanalysis with its emphasis on the adaptive capacities of the ego and a subtle turning away from the shadows of the unconscious. Berne, too, renamed his methodology transactional analysis to distinguish it from psychoanalysis.

Ego psychology was an approach seen to be effective with neurotic patients but unable to reach those with borderline, psychotic, and traumatic disturbances, so it gradually fell out of favor. Bergmann (2000) and colleagues of that era examined the strengths and significant limits of the ego psychological approach that led to demise as a model of any significant contemporary influence within psychoanalysis. There is a certain irony in the fact that while American ego psychology has had no impact in psychoanalysis elsewhere in the world, Berne created a model founded in ego psychology that has found acceptance and enthusiasm around the globe.

Nevertheless, transactional analysis was formed within the framework of the American ego psychology and suffered from similar limits. The living history described in the pages of this book provides a compelling story of subsequent generations of transactional analysts seeking to preserve its core values while expanding its theoretical and therapeutic reach.

Transactional analysis, like most innovative movements in psychotherapy and counseling, was grounded in an idealization of its founder, an idealization that Eric Berne cautioned against in his writing, while all too often reveling in it within his professional alliances. The second chapter provides a lively discussion of Berne's creation of the San Francisco Social Psychiatry Seminar, which gradually evolved into the International Transactional Analysis Association. The tensions between idealization and differentiation come alive in their accounting. In a rather uncanny mirroring of post-war ego psychology, transactional analysis went through a period of isolation from other modalities. As noted by Oates and Deaconu:

> ...the TA world was scarred by two significant phenomena, namely authoritarianism and competitiveness. The consequence of the first was an institutionalization of the theory, generating various protective and self-protective processes in relation to external contributions, thereby leaving little room for potential fertile influences from more recent scientific works. Additionally, competitiveness further led to "conflicting phenomena rather than critical confrontation" (p. 251). We may quite easily infer that this level of power dynamics would have stifled growth inside the community. Hence, for some, the possibility for maturation might have emerged at the intersection between transactional analysis and other psychotherapeutic systems.

Following Berne's untimely death at 60, many of those who worked most closely with him began to splinter into differing "schools" of transactional analysis. Within a few years after his death, the increasingly competitive "schools" of TA began to compete for leadership and validation (Barnes, 1977). In the decades since, there has been a tendency to declare differing models of TA, again linked to the idealization of various leader/innovators, which has too often fostered a competition among models rather than an evolving synthesis of innovations.

It is within this context that Oates and Deaconu present a persistent perspective of great value to the TA community—that of nuanced, curious reflections on the diverse models and applications of TA. They do not advocate one model over another, but rather invite readers into a consideration of the specific questions and innovations advanced by each model. Having presented the fertile ground of Berne's early psychiatric, cultural, and psychoanalytic investigations, they then capture the early, impassioned, innovative spirit of transactional analysis. They go on to describe and critique the varying—and too often competitive "schools" of transactional analysis. While they do not minimize their own critical capacities, they provide a balanced appreciation of the evolutionary and innovative potentials of these models of TA. Most importantly, they situate each of these theoretical/methodological models within cultural and clinical questions of their times. They bring informed, respectful, but challenging critiques of the evolving theoretical perspectives with transactional analysis.

One of the paradoxical tensions within Berne's work was that of his being a psychiatrist/psychotherapist who sought to develop a model that was accessible and useful to anyone who sought to better understand themselves. It may have been to his dismay that he succeeded, finding that his books brought many people seeking TA training who had no clinical credentials to practice psychotherapy. This was "solved" during his lifetime by the creation of the vaguely defined category of "special fields" practices, a solution that was to plague formal training and recognition in transactional analysis for decades. In Chapter 3, Oates and Deaconu step into this aspect of TA history with a true gift for telling a complicated story with clarity and balance. What unfolds is the history of these "special fields" growing into fields of application—psychotherapy, counseling, education, and organizational management—that have contributed to the diversity of TA competencies in practices worldwide.

The subsequent chapters present the diverse approaches to TA theory and practice that emerged following Berne's death at age 60 in 1970. Here again, their strengths as authors are demonstrated as they carefully elaborate models. Too often presented by their own originators as unique ways of thinking and working, drawn in competitive contrast to other models, Oates and Deaconu avoid this trap by situating each approach within the contexts of the specific questions each was attempting to address. In so doing, they circumvent the "schooling" of differing expressions of TA practice and instead foster the sense of a collective voice of dedicated professionals seeking to extend the borders and reach of transactional analysis.

Another limiting consequence of Berne's own personal and professional wounds was a rejection of psychoanalysis, at times to the point of contempt for the whole tradition of psychoanalytic thinking, which had in fact deeply informed Berne. It has been the third generation of transactional analysts who have been able to draw upon contemporary perspectives in psychoanalysis to further deepen the practice of transactional analysis. As captured by Oates and Deaconu:

> This shift in psychoanalysis, in our view, would find an echo in transactional analysis theory and methodology. The first element of resonance would be one about the nature of the mind, namely the fact that it grows in interaction with significant others and that it creates an individual phenomenological experience. A second concordant idea would be that the analyst's subjectivity was not only undeniably present in the clinical process, but that his or her participation was required for facilitating deep characterological change in the patient and for experiencing intimacy and mutuality. Powerful feelings, including love and hate, were no longer something in the patient's psyche to be interpreted and solely

attributed to past relational experiences, but they were fostered by the relational context emerging from the analytic dyad.

A living history of TA psychotherapy succeeds in presenting a lively as well as living history of transactional analysis. Oates and Deaconu conclude, "As we accounted for the multiplicity of changes that TA theory underwent, we could also acknowledge the fact that this is a framework which seems to be resilient enough to accommodate significant shifts in perspective, thereby standing the test of time." The stories contained here are a testimony to that resilience, to the aspiration and vitality of Berne's founding vision.

But the success and importance of this book extend beyond that of being a major historical document for transactional analysis. As someone for whom my library is a beloved and nearly sacred space, to witness the depth and finesse of the authors' wise and respectful reading and research represented in these pages is deeply gratifying.

References

Barnes, G. (1977). *Transactional analysis after Eric Berne: Teachings and practices of three TA schools*. Harper's College Press.

Berne, E. (1947). *The mind in action*. Simon and Schuster.

Begrmann, M. S. (Ed.) (2000). *The hartmann era*. Other Press.

Hartmann, H. (1958). *Ego psychology and the problem of adaptation*. International University Press, Inc.

Acknowledgments

When we embarked upon this exciting venture neither of us knew what would unfold. We were barely out of the perilous insanity of a COVID-19 pandemic, living in different countries, and each of us in the process of quite major life changes. This context functioned as a particular kind of "affective primordial soup" where we both became curious and actively engaged in a process of meaning making. What does it mean to witness the ending of an era? What is it like when the dawn of a new era appears on the horizon? How do changes of this magnitude provoke or unsettle us personally, professionally, and socially?

Those were both provoking and unsettling questions in their own right. They were the seeds from which our writing project emerged. As we immersed ourselves in it, there were many times when it almost seemed we had lost our compass, when ideas refused to form into more consistent structures, or pieces of information remained in the dark. We remained committed to the task and to each other and were rewarded in looking back at a rich time of mutual exploration and curiosity in which we have found much pleasure and delight.

We were enormously supported by the series editor, Bill Cornell, to whom we are much indebted. His light touch and steady guiding hand alongside his encyclopedic knowledge of all things transactional analysis meant that we had a series editor, confident enough in the subject, who offered a gracious encouraging eye. His slight nudges allowed us to develop our own ideas of how to present this view of the continually unfolding history of transactional analysis psychotherapy.

We also want to offer our gratitude to Robin Fryer, the managing editor of the ITAA, who copyedited the first five chapters and patiently taught us how to navigate and reference the Eric Berne archives and Berne's early writing which were published in various journals and a compilation. Due to unforeseen circumstances, Robin had to give up the job of copyediting and we were lucky to find another copy editor, Martin Petitt, who skillfully took over where Robin left off and has been a delight to work with.

In terms of the content of the book, we owe a lot to those individuals in our community who were willing to be interviewed and who offered us insights to help us in our work: Jim Allen, Giles Barrow, Servaas van Beekum, Susanna Bianchini, Leonard Campos, Richard Erskine, Rosanna Giacometto, Linda Gillham, Helena

Hargaden, Sylvie Monin, Rosemary Napper, Trudi Newton, Carla de Nitto, Charlotte Sills, Carol Solomon, Graeme Summers, and Keith Tudor. Each of them gave generously of their time and shared enthusiasm for what we were doing. We are proud to be part of such a community of generous spirit.

It is due to the foresight of Carol Solomon, Marco Mazetti, and Anne Heathcote in their immense work compiling the Eric Berne archives, that we were able to research much of the history. We offer sincere gratitude to them for this treasure trove of information.

Mick Landaiche, Marco Mazetti, and Helen Rowland were invaluable as readers of the final work and very generous in their giving of time and energy to write endorsements. This being our first book, we are genuinely touched by people's enthusiasm and encouragement.

We would have been lost without the guidance of the editorial team from Routledge who showed patience and offered encouragement along the way. And the final icing on the cake was the drawing for our front cover given to us by Daniel Stanciu. We were delighted how he captured the spirit of what we were trying to convey.

And last but no means least thanks must go to our long-suffering partners, who remained alongside us with the lows and the highs inevitably involved in writing such a book.

And now we offer to you, the readers, the fruits of our labors, hoping in some ways that you might be as excited, challenged, stirred, and delighted as we were by our findings and exploration into the context and history of this thriving theory. Our aspiration is that this will contribute further to a community who can think together, as well as to the continuous growth of TA theory and practice.

Abbreviations

BOC	Board of Certification
BOT	Board of Trustees
COC	Council of Certification
EATA	European Association for Transactional Analysis
EBMA	Eric Berne Memorial Award
HUAC	House Un-American Activities Committee
ISYY	I'll Show You Yet
ITAA	International Transactional Analysis Association
MGA	Mathematical game analysis
NCHCA	National Commission of Health Certifying Agencies
SCTA	Social-cognitive approach to transactional analysis
SF	Special fields
SFM	Special fields members
SFSPS	San Francisco Social Psychiatry Seminars
TA	Transactional analysis
TAB	Transactional Analysis Bulletin
TAJ	Transactional Analysis Journal
TGA	Transactional game analysis
TSC	Training Standards Committee
VE	Victory in Europe
WIGFT	Western Institute for Group and Family Treatment

Chapter 1

A Historical Perspective on the Evolution of Transactional Analysis Theory

Context

By way of setting the scene for this book, imagine yourself as a resident of San Francisco in May 1945. The Second World War Victory in Europe (VE Day) was celebrated on May 8, but there was still fighting in the Pacific Theater. It was a strange atmosphere: The war in Europe was over, but there was not yet cause for celebration in the United States. Then came VJ Day (Victory over Japan Day) on August 15, 1945:

> Thousands of revelers, including many young men who had just learned they wouldn't be going to war, poured into the streets. With no planned events—theaters were closed and plans for band performances canceled—drunkenness and chaos ensued. Windows were broken and liquor stolen, and libidos ran unchecked.
>
> (Hartlaub, 2015, para 18)

As we imagine the atmosphere of that day, we can picture the confusion, melancholia, and quite possibly an air of manic positivity. The change would likely have been infusing the air, both as a promise and an imperative to take action. What might you have felt in that circumstance? Restlessness, uncertainty, anxiety, hope? And to whom might you have turned for help understanding such raging emotions?

Even before the end of the war, in a 1943 paper entitled "Group Psychotherapy: A Review of Recent Literature," Giles W. Thomas took a pragmatic approach to consider what was needed for troubled people in those times. He accounted for the fact that psychiatrists were overburdened by their work with both military personnel and civilians due to the war and candid regarding the problem of resources for those in need of psychological help: "With the growing shortage of labor and the need for greater efficiency in all our activities, the functionally incapacitated or partly incapacitated individual becomes a drag on our national effort" (p. 166). Thomas argued that group psychotherapy was efficacious, particularly with psychoneuroses and psychosomatic issues. In comparing types of group psychotherapy, he separated them into two groups, namely, the "repressive inspirational" and "the analytic" (p. 166).

Efficacy aside, it seemed that the choices available to people who needed psychological help at that time were limited. Maybe you would have had no interest in engaging in help from the repressive inspirational approach, which advocated the suppression of troublesome thoughts and a focus on "living life," which Thomas likened to the Christian Science movement. Then again, the analytic approach, which aimed to help people examine repressed aspects of themselves and gain freedom through insight, was costly both in time and money. So where could someone turn?

It seems the San Francisco publishers Simon and Schuster had been contemplating this dilemma, because in May 1945, they approached Eric Berne, a psychiatrist in San Francisco, to write a popular book on psychiatry. We believe that Berne's refreshingly direct, clear speaking would have been welcome in those confusing times, offering people help free of obscure technical language. Maybe they needed ways of understanding themselves and the world around them so that a sense of hope and faith in humanity could be restored. This was no small task.

Eric Berne had moved to the United States from Montreal, Canada, to begin a psychiatric residency at Yale University School of Medicine. Berne, whose birth name was Lennard Bernstein, began training as a psychoanalyst at the New York Psychoanalytic Institute. His didactic analyst was Paul Federn, who was to become highly influential in Berne's thinking and in the development of transactional analysis (TA). Berne's response to Simon and Schuster was that he would write a book on psychoanalysis.

What I have in mind is a book on psychoanalysis which will be suitable for people of high school education and which will interest them; a book, for example, which may be used as a freshman reader in a college, but which will need no professor to elucidate, so that it will be equally suitable for the fireside, the classroom, the women's club, and the lending library (Berne, 1945, para. 6).

In 1947, the new book arrived on the market. It was titled *The Mind in Action*, and Simon and Schuster promoted it as a book that psychiatrists could "wholeheartedly recommend to their patients" (Simon and Schuster, 1947).

This layman's guide was something a potential patient could understand and use to aid in self-discovery. It may have appeared then, as it does to us now, to offer more opportunity and freedom than the narrow choice of cognitive behaviorism incorporated into the repressive inspirational approach or the alternative psychoanalytic approach. Simon and Schuster certainly knew something else was needed when they approached Berne, the founding father of transactional analysis.

The Beginnings of TA Theory

TA as an approach has always appealed to us for its breadth and depth of theory and variety of applications. This section of the book will briefly examine the major texts that Berne wrote in his lifetime, which we believe was cut short before his work was finished.

The publication just described, *The Mind in Action* (Berne, 1947), was comprehensive, ranging from questions such as "Can people be judged by their appearance?" to "How do evil men gain followers?" We find this uncannily relevant at the time we write this chapter. As part of the appendix entitled "Man as a Political Animal," Berne wrote:

> The psychiatrists and the physicists, who are deeply concerned with studying the realities of man and nature, can no longer remain aloof, but must tell the world what they know of its probable future, even at the risk of becoming involved in outside affairs and of being criticized.
>
> (p. 292)

As the publishers stated, many readers would have benefited from this refreshing style of writing, a combination of Berne's philosophical, psychological, and political wisdom. The Appendixes included a discussion of "How Does Intuition work?" (p. 355). In the September prior to the November publication of *The Mind in Action*, Berne presented another new piece of writing to the Los Angeles Psychoanalytic Society. Entitled "The Nature of Intuition" (Berne, 1977f) it was a lengthy paper based on trials that Berne had conducted with his colleagues in an army separation center. In the concluding section of the paper, he wrote, "The intuitive function is part of a series of perceptive processes which work above and below the level of consciousness in an apparently integrated fashion, with shifting emphasis according to special conditions" (p. 30). The studies of these intuitive processes showed that most cases were based on what Berne described as "at least partially on preconscious, sensory observations of the subject" (p. 31).

That paper and seven others, originally published in the *Psychiatric Quarterly*, *The International Record of Medicine*, and the *American Journal of Psychotherapy*, were later gathered together by the International Transactional Analysis Association (ITAA) in 1977 in a book entitled Intuition and Ego States (Berne, 1977e). It tells the fascinating story of the early development of TA. From the outset in his paper on intuition, we can see that Berne was no ordinary psychiatrist and no ordinary training psychoanalyst. It was interesting to us that throughout those early papers, he referred to psychotherapists more than to psychoanalysts, perhaps with an as yet unknown (latent), as Berne would have described it, sense of the way his career path would change. In those papers, we can see the sheer breadth of Berne's curiosity as well as his scholarship. Gregory Bateson, the renowned anthropologist and cyberneticist, for instance, is said to have described Eric Berne as one of the few people he had met who knew ancient Greek and "not just in the sense of having memorized the declinations and other grammatical details, but who could really use ancient Greek texts as a source of information and reference" (Berne, 2010, p. 170).

What also emerges is Berne's interest in a particular aspect of the human psyche that operates outside awareness yet represents something ontologically different from the repressed unconscious, which had constituted the main focus of attention of psychoanalysis at the time.

Berne carried the theme of intuition on in his paper "Concerning the Nature of Diagnosis" published in 1952 in the *International Record of Medicine* (and later republished: Berne, 1977b). In it, we catch a glimpse of Berne already making the complex process of diagnosis into something more digestible by suggesting that "every normal individual is able to make diagnoses by inspection" (p. 48). He argued that an experienced clinician's diagnosis is "a function of skill, keenness, and experience, rather than the result of the deliberate application of a collection of formal criteria" (Berne, 1977b, p. 35).

This was certainly evident in the conversations that we have had with people who knew Berne personally. A number of them spoke about his capacity to know people deeply from the inside–out, to reach places that others could not reach. Some experienced Berne being able to access their most vulnerable parts, parts they thought were hidden. In contrast, others spoke of feeling personally unknown by Berne despite spending time with him, although they appreciated his "razor-like focus." Everyone agreed that he had an inordinate capacity to see patterns and see them at a distance. We wonder if Berne's lucid eye as a clinician sometimes penetrated and astutely "inspected" the world of the other in a way that took priority over the more interpersonal dimensions of the encounter.

The capacity to see patterns was evidenced in a paper titled "*Concerning the Nature of Communication*" published in 1953 in the *Psychiatric Quarterly*. In this paper, we can see Berne's capacity to scan the horizon and to discern patterns. He referenced cybernetics as a theory relating communication systems to physical and engineering aspects of devices such as calculators and computers. He noted, however, that while the focus for mathematicians and engineers in cybernetics would be on the precision of the communication between machines, with human beings "the notion of a precise message … is psychologically inconceivable" (Berne, 1977a, p. 51). In this early paper, we find the beginnings of Berne's thinking about what may be communicated ulteriorly, something he referred to as "latent communication," which rests mainly on the implicit, often non-verbal messages being exchanged. Berne wrote that communications are only understood when there is a change in the psychic energy of the recipient, thereby signaling that the latent meaning of the message was processed.

Sadly, at the same time when Berne was writing his paper on the nature of communication, his own psychic energy was altered when he was called to testify before the House Un-American Activities Committee (HUAC), which was established to investigate allegations of communist activity in the United States. Steiner (2010) wrote about that time as follows:

> Berne had experienced severe persecution in the anti-communist era of the late 1940s and early 1950s in the United States. He was investigated and interrogated, and he lost his government job and his passport because he signed a

petition of the citizens committee to preserve American freedoms in 1952, a petition critical of the treatment of certain scientists the government suspected of left-leaning tendencies.

(p. 212)

Berne's energy for writing and talking about politics changed after that, such that the reprint of *A Mind in Action* in 1957 had the political chapters removed. The book was also retitled *A Layman's Guide to Psychiatry and Psychoanalysis* (republished: 1971).

Berne had continued his emphasis on the importance of intuition in a 1955 paper originally entitled "Intuition IV: Primal Images and Primal Judgment" (later republished: Berne et al., 1977g). He seemed to be ahead of his time and had he lived longer he might have had an animated conversation with Wilma Bucci. She wrote a paper in 2011 entitled "The Interplay of Subsymbolic and Symbolic Processes in Psychoanalytic Treatment: It Takes Two to Tango—But Who Knows the Steps, Who's the Leader? The Choreography of the Psychoanalytic Interchange." There are remarkable similarities between some of Berne's work and Bucci's, although those papers were written over 50 years apart. For example, Berne in 1952 wrote:

A beginner dances the rhumba by remembering to put one foot here, then one foot here, and so on, and by this additive process he gets along in an awkward way. After a while he no longer needs to remember, and as a result he dances a smooth, well-integrated rhumba without thinking about it.

(Berne, 1977a, p. 47)

For her part, in 2011, Bucci wrote, "Argentine tango and the teaching of tango present optimal examples of processes that are systematic and subsymbolic, that occur within awareness and underly the intersection of organization and interpersonal communication" (Bucci, 2011, p. 51). Berne's ideas around the nature of the human psyche, the unconscious, and the intuitive process from 1952 would have found a welcome alongside Bucci's descriptions of systemic and subsymbolic processes.

Similarly, there is a resonance between Berne's work and Donnel Stern's (2003) ideas on unformulated experience:

Thoughts need not be sublime, nocturnal, or psychotic to be unbidden. As a matter of fact, surprise is not the exception, but the rule. The "unconscious thought" revealed in artistic inspiration and creative dreams is not as unusual or mysterious as it seems. These events are best understood as particularly graphic and dramatic instances of a process that occurs with regularity, and in waking hours as often as in sleep.

(p. 73)

In Berne's (1977c) next paper on intuition, published as *"Intuition V: The Ego Image,"* we see the introduction of the best-known building block of transactional analysis theory: ego state theory. This paper was published in 1957 after Berne's formal application for membership in the San Francisco Psychoanalytic Institute was turned down with a recommendation that he reapply in a few years. In the paper, Berne's proclivity to expand on psychoanalytic ideas rather than contest them is evident in his attempt to describe different aspects of clinical experience. In a letter to the San Francisco Psychoanalytic Institute after his membership was deferred, his frustration is evident: "My impression is that there have only been two or three real advances in psychoanalytic thinking in the seventeen years since 1939, as compared with the similar periods 1922–1939" (Berne, 1956, para. 1). Berne took the deferral stoically and it was clear from the same letter that it was not going to interfere with his desire to advance psychoanalytic thinking and to keep sharing his ideas with colleagues. He offered two statements and posed two questions to the organization:

> I am sure it is not your intention to cut me off from any sources of scientific information and from association with my colleagues. If this is true then how do I go about without humiliation attending local, regional, national and international meetings?
>
> (1956, para. 6)

> I doubt that my loss of status will affect my "publishability," if I have something worthwhile to say that I would call psychoanalytic in a psychoanalytic journal. But since some of you are on editorial boards, any comments you might have to make about this would be appreciated.
>
> (1956, para. 7)

Berne demonstrated his tenacity in his research, his determination to develop ideas and keep learning, and his prolific writing and capacity for recording and laying down in history the expansion of his thinking as it progressed.

Once more, it appears that the act of gaining clinical knowledge would take priority for Berne at the expense, perhaps, of the interpersonal realities of his life at the time.

The Development of Ego State Theory

Berne started his psychoanalytic training with Paul Federn in 1941. Federn's influence can be seen throughout Berne's early development of transactional analysis. In a 1934 paper entitled "The Awakening of the Ego in Dreams," which was later revised by Federn and translated by Edoardo Weiss (Federn, 1952), Federn postulated a basis for ego psychology. He provided three definitions of the ego that we believe Berne took forward in his own understanding and development of ego states:

- The descriptive: "The 'ego' is the lasting or recurring psychical *continuity* of the body and mind of an individual in respect of space, time and causality" (Federn, 1952, p. 94).
- The phenomenological: "The ego is felt and known by the individual as a lasting or recurring *continuity* of the body and mental life in respect of time, space and causality, and is felt and apprehended by him as a unity" (p. 94).
- The metapsychological: "The basis of the ego is a state of psychical cathexis of certain independent bodily and mental functions and contents, the cathexes in question being simultaneous and interconnected and also continuous. The nature of these functions, and the centre around which they are grouped are familiar" (p. 94).

Federn had developed his ideas around ego boundaries through extensive study on changes in states of the ego in the processes of falling asleep, dreaming, and awakening. In these ideas on the ego boundary, he distinguished between emotions experienced at the ego boundary and those that seized the whole ego. For example, anger would be experienced at the ego boundary, that is, "I have anger," whereas rage is experienced in the entire ego, that is, "rage has me."

In the "*Intuition V: The Ego Image*" paper, Berne (1977c) referred to Federn in his differentiation between the mature ego (the "adult") and the troublesome feelings that Federn had identified as delusions and "the revival of an archaic ego state" (p. 10).

Another paper entitled, "Ego States in Psychotherapy," showed Berne (1977d) stressing the importance of research in psychotherapy and describing his new approach as one that "seems to find its most useful application in just those cases where other methods of psychotherapy are generally considered to be the most difficult or least effective" (p. 121). The paper provided the first diagrams of ego states and showed Berne's continuance of Federn's work on ego state boundaries. The diagram showed two ego states with an overlap between Child and Adult ego states. Berne wrote:

> The process of clearly differentiating ego states, which may be conveniently called "structural analysis," should be clearly distinguished at this point from two of its therapeutic relatives. It is different from an "ego" vs. "id" approach ... The "Child" is not synonymous with the id, but is a complete ego state in itself, with its own psychic structure.
>
> (p. 125)

Berne's goal in treatment was to engage patients in freeing themselves from "contamination by archaic attitudes" (p. 125), thereby strengthening their mature ego, in Federn's terms.

Further observation led Berne to describe the internal dialogue in a patient who had come to him with a gambling problem as a "trialogue" (Berne, 1977d, p. 127). Here, we see the identification of a "parent" ego state. The ego is, therefore, no longer considered a bipartite structure but a tripartite one. Berne was clear to reference Federn's work, underscoring that it was his own emphasis and development of the concepts that were new, not the concepts themselves.

Berne (1977d) suggested in his paper that these ego states are "not merely neologisms for the superego, ego, and id of Freud (1949) but complete ego states in themselves" (p. 131). He suggested that capitalizing Parent, Adult, and Child would make things clearer. The Child ego state, for example, is not unorganized like the id but has a structure and organization of its own, as does the Parent ego state. Further differentiation occurred as Berne outlined a P inside the Parent ego state as the grandmother (p. 131), the A in the Parent ego state as the mother's distorted or undistorted view of reality, and a C in the Parent ego state as the mother's fixated archaic ego states. The Parent, Adult, and Child contained in the Child ego state were described as archaic ego states within the Child ego state to which a patient may return according to what has been fixated. This view corresponds with approaches theorized by developmental psychologists, such as Piaget, whom Berne referenced in his writings. Berne stated that although his new approach could be taught easily, the practitioner would develop more expertise and advantage in working with patients by "clarifying the boundaries between his own ego states" (1977d, p. 134).

By 1958, Berne had further developed his theory of transactional analysis in a paper published in the *American Journal of Psychotherapy* entitled "Transactional Analysis: A New and Effective Method of Group Therapy" (1958b). In it, he further developed the theory from structural analysis of ego states through what he called simple transactional analysis (i.e., analysis of transactions between members of the group) to the more complex analysis of games (whereby group members were encouraged to gently identify and demonstrate to each other what was happening), through to script analysis, which Berne defined as the ultimate goal of transactional analysis.

In a fascinating paper written in 1958, "Principles of Transactional Analysis" (1958a), sourced from the Eric Berne Archive, Berne was keen to emphasize how his new approach was being "systematically tested by fifty therapists in Northern California" (p. 1). In the paper, Berne referred to ego states being derived from psychic organs. He also described how the anatomy and physiology of these psychic organs were revealed by the Penfield (1954) experiment whereby electrical stimulation was applied to the cerebral cortex of patients. When the electrical stimulation was applied, the patient would report complete ego state experiences, that is, memories that included intricate details such as sound, movement, and color. Berne also wrote about a colleague interviewing a patient's father and in that process corroborating that the patient had exactly reproduced his father's fixated paranoid ego state.

One of the people we interviewed as part of our research for this book had attended one of Berne's therapy groups. Their experience was of watching a "cowboy in action." When we questioned the meaning of this, they and others we spoke to explained that "a cowboy is a straight shooter." They reported that Berne's interventions were incisive and direct, although quiet. They stressed that one of Berne's main values was that people should speak in a language that an 8-year-old child would understand. Berne's approach in private practice was to see his patients both individually and in a group. This meant that he knew people more personally as well as helping them interpersonally. It was their experience that everyone in the group felt deeply known and acknowledged by him.

For Berne, theory was a living organism, always shaped in an intimate dialogue with his clinical practice. Therefore, he would continuously experiment with various aspects of the psychotherapeutic frame and methods of intervention. An example of this was the active group therapy program at Mount Zion Hospital developed under his supervision beginning in the mid-1950s. There was also a weekly seminar group open to professionals. They were so popular that participants asked if the seminars could be run after working hours for those who could not attend the group at the hospital. This led to Berne holding seminars at his office, the attendance at which grew rapidly.

A Systemic Individual and Social Psychiatry

In his 1961 book, *Transactional Analysis in Psychotherapy: A Systemic Individual and Social Psychiatry*, Berne thanked people who attended the seminars for their part in the development of the most dynamic aspects of transactional analysis theory. The book is a comprehensive textbook in which Berne worked from the outset to provide an outline of his theory to that date, beginning with a definition of an ego state theory. Berne explained that the book had been published because there was a growing need for him to provide lectures and reprints of his articles, as well as enter into correspondence (which can be seen in the many letters from this time in the Eric Berne Archive). In the book, Berne explained briefly that he had parted company with orthodox psychoanalysis on "friendly terms" (p. 13) and made clear that his idea of ego function differed from that of many psychoanalysts but followed most closely Federn (1952) and Weiss (1950).

Referring again to Penfield's experiment, Berne (1961) stressed how it showed that "two different ego states can occupy consciousness simultaneously as discrete psychological entities distinct from each other" (p. 17). He also emphasized how in the experiment, the patient's past was evoked as a vivid reliving of the experience in the present with the original intensity. He likened it to the work in which LSD had been used to enhance psychotherapeutic work:

> More recently Chandler and Hartman ... working with LSD-25, have demonstrated the striking similarity between the pharmacological reactivation of archaic ego states and that obtained through electrical stimulation of the cortex, although like Penfield, they do not employ the term "ego state" itself. They describe the same simultaneous experiencing of two ego states, one oriented

toward the current external and psychological reality, the other a "reliving" (rather than mere recall) of scenes dating back as far as the first year of life, "with great vividness of color and other detail, and the patient feels himself to be back in the situation and experiences the affects in all the original intensity." (p. 19)

Berne differentiated transactional analysis from other psychotherapy approaches that offered reassurance, suggestion, or confrontation and from nondirective approaches, within which he included psychoanalysis, emphasizing that the goal of structural analysis, which he emphasized was to precede transactional analysis, was to "establish the predominance of reality-testing ego states and free them from contamination by archaic and foreign elements" (p. 22). The distinctions described here mainly serve clinical purposes in the sense that they support the practitioner in making appropriate judgments regarding methodology and intervention modalities. In our reading, they are not aimed at conveying absolute truths or making evaluations about which is the "best" way to do psychotherapy.

Part I of Berne (1961) book, entitled "Psychiatry of the Individual and Structural Analysis," further defined ego state theory. Berne focused on the structure of the personality in ego state terms, how this functions in relation to stimuli, the flow of cathexis, ego state boundaries, the function of the personality, and problems that may persist in shifts from one ego state to another.

Part II focuses on "Social Psychiatry and Transactions." The first of these chapters, "Social Intercourse," outlines a theory of social contact with an emphasis on stimulus and recognition, the structuring of time to satisfy structure hunger, and the influences of programming and social intercourse where the concept of games is introduced. Further chapters outline the analysis of transactions, games, scripts, and relationships.

In Part III, titled "Psychotherapy," Berne (1961) clearly defined the therapy of functional psychosis, giving clear definitions of his thinking on active and latent psychoses in terms of ego state boundaries. He made clear that in active psychosis: (1) Psychotherapy should be initiated only during periods of minimal confusion and (2) no active psychotherapeutic moves should be made until the patient has had a chance to appraise the therapist, which they should be given the opportunity to do (p. 141). Berne's respectful attitude toward his patients provided a solid foundation on which the ethos of transactional analysis was built. Transactional analysis practitioners today hold high the values of mutual respect and open communication.

In the subsequent chapter in Part III, Berne (1961) outlined the four possible goals in the therapy of neurosis: symptomatic control, symptomatic relief, transference cure, and psychoanalytic cure (p. 153). He wrote that "transactional analysis, game analysis, and script analysis were a good foundation for subsequent psychoanalytic work" (pp. 163–164) and outlined that "the unfolding of the script is the substance of the psychoanalytic process. The transference consists not merely of a set of interrelated reactions, a transference neurosis but of a dynamically progressive transference drama" (p. 164).

In the final section of Part III, Berne (1961) focused on group therapy. His lecture to the American Group Psychotherapy Association at their annual meeting in 1957 had clearly been well received and was entitled "Transactional Analysis: A New and Effective Method of Group Therapy" (later published in the *American Journal of Psychotherapy*—1958b). By 1960, it was clear that he was quite involved with the association in setting up a therapy program for the seventh annual meeting. In this part of his 1961 book, Berne outlined the objectives of group therapy as carrying the patient "through the progressive stages of structural analysis, transactional analysis proper, game analysis and script analysis until he attains social control" (p. 165).

Psychotherapists today can benefit from Berne's emphasis on the importance of the therapist undergoing structural analysis and game analysis to work out their own motivations for running a group. As with all the chapters in the 1961 book, Berne brought the theory alive with his patient vignettes. As we write this book in the 2020s, we are aware of the starkness of the language Berne used when describing patients and remind ourselves of the context and tendencies of the times. Like Thomas, Berne was keen to find ways of working that were more efficient. It seems paradoxical that in the present times, the psychological language used in Berne's writings appears so medically oriented, although the approaches themselves are humanistic and refreshingly egalitarian.

In terms of group therapy, Berne's (1968b) introduction of "staff–patient staff" conferences was quite innovative and profoundly humanistic:

> The staff-patient staff conference first attacks the established sociological roles of "therapist" and "patient" and substitutes a bilateral contract with rational exceptions. Everyone is treated as a "person" with equal rights on his own merits. Thus, the patients have as much right to hear what the staff has to say as the staff has to hear what the patients have to say and if the staff have the courtesy to remain silent while the patients are talking, the patients are expected to extend a similar courtesy to the staff.
>
> (p. 12)

Part IV of Berne's (1961) wide-ranging book is entitled "Frontiers of Transactional Analysis." In it, he further extrapolated into a finer structure of the personality and advanced structural analysis into a second-order structure of the Parent and Child ego states similar to the way he did in his 1957 paper "Ego States in Psychotherapy" (Berne, 1977d).

Following that, he wrote about the therapy of marriages, stating that a group that included four married couples had been one of his most stimulating experiences to that point. In a rare insight into his internal emotional landscape, he wrote:

> Nothing is more edifying and touching to the onlooker than the expression of deep and real love between two human beings, especially when there are others present who are equally moved. Speaking rhetorically, whoever has been

saddened by loss of confidence in the essential goodness of people should attend such a group. And sometimes it is the sickest people who give the most beautiful pictures of their souls.

(Berne, 1961, pp. 212–213)

In the closing chapters of *Transactional Analysis in Psychotherapy*, we are reminded that TA is a theory that is still a work in progress. In Chapter 19, Berne referred to regression analysis as being in an embryonic state, and in Chapter 20, he referred to practicing the procedure for no longer than four years. In the final chapter, "Theoretical and Technical Considerations," in a section called "Psychic Apparatus," Berne examined ambiguities and complexity in structural analysis, for example, how internal, external, and probability programming will influence ego states and how ego states will be further divided into structural and functional aspects, the structure more akin to anatomy and the function more akin to physiology.

Despite the relative newness of this theory, Berne (1961), book stands as proof of his commitment to taking a scientific approach to the advancement of psychotherapeutic knowledge. His emphasis was on articulating a coherent system of understanding the human psyche, one that stands the test of internal, as well as external, validity.

An Intense Period of Growth

The publication of the first *Transactional Analysis Bulletin* occurred in 1962. It was published quarterly to keep people up to date with the happenings of the San Francisco Social Psychiatry Seminars, which had been meeting for five years at that point. From contemporary issues of the *Bulletin*, it is clear how active members of the seminars were in discussing, promoting, and continuing to develop transactional analysis theory and practice. In the first issue, there is an advertisement for a "101 Introductory Social Dynamics" course. It was advertised as "A Theoretical Introduction to Group Dynamics, Structural Analysis, and Transactional Analysis" and was based on Berne's (1961) *Transactional Analysis in Psychotherapy*.

It is clear from the issues of the *Bulletin* from that time that the San Francisco Social Psychiatry Seminars were an excellent breeding ground for Berne's writings, as the 101 course and the discussions that followed were presumably the foundation of the book *The Structure and Dynamics of Organizations and Groups* (first published in Berne, 1963). The aim of the book was to offer "a systematic framework for the therapy of ailing groups and organizations" (Preface, p. vii). The book follows a familiar pattern and is divided into four parts. In the beginning, Berne analyzed the sequence of what needs to happen in establishing a group. He emphasized two phases: the preliminary phase and the organizational phase, during which the structure of the group is formed.

Part II, "The Group as a Whole," offers a detailed examination of the structure and dynamics of groups. Berne's (1963) focus there was not just on psychiatric and psychotherapy groups but on all groups. His focus was on the health of a group and the importance of its survival, so he highlighted factors that might threaten the group, such as external pressures and internal agitation. Berne wrote that "all the work of any group falls into three categories: the group activity, the external group process and the internal group process" (p. 78) and that "the existence of a group is continually in jeopardy if it cannot mobilize enough cohesive force to support all three kinds of work" (p. 78). His emphasis on group culture, the group cannon, and leadership is significant and far-reaching and can be seen to be deeply embodied in his own life experience. The following excerpt from *A Montreal Childhood* (Berne, 2010) describing his time in the Boy Scouts shows Berne's keen interest in group work from a young age:

> I soon rose from tenderfoot to patrol leader, and it was in that run-down philanthropic center that I first experienced politics, leadership, and social work. The politics consisted of maneuvering to get all the most literate recruits into my patrol, which I carried out successfully. The leadership consisted of making sure that my patrol was the best in everything, and that too came off well. The direct result of this was the social work. One day the scoutmaster, A. M. Ravitch, called me away from his knot-tying to consult with me on the platform. Mr. Ravitch confided that there was an orphan boy, Jim Jassby, who had been getting into trouble, and the authorities thought the Boy Scouts might help straighten him out. Would I like to include him in my patrol, which had such a good record?
>
> (p. 115)

From reading about this early experience of politics, it was touching to find in the Eric Berne Archive a letter that Berne had written to then-US President John F. Kennedy congratulating him and his wife and describing them as a literate couple holding a "historical perspective on Fascism and Communism" (Berne, 1962a, para. 1). This was clearly a reference to Berne's unfair trial by the House Un-American Activities Committee when there was an almost paranoid anti-communist stance in the United States during the Cold War. In his letter, Berne referenced a certain General Walker, who was accused of promoting his extreme right personal political opinion to his troops. In context, we can view this as Berne's sharing his perspective on organizations and groups:

> It should be made unequivocally clear ... that the Armed Forces are part of the group apparatus and not of its policy-making leadership, that they are there to serve, but not to criticize nor tamper with the duly elected civilian government.
>
> (para. 3)

This is a description of how an exclusive focus on the external process of a group (the nation, in this case) can be detrimental to internal group processes (such as the status and freedom of particular members of the group) and, potentially, to group activity (the unobstructed development of scientific knowledge, for instance).

In Part III of *The Structure and Dynamics of Organizations and Groups*, Berne (1963) brought his previous work into analyzing the individual in the group, using the apparatuses of transactional analysis, including analysis of transactions, games, and script. In this section, he began to expand (though minimally) on the idea of protocol and palimpsest. Here, we also see that Berne emphasized the importance of social contact and time structuring for individuals and how this can be found in groups. He outlined that individuals will bring their provisional group imago—that is, their own "mental picture of what a group should be or is like" (p. 92)—before entering the group and that they will make certain adjustments according to how flexible and adaptable they are. The individual will be impacted by the social customs and patterns of the group along with specific goals. He emphasized that individuals need to know how they fit into the leader's group imago before they will initiate of their own accord. He accentuated that the group imago and the group script will go through phases of adjustment.

In Part IV, entitled "Applied Social Psychiatry," Berne (1963) wrote about the group dynamics of group psychotherapy and provided important information about ailing groups, finalizing the book with a chapter entitled "Management of Organizations."

In the chapter on group psychotherapy, Berne (1963) stressed the importance of organization and preparation, recommending further diagrams: A location diagram that included rosters, schedules, timings, and the arrangement of the room; an authority diagram that emphasized the difference between groups in private practice and those under federal jurisdiction whereby the case of a patient might become a national issue; and a structural diagram that Berne used to recommend thoughtfulness regarding group leadership and considerations that need to be accounted for if the group is tape-recorded and if there is a co-leader. With regard to group imagoes, Berne suggested that clarification of individual group imagoes is the aim of the group and went on to propose that using transactional analysis in group therapy "raises the theoretical efficiency of this treatment to 100 per cent" (p. 177).

The chapter on ailing groups, with vignettes of an ailing clinic and an ailing therapy group, brings alive the theory in the previous chapters. Using the diagrams he had suggested in previous chapters, Berne highlighted procedures that had worked and those that had not worked. Examination of the structural dynamics diagrams and the group imagoes underscored the need for ruthless examination of the leaders' motivations. Berne ended this part of the book with a summary of the six basic diagrams exemplified in a story about a little boy wanting to start a club in his house who later became a group therapist (Berne, 2010, p. 51).

Berne's attention to the motivation of the group therapist was further corroborated by a large research project conducted in the late 1960s and reported by Lieberman et al. (1973). Two transactional analysis groups were analyzed, with one deemed successful and one not. The successful group, led by a well-known psychiatrist and an expert in transactional analysis, was ranked first and equal with another group of 17 groups studied. The leader of the group was ranked first in terms of participants' satisfaction with their learning. The second transactional analysis group studied was considered unsuccessful with exceptionally negative feedback. It tied for last in terms of being a turn-off. The leader was ranked 14 out of 15 (last) leaders in terms of competence. When he was interviewed after the group ended, the leader agreed that the group had been unsuccessful and put that down to "poor structure" (p. 58). Modern sensibility and research today suggest that the therapeutic relationship (Strupp, 2001) is as powerful if not more so than the particular treatment method a therapist is using. This is in stark contrast to some of the claims made by Berne regarding the effectiveness of transactional analysis.

The Best-Seller

Soon after the publication of *The Structure and Dynamics of Organizations and Groups* came the publication of *Games People Play: The Psychology of Human Relationships* (Berne, 1964). The book is credited with bringing transactional analysis into the limelight. The idea for it came because participants in the San Francisco Social Psychiatry Seminars were often thinking of new names for games, which helped them understand their work with individuals and groups. So students and lecture audiences had asked Berne to write a catalog or thesaurus of games. Berne dedicated this book to his patients and students, "who taught me more and more and are still teaching me about games and the meaning of life" (Dedication). Berne designed the book to be a sequel to *Transactional Analysis in Psychotherapy* and emphasized that the book could also be read independently.

Berne also took pains to acknowledge and differentiate his work from the work of mathematicians, who were also working with game analysis, and he recognized that some terms (e.g., payoff) were shared in the *Transactional Analysis Bulletin* (1962b, p. 24). In the *Transactional Analysis Bulletin* (Publications, 1964, p. 112), it was stated that there had been vigorous negotiations with the publisher, who had originally turned down the book. Berne apparently brokered a deal whereby if he could sell 500 copies on his own, then Grove Press would publish it (W. Cornell, personal communication, June 10, 2022). Berne's determination proved successful as he sold the book to attendees at the San Francisco Social Psychiatry Seminars as a "Limited Edition *Transactional Analysis Bulletin*, Supplement #2" for $5.

In the introduction, Berne (1964) outlined the theory of social intercourse and his ideas that stroking, although it may be "used as a general term for physical intimate contact" (p. 18), may be extended to denote recognition of another. Game theory, he extrapolated, is based on the principle that "any social intercourse whatever has a biological advantage over no intercourse at all" (p. 15). The Introduction is a neat summary of hungers, stimulus, recognition, and structure and how material, social, and individual programming leads to the inevitable games involved in social contact. The short introduction also incorporates the advantages of games revolving around somatic and psychic equilibrium, and Berne wrote that "significant social intercourse most commonly takes the form of games" (p. 6).

In the promotional brochure, Grove Press (1964) outlined that

> noting that people tend to live their lives by consistently playing out certain "games" in their interpersonal relations, the author of *Transactional Analysis in Psychotherapy* here provides us with a startling new way to diagnose neurotic behavior. Written in non-technical language and designed to entertain as well as to educate, *Games People Play* is an invaluable source book for therapists, teachers, and parents, as well as of great interest to the general reader.

The book breaks games into seven major classifications: life games, marital games, party games, sexual games, underworld games, consulting room games, and good games. Each classification is then subdivided into further named games.

Games People Play took the United States by storm, and spent over 100 weeks on the *New York Times* best-seller list. Some reviews were more critical, such as Papowitz's (1967) comments in the *American Journal of Psychoanalysis*:

> The principal defects of transactional analysis, as presented in *Games People Play*, are oversimplification and superficiality. To study human behavior motivation almost exclusively in interpersonal terms is to ignore the vast realm of the intrapsychic. Few would deny the impact of other people on our psychic lives, but to maintain that the principal motivations governing our emotional lives are the advantages to be gained from social intercourse is to brush off lightly the profound insights that psychoanalysis has made possible.
>
> (p. 219)

At the end of his review, however, Papowitz wrote:

> To the extent that the book is used by readers to improve their gamesmanship it will be innocuous, but to the extent that it will help people take any interest in their own game-playing and encourage self-awareness, it can be very valuable. It is likely that many readers may be encouraged to enter analysis themselves. While analysts may find an interesting new perspective on interpersonal psychological phenomena, this book is primarily for the layman.
>
> (p. 219)

Much discussion about this last comment occurred in the San Francisco Seminars because Berne had originally intended that the book would not be for laypersons but for transactional analysis group therapists. Berne (1965) wrote in the *Transactional Analysis Bulletin*:

> Some people had hinted that it would be good form for the author to express horror at this crass invasion of scientific discipline, but he does not share either what Joseph Alsop calls "The modern specialist's curious loathing for the

intelligent general reader" or the feelings of the two psychoanalysts who have forbidden their patients to read the book.

(p. 81)

In fact, it appears that Berne rather enjoyed the media attention. He wrote of himself and some colleagues enjoying the prototype of the board game based on *Games People Play* that a popular board game manufacturer had commissioned, and he wrote a three-act musical comedy (Berne, 1967). Reading the script for the musical comedy in the Eric Berne Archive, we wondered if, in fact, Berne had collaborated with Joe South on the popularized song "Games People Play" (South, 1968). The script for the potential musical showed the lyrics of a song "Oh the games people play, they play them night and day, you think they're talking straight until you have to pay" (p. 5 para, 3). Joe South's (1968) lyrics read: "Oh the games people play now, every night and every day now, never meaning what they say now, never saying what they mean."

Berne's response to his critics, published in the *Transactional Analysis Bulletin* (1966b), was clear:

If psychiatry is for all of the people then all of the people should be told about it not in a form which all but a few may consider stale but in a form they most desire and which they are most willing to listen to.

(p. 132)

And there is still more. Only two years after *Games People Play*, Berne published *Principles of Group Treatment* (1966a). In the foreword, he explained the rationale for the book, emphasizing that it is about group treatment rather than group therapy. The main distinction, he wrote, is that in group treatment, the therapist's primary focus is on "curing patients" (p. 4). Group therapy can incorporate group treatment, but not all group therapy is group treatment. Berne also described the book as a "systematic treatise on the use of transactional analysis in groups" and explained that the book was a response to

a large number of people who have observed the writer's groups or have heard him discuss them [and] want more information about why he does what he does, especially when he does what other therapists would do, or does not do, what others therapists would.

(p. vii)

It is an inclusive book, including some of what was covered in *The Structure and Dynamic of Organizations and Groups* (Berne, 1963) but expanded in more detail.

Berne (1966a) wrote about his first experience of running a group at an army hospital where soldiers who had no access to liquor had taken to imbibing shaving lotion. He called a meeting of the soldiers to discuss the issue, and they appreciated the opportunity so much that it turned into a daily meeting sanctioned by the War Department.

The first part of the book serves as an incredibly well-thought-through and detailed handbook. Berne outlined what to consider and how to prepare for running a treatment group. He outlined clearly defined contracts—the professional contract, the psychological contract, and the organizational contract—as well as the organization's needs and the authority diagram described earlier. Berne's emphasis on the therapist's responsibility not only to his patients but to the organization and ultimately to self-examination was clearly underlined.

> Optimally, the therapist should have had not only didactic training, but also personal experience as a patient in both individual and group therapy. These are the best preparations for attaining the degree of self-awareness necessary to have a full grasp of what is happening in his groups.
> (Berne, 1966a, p. 21)

The section on methods of treatment is well-researched. Berne (1966a) mentioned the article by Thomas (1943) referred to earlier in this chapter, and Berne's interpretation was that the repressive inspiration groups involve much more the Parent ego state and the analytic groups the Adult ego state.

Berne (1966a) wrote about four types of patient transactions:

> Patient I says: "I read an article on group therapy, and it said we were supposed to do the talking."
> Or Patient II says: "What are we supposed to do here?"
> Or Patient III says: "I hate to break this silence, it seems almost sacred."
> Or Patient IV says: "I'm sorry I was late." (p. 101)

He then described how various groups would deal with these patients. The various groups, as Berne categorized them, were supportive therapy, group analytic therapy, psychoanalytic therapy, and TA. Berne offered a critique of the various approaches, suggesting that transactional analysis was proving to be a favored approach. He was also keen to underline that

> comparison between various forms of psychotherapy is always open to serious criticisms. One principle which should not be neglected, however, is that only people who have an intimate acquaintance with a technical instrument are competent to pass judgment upon it. A transactional analyst who had not had formal education in psychoanalysis would not consider himself competent to judge the latter, and psychoanalysts should be expected to show the same courtesy toward transactional analysis.
> (p. 135)

The following sections of the book cover group dynamics, revisiting some of the concepts in *The Structure and Dynamics of Organizations and Groups* and representing diagrams showing seating, authority, internal and external boundaries, internal and external group processes, the group imago, and transactional diagrams.

In his chapter on teaching, Berne (1966a) outlined a wide-ranging three-year curriculum covering didactic teaching, clinical presentations and observation, and practical group leadership (p. 161). He emphasized that the syllabus should include education on a wide variety of "schools" or approaches to group psychotherapy, listing ten different approaches. The quotation below is strikingly relevant to students and trainers of transactional analysis today:

> The student should remember that proportionately, there were just as many intelligent people in the world in the old days as there are now. Many of them were relatively isolated as thinkers, and had the additional advantage of being unhampered by the demands of methodological and material technology and the need for academic and journalistic compliance.
>
> (pp. 200–201)

The next chapters in the book are devoted to a thorough explanation of transactional analysis as applied to group treatment and group psychotherapy. Berne offered a convincing argument emphasizing that transactional analysis, which grew out of group therapy, is more effective because it requires a shorter training period (although just as thorough) than psychoanalysis and that it is applicable to a wider range of psychiatric patients.

The major concepts of transactional analysis theory are outlined under the subheading "The Formal Aspects of Transactional Analysis" (Berne, 1966a, p. 219), and the eight therapeutic operations that are introduced for the first time are described under "Basic Techniques" (p. 233). In a subtitled section called "Learning to Operate," Berne amusingly wrote that a beginner therapist might well learn the process by numbers and that the ultimate aim is for the numbers to "coalesce into a single skilled sequence" (p. 250). Berne outlined eight therapeutic operations with a careful explanation of each. His astute observational powers and clarity was evident as he carefully outlined the procedures of interrogation, specification, confrontation, explanation, illustration, confirmation, interpretation, and crystallization (pp. 233–247). Each operation is clearly explained with caution about which kinds of patient may or may not respond well, always with Berne respecting the patient in mind. The clear way he described the processes has stood the test of time.

Berne (1966a) also offered three important notes of caution:

1. Never get ahead of the clinical material offered by the patient. Preferably stay three steps behind …
2. Never miss a legitimate chance to forge ahead.
3. Never push against resistance except for testing purposes based on a well-thought-out concrete hypothesis. (pp. 247–248)

In this chapter, Berne reminded us that the main goal of any psychotherapeutic operation is to "cure the patient" (p. 256). He also offered further guidelines in the form of questions that therapists need to ask themselves before deciding which interventions or operations to use. Berne followed with an illustrative example of how Dr. Q (Berne himself) used the therapeutic operations in interventions.

In the next section, "The Transactional Theory of Personality," Berne (1966a) wrote regarding child development and the family culture from birth to 4–7 years, at which point children are making decisions and compromises in life. He then offered a case study to demonstrate the decisions and the life script of Rita. He also briefly mentioned that the "protocol (or original version)" (p. 267) of her life script was written by her seventh year and played out as a "palimpsest" (p. 267) in her adolescence. Berne described the ruthless adaptation of Rita's script in her marriage as "the Broadway Version" (p. 267). He went on to explain the "constancy of games" (p. 267), which support the life script, and that "every game, script and destiny" (p. 270) is based on one of four life positions: "I am OK, you are OK," the intrinsically constructive; "I am OK, You are not-OK," the essentially paranoid; "I am not-OK, you are OK," the depressive; and "I am not-OK, you are not-OK," the futile and schizoid (p. 270).

In a section entitled "Clinical Accompaniments," Berne (1966a) described possible ways that patients might try to relieve their despair, maybe by playing games, seeking oblivion in alcohol or drugs, or quitting therapy. This stage is marked by confusion, and as the work progresses, the patient has to face "the archaic fears previously warded off by playing games" (p. 278).

Berne (1966a) summarized this section by contrasting "two kinds of therapeutic goals": one that aims to make progress, and transactional analysis, where the aim is to "get well" (p. 290). Berne expressed a belief that "every human being is born a prince or a princess; early experiences convince some that they are frogs, and the rest of the pathological development follows from this" (pp. 289–290). The goal of transactional analysis is to transform frogs back into princes and princesses. It is our understanding that Berne's view of cure involved patients reclaiming parts of themselves that have been silenced or otherwise made inaccessible.

Berne (1966a) devoted the next section of the book to a thorough examination of "The Relationship Between Transactional Analysis and Other Forms of Treatment" (p. 292). He was mostly respectful of the other forms of treatment, which included psychoanalysis, existential analysis, Gestalt therapy, psychodrama, supportive therapy, and group analysis. Each one was compared and contrasted to transactional analysis. Supportive therapy was the only one of which Berne was overtly critical, believing it to be somewhat patronizing.

Berne (1966a) could not quite conceal his wry wit in comparing psychoanalysis and transactional analysis when, in reference to the transferential relationship, he wrote that a psychoanalyst would say, "If you come regularly and tell father everything according to the procedure he prescribes, then your cure will be forthcoming" (p. 304), whereas a transactional analyst would say, "If you get better first and give up your symptoms, then you may come if you wish and talk to father for an hour each day" (p. 302).

Chapter 14 addresses games that would be played in groups. Of note are Berne's (1966a) definitions of types of therapists and the games they bring to groups. These games have similarly amusing names and show Berne's cynicism and acerbic wit. They include Phallus in Wonderland, The Delegate, The Smiling Rebel, The Jargon Juggler, The Conservative, and The Hypochondriac. Berne suggested amusing ways that a supervisor should approach these therapists. For example, with the Delegate therapist who feels like he is throwing "pearls before swine," the supervisor needs to tell him it is more like "doing twirls without a spine" (p. 338).

Berne (1966a) concluded *Principles of Group Treatment* with a chapter on "Diagnostic Categories." He gave a short synopsis of diagnostic terms taken from the *American Handbook of Psychiatry* (Arieti, 1959). It is interesting to note that at that time, homosexuality was considered a sexual deviation and listed as a psychiatric diagnosis. As a consequence, Berne included it among the categories he listed. It was not until 1973 that the American Psychiatric Association voted to remove homosexuality from the *Diagnostic and Statistical Manual of Mental Disorders* (1973) and as late as 1990 when "the World Health Organization removed homosexuality per se from the International Classification of Diseases" (Drescher, 2015, p. 571).

In this concluding chapter, Berne (1966a) applied game analysis to each of these diagnostic categories. At the end of the chapter, there is a rather spurious list of suggestions that Berne described as "hints or aphorisms" (p. 357). They included suggestions such as, "The recumbent patient is more impressed by your competence than by your virtuosity. It does not reassure him to be treated like a violin" (p. 358).

In G. C. Heller's (1967) review of *Principles of Group Treatment* in *The British Journal of Psychiatry*, he wrote:

> The author, a trained psychoanalyst who is not a member of any psychoanalytic society, has come to terms with both psychoanalysis and applied existentialism. He incorporates the mechanistic concepts of the former and the ethical values of the latter in his own therapeutic philosophy. To shrug this book as an exercise in groupmanship would label the reader as an incorrigible square. Dr. Berne's book is neither wooly nor superficial. It is scientific eclecticism *par excellence* and a joy to read.
>
> (p. 458)

Berne published one more book in 1968 before his untimely death from a heart attack in July 1970 at the age of 60. It was a children's book entitled *The Happy Valley* (Berne, 1968a), which it appears he had been incubating since 1948 when it was looked on unfavorably by publishers.

In November 1970, after Berne died, *Sex In Human Loving* was published by Simon and Schuster. Berne had made modifications in December 1969 following feedback from some of his female readers, whom Berne referred to as "liberated women." They objected to some of the "male chauvinism" in the book, and he considered their points "well taken" (p. xv). The book was published with material from a series of lectures Berne had delivered as part of the 1966 Jake Gimbel Sex Psychology Lectures.

Berne's (1970) playfulness, which could be described as schoolboy humor and dry wit, came through in the book and in the lectures, where he played with words, turning words such as "fuck" into "cuff."

> Cuff is the only word in the English language that gives the full feeling, excitement, slipperiness, and aroma of the sexual act. Its lascivious "f" sound also helps to give it a realistic punch ... [Other synonyms] carefully avoid the idea of excitement and lust, and even more carefully avoid one of the most primitive and powerful elements in sex, which is smell. Cuff takes in all of these, just as a child does, because it starts off as a child's word.
>
> (p. 22)

Transactional analysis concepts are cleverly scattered throughout the book, with a chapter on sexual games and specific reference to time structuring in a section entitled "Sex Organs in Time-Structuring."

In an attempt to make the lectures more readable, Berne (1970) altered the original material to make it seem like he was writing or speaking to just one person. He used the *noms de plume* of "Cyprian St. Cyr" as an author who was writing letters to his wife's maid while he was traveling and Dr. Horsley as St. Cyr's friend. In a section entitled "Afterplay" (p. 216) in Chapter 8 titled "A Man of the World" (p. 233), Berne used short sayings from these two fictional characters.

It is poignant to read the final paragraph of the book, which was written so close to Berne's death:

> A star is the glowing light inside the other person, distantly seen, brave soul's tiny flame, too bright to approach without great courage and integrity. Each person lives alone in inner space, and intimacy is out there. Intimacy is outer space, and if that's where you are, you don't say "Cuff you!" to a star.
>
> (Berne, 1970, p. 246)

It was also interesting to find that the contract signed with Simon and Shuster for the book included signatories under Berne, 1967 trust for his children, Peter Berne and Ellen Berne Finkle, even though the contract was dated April 1970, some months before Berne's death.

In a memorial article in the Eric Berne Archive (sadly undated and source unknown) written by Gary Gregg there is a banner showing "Eric Berne—A Drive to Simplify and Make It." We wonder if this might have been a fitting epitaph. In the obituary, Gregg wrote:

> Berne soon found himself on the pages of *Life* and *Newsweek*, and further estranged from many fellow psychiatrists who charged that he oversimplified and argued that psychiatry needed a language that both therapist and patient could understand. He continued to set high standards for himself and grew quick to anger psychiatrists who moaned in staff conferences about why they couldn't

cure their patients. "I think Freud would consider most analysts today nothing but picture hangers" and when the Psychoanalytic Institute offered him the membership he had long sought, he declined with thanks.

(Gregg, n.d.)

The Testament

Berne's (1972) final book, *What Do You Say After You Say Hello? The Psychology of Human Destiny*, which was published posthumously, originally had the title *Script Analysis in Psychotherapy*. It is a popular book among professionals and laypeople alike and was described in a review in the *New York Times* by James Gordon (1972), a psychiatrist with the National Institute for Mental Health, as follows:

> Eric Berne's last book, "What Do You Say After You Say Hello?," published two years after his death, is more interesting and ambitious than his best-selling "Games People Play," and it reveals, as that book did not, both the modest value and the profound limitations of Berne's creation, Transactional Analysis.
>
> (p. 44)

Berne's own words described the book as follows:

> In order to say Hello, you first get rid of all the trash which has accumulated in your head ever since you came home from the maternity ward, and then you recognize that this particular Hello will never happen again. It may take years to learn how to do this ... Mostly, this book is about the trash: the things people are doing to each other instead of saying Hello.
>
> (p. 4)

In our view, the book seems to articulate Berne's existential views and dilemma. In his words, "This childlike question, so apparently artless and free of the profundity expected of scientific inquiry, really contains within itself all the basic questions of human living and all the fundamental problems of the social sciences" (Berne, 1972, p. 3). In trying to grasp the meaning of why people talk to each other, Berne wrote that "to say Hello is to see the other person, to be aware of him as a phenomenon, to happen to him and to be ready for him to happen to you" (p. 4). To do this, one needs to move through "the trash" (p. 4), as Berne described those rather dark aspects of being human. In our reading of Berne, we take his words as a sort of plea that he makes to the practitioner to make space within himself to receive his patient so that the two can eventually greet each other.

The book proceeds in Part I with an introduction to transactional analysis through a vignette about a patient who is nearing the end of his life and the interactions he has with his fellow patients. Berne then reflected on the subtleties of a handshake and on friendship.

The theory is introduced in Chapter 2 with an overview of the foundations of transactional analysis: structural analysis, transactional analysis, time structuring, and scripts,

> This book provides a much more comprehensive outline of script theory, and in Part II, entitled "Parental Programing," Berne (1972) explained that "each person decides in early childhood how he will live and how he will die, and that plan, which he carries around in his head wherever he goes, is called his script" (p. 31). In this section, the first chapter, called "Human Destiny," provides a more detailed understanding of script through a number of vignettes. This is followed by Berne likening the idea of script to Greek drama and Greek myth with a well-defined outcome.

> The following quote demonstrates Berne's (1972) skepticism and makes us wonder just what he was carrying around in his own head so near his untimely death. At the same time, we appreciate that there is an honesty and vulnerability in the statement:

> The patient fights being a winner because he is not in treatment for that purpose, but only to be made into a braver loser. This is natural enough, since if he becomes a braver loser, he can follow his script more comfortably, whereas if he becomes a winner he has to throw away all or most of his script and start over, which most people are reluctant to do.
>
> (p. 32)

This section continues with an elaboration of script theory told through myths and fairy tales; we note throughout Berne's writing his skill at making the theory come to life through examples that people understand, although some of the language has not stood the test of time and would currently be considered offensive.

Further chapters follow the chronology of how the script is formed, including prenatal influences, early developments, and the "plastic years" (p. 100) between 2 and 6 years of age. Here, Berne (1972) introduced the idea of a "Thinking Martian," which refers to a being who "has to tell it like it is" (p. 40). Further chapters define the apparatus of script such as the payoff and parental patterning and script equipment, which Berne described as "the nuts and bolts from which the script apparatus is built, a do-it-yourself party kit supplied by the parents and partly by the child himself" (p. 128).

Throughout most of the book, Berne (1972) used the name "Jeder" (p. 65) to represent "every human being in every soil or clime" (p. 65). He takes the reader through the developmental stages to Chapter 10, poignantly entitled "Maturity and Death." We can see the influence of Eric Erikson on Berne, and in this book, he paid tribute to Erikson as the "most active psychoanalyst in making systematic studies of the human life cycle from birth to death" (p. 58).

It is poignant to read Berne's view on life expectancy and script because he suggested that individuals whose parents died young will be influenced by their own view of their life expectancy. Berne's relatively early death might well have been influenced by his parents' limited longevity.

In writing about the posthumous scene, Berne (1972) appeared to write of himself as Jeder in a success script:

> Jeder has built up a large organization, or left a large body of work, or a lot of children and grandchildren, and he knows that his life production will survive him and that those connected with it will see him to his grave.
>
> (p. 196)

Chapter 10 also includes Berne's view on the testament and how this might relate to a person's script payoff: "Whatever the person's fantasies about what will happen after his death, his will or his posthumous papers offer the last chance for a payoff" (p. 198). What is evident from Berne's posthumous papers is an ongoing lively engagement with the theory and development of transactional analysis, a positive payoff indeed.

Parts III and IV further elaborate on the script in action and the script in clinical practice. In Part V, Berne (1972) answered objections that had been raised about the theory of script from various points of view (spiritual, philosophical, rational, doctrinal), which he wrote can be religious or psychoanalytic.

> The psychoanalytic objections are Jesuitical ones. As a doctrine, script analysis is not independent of or irrelevant to psychoanalysis, it is an extension of it, and hence is regarded by some as anti-analytic and as, in effect, not paganism, but a heresy within the doctrine itself.
>
> (p. 399)

Berne continued to answer empirical, developmental, and clinical objections in a similar way, laying out the objections and answering as to how script theory overcomes them. In his answer to the clinical objection that the patient cannot be cured by accessing conscious material alone, he wrote:

> There is no proscription against the script analyst dealing with unconscious material (that is, some of the primal derivatives of the original castration fear and the original Oedipal rage) if he is equipped to do so. And he will do so, because, of course, it is these very experiences which form the basic protocol for the script.
>
> (p. 404)

In his article "What Do You Say If You Don't Say 'Unconscious'? Dilemmas Created for Transactional Analysts by Berne's Shift Away from the Language of Unconscious Experience," Cornell (2008) described some of his personal conversations with those who had known Berne and had attended the San Francisco Seminars.

> Claude Steiner (personal communication, October 12, 2006) wrote that Berne's definitive statement on the matter was that unconscious was a PA [psychoanalytic] concept that should be used carefully and conscientiously (as should other PA concepts such as masochism or transference) in the fully psychoanalytic meaning—namely "dynamically repressed unconscious"—rather than all the obvious biological processes that are indeed out of awareness, but not unconscious in the PA sense. Scripts were also not unconscious in the PA sense but merely often (but not always) out of awareness.
>
> (p. 95)

Berne, ever the self-proclaimed scientist, completed his extraordinary final book with two chapters, one concerning methodological problems in which he warned against the Procrustean tendency to try to make the patient fit the data, the other offering checklists recommended by his colleagues at the San Francisco Seminars. He strongly advocated that clinicians listen to the patient to get the idea of their script, only making inferences with verification from the patient, and offered a conceptual grid to use in standing up to methodological questions.

The final chapter of *What Do You Say After You Say Hello?* culminates in a collection of checklists that had been recommended by colleagues Claude Steiner, Martin Groder, and Stephen Karpman. There is an extensive script checklist, which could be used as a psychiatric interview, followed by a condensed checklist that Berne suggested should be used not instead of a full psychiatric interview but as an adjunct. Finally, there is a therapy checklist designed to be used as a quantitative way of estimating the efficacy of the questions. There are 40 questions altogether, and it was thought that the patient was cured if they could answer yes to all of them.

Prior to the Glossary, there is an Appendix. Much like the list of suggestions that Berne wrote at the end of *Principles of Group Treatment*, Berne's (1972) stated intention was as follows: "These few suggestions are offered out of courtesy, in order to make good on the title of this book and are intended only to stimulate the reader's ingenuity" (p. 441).

Speculation as to what else Berne may have left the transactional analysis community is interesting to consider. Cornell (2020) wrote that

> as I have come to understand it, the origins of transactional analysis and all of its generativity were born in the midst of Berne's narcissistic woundings at the hands of the psychoanalytic establishment and an unresolved ambivalence that I think came to haunt transactional analysis.
>
> (p. 167)

In the July 1970 edition of the *Transactional Analysis Bulletin* (*TAB*), published immediately after Berne's death, Warren Cheney wrote:

> Many of us who knew him well are still under the spell of his loss and, so soon after the event, find it difficult to place his passing into significant perspective. This issue of the *TAB* was the last he and I worked on together. Its content this time thus reflects essentially his choice of material. Hence his name remains on the masthead as Consulting Editor.
>
> (1970, p. 74)

The *Bulletin* then continued with a lengthy transcript of one of the staff–patient staff groups that Berne had run at St. Mary's Hospital in San Francisco.

To end this chapter of our book, we found this paragraph in Gordon's (1972) review of *What Do You Say After You Say Hello?* very suitable for purposes in this book as a whole and as a link to upcoming chapters:

> In short, the system that Eric Berne created has become an important social phenomenon, offering therapy to many thousands and providing advice and counsel to millions more. It is for this reason that faults one may have excused in Berne's books must be examined more closely. The style of the master as well as the substance of his arguments are now hardening into powerful dogma in the minds and work of his followers.
>
> (p. 46)

As you move through the remaining chapters in this book, you will read that transactional analysts worldwide have and are still working to prevent what Gordon (1972) feared: that "TA winds up being a hermetic system—defensively, self-righteously complete, dangerously closed to outside criticism and change" (p. 44).

References

American Psychiatric Association. (1973). *Homosexuality and sexuality orientation disturbance: Proposed change in DSM-I 6th printing, page 44*. APA Document Reference No. 730008.

Arieti, S. (Ed.). (1959). *American handbook of psychiatry*. Basic Books.

Berne, E. (1945, August 1). [Eric Berne Letter to Henry Simon 1945-08-01]. UC San Francisco, Library, Special Collections, Berne (Eric L.) Collections. https://calisphere.org/item/7b30d3c3-17e4-4486-83eb-ada9faf9a031/

Berne, E. (1947). *The mind in action*. Simon and Schuster. https://archive.org/details/in.ernet.dli.2015.191179

Berne, E. (1955). Intuition IV: Primal images and primal judgment. *Psychiatric Quarterly.* 29, 634–658.

Berne, E. (1956, 1 November). [Eric Berne letter to the San Francisco Psychoanalytic Institute]. UC San Francisco, Library, Special Collections, Berne (Eric L.) Collections. https://calisphere.org/item/c21b73b1-4eac-4ab0-823d-b75e54ecb4d5/

Berne, E. (1958a). *Principles of transactional analysis*. UC San Francisco, Library, Special Collections, Berne (Eric L.) Collections. https://calisphere.org/item/6d5d36f8-4fcb-47e5-a4ae-5c2b7b6f6a8b/

Berne, E. (1958b). Transactional analysis: A new and effective method of group therapy. *American Journal of Psychotherapy*. 12:4, 735–743.

Berne, E. (1961). *Transactional analysis in psychotherapy: A systemic individual and social psychiatry*. Grove Press.

Berne, E. (1962a, January 29). [Eric Berne letter to U.S. President John F. Kennedy]. UC San Francisco, Library, Special Collections, Berne (Eric L.) Collections. https://calisphere.org/item/0441d4d5-8def-4358-9bb0-41ffe78f83b5/

Berne, E. (1962b). Research terminology. *Transactional Analysis Bulletin*. 1:3, 24.

Berne, E. (1963). *The structure and dynamics of organizations and groups*. J. B. Lippincott; Grove-Evergreen Press.

Berne, E. (1964). *Games people play: The psychology of human relationships*. Grove Press.

Berne, E. (1965). The public eye. *Transactional Analysis Bulletin*. 4:16, 81.

Berne, E. (1966a). *Principles of group treatment*. Oxford University Press.

Berne, E. (1966b). The public eye. *Transactional Analysis Bulletin*. 5:18, 132.

Berne, E. (1967). *Games people play: A musical comedy in three acts*. Eric Berne Archive, UC San Francisco, Library, Special Collections, Berne (Eric L.) Collections. https://calisphere.org/item/c7cceeb7-ebd5-4444-b7a3-e427831c7d93/

Berne, E. (1968a). *The happy valley*. Grove Press.

Berne, E. (1968b). *Staff–patient staff conferences*. Eric Berne Archive, UC San Francisco, Library, Special Collections, Berne (Eric L.) Collections. https://calisphere.org/item/8cf14477-194b-45fb-b993-69daded52f94

Berne, E. (1970). *Sex in human loving*. Simon and Schuster.

Berne, E. (1971). *A layman's guide to psychiatry and psychoanalysis*. Penguin. (Original work published 1957)

Berne, E. (1972). *What do you say after you say hello? The psychology of human destiny*. Grove Press.

Berne, E. (1953/1977a). Concerning the nature of communication. In E. Berne, *Intuition and ego states: The origins of transactional analysis* (P. McCormick, Ed.) (pp. 33–65). TA Press. (Original work published 1953)

Berne, E. (1977b). Concerning the nature of diagnosis. In E. Berne, *Intuition and ego states: The origins of transactional analysis* (P. McCormick, Ed.) (pp. 33–65). TA Press. (Original work published 1952)

Berne, E. (1977c). The ego image. In E. Berne, *Intuition and ego states: The origins of transactional analysis* (P. McCormick, Ed.) (pp. 99–119). TA Press. (Original work published 1957)

Berne, E. (1977d). Ego states in psychotherapy. In E. Berne, *Intuition and ego states: The origins of transactional analysis* (P. McCormick, Ed.) (pp. 99–119). TA Press. (Original work published 1957)

Berne, E. (1977e). *Intuition and ego states: The origins of transactional analysis* (P. McCormick, Ed.). TA Press.

Berne, E. (1977f). The nature of intuition. In E. Berne, *Intuition and ego states: The origins of transactional analysis* (P. McCormick, Ed.) (pp. 1–31). TA Press. (Original work published 1949)

Berne, E. (1977g). Primal images and primal judgment. In E. Berne, *Intuition and ego states: The origins of transactional analysis* (P. McCormick, Ed.) (pp. 1–31). TA Press. (Original work published 1955 as Intuition IV: Primal images and primal judgment)

Berne, E. (2010). *A Montreal childhood* (T. Berne, Ed.). Editorial Jeder.

Bucci, W. (2011). The interplay of subsymbolic and symbolic processes in psychoanalytic treatment: It takes two to tango—But who knows the steps, who's the leader? The choreography of the psychoanalytic interchange. *Psychoanalytic Dialogues.* 21:1, 45–54. https://doi.org/10.1080/10481885.2011.545326

Cheney, W. D. (1970). Eric Berne 1910–1970. *Transactional Analysis Bulletin.* 9:35, 73–74.

Cornell, W. F. (2008). What do you say if you don't say "unconscious"?: Dilemmas created for transactional analysts by Berne's shift away from the language of unconscious experience. *Transactional Analysis Journal.* 38:2, 93–100. https://doi.org/10.1177/036215370803800202

Cornell, W. F. (2020). Transactional analysis and psychoanalysis: Overcoming the narcissism of small differences in the shadow of Eric Berne. *Transactional Analysis Journal.* 50:3, 164–178. https://doi.org/10.1080/03621537.2020.1771020

Drescher, J. (2015). Out of DSM: Depathologizing homosexuality. *Behavioral Science.* 5:4, 565–575. www.ncbi.nlm.nih.gov/pmc/articles/PMC4695779/

Federn, P. (1934). The awakening of the ego in dreams. *International Journal of Psychoanalysis.* 15, 296–301.

Federn, P. (1952). *Ego psychology and the psychoses* (E. Weiss, Ed.). Basic Books. (Original work published 1934)

Freud, S. (1949). *An outline of psychoanalysis.* Norton.

Gordon, H. S. (1972, 1 October). [Review of the book *What do you say after you say hello? The psychology of human destiny*, by Eric Berne]. *New York Times Book Review.* 44.

Gregg, G. (n.d.). [Eric Berne memorial article]. UC San Francisco, Library, Special Collections, Berne (Eric L.), Collections. https://calisphere.org/item/134f6ff4-d1f4-4d53-9e35-ef2214e149fd

Grove Press. (1964). Brochure for *Games people play: The psychology of human relationships*, by Eric Berne. UC San Francisco, Library, Special Collections, Berne (Eric L.) Collections. https://calisphere.org/item/fa08bcc9-6965-4894-b82f-ca89b49bfbc7/

Hartlaub, P. (2015/2019, 9 May). San Francisco during World War II: A city that sacrificed. *San Francisco Chronicle Vault.* (Original work published 2015). www.sfchronicle.com/oursf/article/Our-SF-The-end-of-World-War-II-and-a-city-that-6237046.php

Heller, G. C. (1967). [Review of the book *Principles of group treatment* by Eric Berne]. *The British Journal of Psychiatry.* 113:497, 458. https://doi.org/10.1192/bjp.113.497.458

Lieberman, M. A., Yalom, I., & Miles, M. (1973). *Encounter groups: First facts.* Basic Books.

Papowitz, E. B. (1967). Games people play. By Eric Berne. *American Journal of Psychoanalysis.* 27:2, 218–219.

Penfield, W. (1954). *Epilepsy and the functional anatomy of the human brain.* Little, Brown and Co.

Publications (1964). *Transactional Analysis Bulletin.* 3:9, 112.

Simon and Schuster. (1947, 13 November). [Letter announcing publication of *The Mind in Action*]. UC San Francisco, Library, Special Collections, Berne (Eric. L.) Collections. https://calisphere.org/item/109bf760-71e8-49f4-8081-7d104a3f70e2/

South, J. (1968). Games people play. On *Introspect.* Capitol.

Steiner, C. M. (2010). Eric Berne's politics: "The great pyramid. *Transactional Analysis Journal.* 40:3–4, 212–216. https://doi.org/10.1177/036215371004000306

Stern, D. B. (2003). *Unformulated experience: From dissociation to imagination in psychoanalysis.* Analytic Press.

Strupp, H. H. (2001). Implications of the empirically supported treatment movement for psychoanalysis. *Psychoanalytic Dialogues.* 11:4, 605–619. https://doi.org/10.1080/10481881109348631

Thomas, G. W. (1943). Group psychotherapy: A review of the recent literature. *Psychosomatic Medicine.* 5, 166–180.

Weiss, E. (1950). *Principles of psychodynamics.* Grune and Stratton.

Chapter 2

Growth, Challenge, and Expansion of the Theory

Keeping in mind Gordon's (1972) review of *What Do You Say After You Say Hello* (Berne, 1972), with its cautionary tone regarding the potential for transactional analysis to become "an hermetically sealed system" (p. 44), this chapter examines the burgeoning popularity of TA in the 1950s and 1960s. Imagine yourself at the beginning of this era with the excitement over this new treatment.

It was in the early 1950s that Eric Berne invited his close friend and colleague David Kupfer to join him in supervising a social worker. Gradually, the two of them invited others to join.

This became what was called "the Seminar." The attendance for the next year or so ranged from 5 to 15 people. Gradually, Berne began to present his ideas about the structure of the personality and the subsequent materials in TA. Except for the book on group techniques, every chapter in Berne's books was thoroughly rehashed, edited, and changed in this first seminar. Later, for personal reasons, Berne decided to commute to San Francisco and start another seminar there (Kupfer, 1971, p. 62).

As described in our previous chapter, Berne had been running weekly public seminars at the Mount Zion Hospital in San Francisco. When asked if these could be held after working hours so more people could attend, Berne ran them on Tuesday evenings from his office. The first meeting was held in 1958, and within six months, the attendees had risen from 6 to over 40.

In another six months, the rising numbers and the variety in attendees' level of knowledge meant that it soon became too unwieldy to run in Berne's office. Therefore, it was decided that an organization should be established. It was called the San Francisco Social Psychiatry Seminars (SFSPS) and eventually formed the basis of today's International Transactional Analysis Association (ITAA). At that time, it was important to the founders that care was taken to avoid titles like "institute" or "society" because those were considered to be pretentious (Berne, 1963, p. 45).

Dr. Kenneth Everts, the first president of the ITAA after Berne's death, was quoted as saying, "It was the first time in my psychiatric practice that I had found a psychiatrist that would take in nurses, social workers, [and] probation officers and I thought wow!" (Jorgensen & Jorgensen, 1984, p. 164).

There was, indeed, openness in the seminars to anyone who could learn and apply transactional analysis. Yet, soon the design of the seminars was changed so that there would be an introductory course entitled a "101" and advanced seminars "202" for those attendees more familiar with TA. Attendees of the 202 were required to have a degree in medicine or the social sciences or to be registered for advanced study at a recognized university. Here, we see the beginnings of the tiered structure of the current TA community worldwide.

Numbers grew, and several people devoted time and energy to the seminars, something that Jorgensen and Jorgensen (1984) likened to a "crusade" (p. 171). The Jorgensens were a couple who had attended a TA family therapy group in Carmel and later wrote *Eric Berne: Master Gamesman. A Transactional Biography*. They depicted Berne as a complex character, having interviewed his wives, friends, and colleagues. Not everyone appreciated their book. A critical review suggested that it would be enjoyed by gossipers and that they placed too much emphasis on the reports from Berne's first wife (Wax & Knapp, 1985, p. 236).

In 1960, with an ever-increasing number of participants, it became necessary for financial considerations to be on a more formal footing, and the seminars became a nonprofit educational corporation. Before this time, any funds that had accumulated from the fees of those attending were absorbed by the fostering of a young fatherless boy in Crete who was referred to as "George, our sponsored orphan in Crete" ("George," 1962, p. 3).

In 1962, the first *Transactional Analysis Bulletin* (*TAB*) was produced with the purpose of "keeping interested parties current with the scientific, educational and personal activities of the San Francisco Social Psychiatry Seminars" ("Volume 1," 1962, p. 2), and the SFSPS was granted tax-exempt status.

Nine volumes of the *Transactional Analysis Bulletin* were published quarterly in January, April, July, and October each year from 1962 to 1970. Each one states the purpose of the *Bulletin*, where contributors should send their offerings of "personal and organizational notes, letters to the editor, brief accounts of clinical, scientific, or teaching activities, and short summaries of newly discovered transactional games or other original observations" ("Contributors," 1962, p. 2). There is also information regarding subscriptions and a list of directors and at-large members.

Throughout the nine volumes, a phenomenal range of applications demonstrated how transactional analysis was being practiced. The manic excitement of the times is evident. The contents page of each *TAB* lists a range of news, the scientific proceedings where topics of the advanced seminars are listed, articles on social dynamics, clinical notes, theory, an illustrative situation, and other activities. (All the *Transactional Analysis Bulletins* can be accessed through the Eric Berne Archive collection at www.ericbernearchives.org.)

In the *TAB*, the illustrative situations or "living problems," as they were called, is where we are introduced for the first time to Cyprian St. Cyr, Berne's *nom de plume* (which we referred to in Chapter 1). In future issues for the *Bulletin*, we meet other characters, including St. Cyr's friend Dr. Horsley and St. Cyr's family members. Berne's practice of using pseudonyms was evident from his student days, when he wrote for the McGill medical undergraduate journal in various voices, including Count Lennard Gandalac and Ramsbottom Horseley. It is unclear why Berne chose to do this. It might be an example of his quirkiness, or perhaps he felt he could take more risks by writing in that way.

For example, in the Cyprian St. Cyr voice, Berne could more subtly encourage people to think about the power of transactional analysis and reinforce a message while maintaining seriousness in the seminars in discussing how TA was used in casework and groups. The stories of these characters serve almost like parables in ancient religious texts. They offer stories by which teaching is illustrated. For example, Cyprian St. Cyr wrote of one of the 12 children of Snodgrass, who came to talk to R. Horsley, the Sage of the Ozarks. You can also see here the precursor of Berne's (1972) posthumous book *What Do You Say After You Say Hello?*

> "Why do you think I've lost my zest for life?" he asked one evening.
> "It's because you don't know how to say 'Hello'" replied Horseley.
> "Oh, I know how to say 'Hello,'" protested Snodgrass. "I know just how to con people when I say 'Hello,' and everybody likes me."
> "Do you know how to look at grass?" asked Horseley
> "Funny you should ask that. Just the other day I was lying in a field and for the first time since I was a boy I really saw the grass."
> "Were you conning the grass?"
> "No that's just it."
> "Well, it's as hard to say 'Hello' as it is to see grass," said Horseley.
> "Come back in five years, after you've learned to say 'Hello,' and we'll talk about what you do after that."
> Question: "Which is harder, to say 'Hello' or to see grass?"
>
> (St. Cyr, 1965, p. 80)

After the publication of *Transactional Analysis in Psychotherapy* (Berne, 1961), many people who attended the San Francisco Social Psychiatry Seminars reported being astounded by Berne's new ideas. Many traveled some distance and would take the theory back to where they were working. Pat Crossman, working in England for the National Health Service, saw Berne's ideas in this 1961 book as a powerful way through the challenges that mental health workers faced in the United Kingdom. She is quoted in the Jorgensen's biography as follows:

> I read it while I was working in a therapeutic community where all hell was breaking loose. Doctors were attacking each other; everything was in uproar. I took my book on Transactional Analysis and began sharing it with patients, much to the consternation of my colleagues and superiors. That's when I realized it was so powerful.
>
> (Jorgensen & Jorgensen, 1984, p. 167)

Pat Crossman met Berne in 1964 and attended the seminars until 1969. She was one of the women considered to be part of what came to be known as "the inner circle" (Jorgensen & Jorgensen, 1984, p. 168). She acted as a co-therapist and as a locum group therapist for Berne when he was traveling.

Although the seminars were an important breeding ground for developing ideas around TA theory, the interpersonal dynamics were more complex and uncomfortable for some. This is especially highlighted by the women who attended. Sexism abounded generally in that era, and the seminars were no exception. The women who attended the seminars were referred to as "the dancing girls" or "dance hall girls" (English, 2010, p. 206). It is evident from reports (Crossman cited in Cornell, 2008, p. 94; James cited in Jorgensen & Jorgensen, 1984, p. 200) that these strong and forthright women could somehow discern what they could learn from Berne and others in the seminars and differentiate it from the insulting attitude and lecherous behavior that prevailed toward women at the time. Muriel James said this:

> For about two years I felt furious at the seminars because women were expected to be "dancing girls" and not much else. I had decided I wanted to learn from Berne whether or not I would be listened to ... However, it was interesting being around a genius in spite of the games, or maybe, because of them ... Berne encouraged the excitement of sibling rivalry ("I'm brighter than you") with the small group of men, because it made him feel important.
> (James, in Jorgensen & Jorgensen, 1984, p. 200)

Debate and rivalry are close companions, a debate being the process of examining reasons for and against and rivalry being an effort to win. Berne's interest in poker playing and in mathematical game theory may indicate that the distinction at the seminars between debate and rivalry was blurred; contention, it seems, was considered a sport in the San Francisco Social Psychiatry Seminars.

The distinction Berne made between mathematical game analysis (MGA), also popular at the time, and transactional game analysis (TGA) was "MGA states what he might do to win, TGA says what he will do to lose" ("Research Terminology," 1962, p. 24).

There is a consensus that Berne developed his thinking out of his own frustration with what was being taught at the time in psychoanalytic training. Berne, as well as being extremely intelligent, was impatient for results and believed that therapists should have cure as the focus. Making progress was not enough, and he was not alone in his frustration with the way that psychoanalysis was being taught and practiced. Fanita English, a seminar attendee, had also grown tired of psychoanalytic methods. She referred to misogyny in psychoanalytic practice and impatience at the slow process. She was given *Transactional Analysis in Psychotherapy* by a colleague.

> Jack and I weren't exactly friends, and he gave me the book with the disparaging remark "You'll like this, it's from someone who criticizes psychoanalysis like you do." So I took it, very sceptically. But once I started reading, I couldn't stop all night long. This "transactional analysis" was revolutionary for me.
> (Röhl, 2021, p. 111)

After meeting Berne for the first time, when he made a lewd proposal to English (English, 2010, p. 205), she kept him physically at arm's length while continuing to enjoy his ideas and offer her own appropriate challenges to the theory, which in time he came to appreciate.

English was not the only TA person who felt concerned at the lascivious behavior of some of the San Francisco seminar attendees. One person we interviewed remembered with regret that some of Berne's followers would spread the word of TA in a fashion that promoted TA as a system where you might "get rich quick and have fancy cars and women on your arm." English wrote of being invited to dinner with Berne and his four "Horsemen" (English, 2010, p. 206), Berne's favorite male colleagues from the seminars, and of being the subject of many off-color in-jokes between the men, with Berne joining in rather than supporting her as his guest.

What is particularly striking in the issues of the *TAB* is both the excitement of the era and the level of certainty with which Berne and the attendees spoke and wrote. In response to the invitation to write about game discoveries, new games were constantly being paraded and discussed, such as, "Pay Back—An Asthma Game" (Matson, 1968). It seems that almost every aspect of human suffering could be categorized in game theory with a heavy emphasis on the need for behavioral change. Little or no attention was given to the meaning of the suffering or the possible unconscious motivation of games. The hopefulness in cure and speedy results meant that assumptions were made that awareness of a person's unhelpful habits could be easily accessed and that relief would be found in the new knowledge. Underneath the vocabulary used in game theory lies what could be termed a paranoid vulnerability (W. F. Cornell, personal communication, June 10, 2022), indicated by the use of American terms connected with the mafia: con, gimmick, and racket.

What is also evident is the breadth of TA application. The *Transactional Analysis Bulletin* contains many early articles on a vast range of subjects, for example, "The Face Game: Transactional Analysis Applied to Zen" (Harding, 1967) and news on various groups across the globe. In 1966, there were eight groups in California, groups in 30 other states in America, as well as groups in Canada, Costa Rica, and England.

There were many examples of people grappling with the kinds of questions which we as transactional analysis practitioners, teachers, and students ask today.

> Pat Crossman solved the vexing question of how to diagnose the Child acting like a Parent, from a true Parental ego state. The Child acting like a Parent is saying, "How'm I doing?" while the true Parent doesn't care how he's doing, he just says whatever it is he has to say no matter how poorly thought out or ineffectual it is, or on the other hand, sees that the offspring are taken care of no matter whether others like it or not. Berne summarized this by saying that the Child acting like a Parent is a three-handed transaction agent, respondent and actual or fantasized onlooker; while the true Parent's transactions are two-handed: agent and respondent.
>
> (Steiner, 1967a, p. 67)

The *Transactional Analysis Bulletins* show many attendees working together and across different branches of the San Francisco Social Psychiatry Seminars. There is also evidence of how transactional analysis could be combined with conjoint family therapy, behavior modification, and Gestalt therapy. The rich discussions and explorations as well as the rivalry and competition that was within the seminars also operated between transactional analysis and the wider psychotherapeutic world.

In light of Gordon's (1972) caution, it is unfortunate that there was too often an attitude at the Seminar that TA was superior. For example, there is an instance in which a seminar presenter used TA and techniques from Satir's conjoint family therapy approach. Satir had previously been invited to present her theory at The Seminar in 1962, and three years later, Donald Young described his work using Satir's approach.

> Young presented a taped interview with a father, mother, daughter 17, and son 10. He skillfully "captured" the son and isolated him from the enveloping games of the other members. He then dissected out single transactions concerning the boy's behavior at meal times. Young did not use TA and his approach was more like that of Satir. It was felt that the extrapolative value of the experience to the family would have been greater with explicit use of TA and game analysis.
>
> (Young, 1965, p. 48)

In the same year, TA and Gestalt therapy were being considered to be useful alongside each other, as they were believed to have much resemblance. At the Sixth Summer Conference in 1968, a discussion between Jack Dusay and Fritz Perls was offered. The idea was for them to discuss the similarities and differences between TA and Gestalt. The discussion was reported as Fritz Perls treating Jack Dusay as a patient instead of a discussant. The following similarities and differences were reported, with the audience "contributing what the chairman called 'absurdities and obscenities'" ("TA and Gestalt Therapy," 1968, p. 79) due to their frustration with the process.

> Two main points of comparison seemed to emerge. One, where TA seeks to interpose the Adult between the Parent and Child to ward off irrational domination and to secure autonomy, Gestalt views the resolution of such internal conflict as a process in which the "underdog" assimilates and "chews up" the "top dog" to achieve an integrated whole. Two, where TA's goal is Adult control for the appropriate expression of feelings, Gestalt's emphasis is upon "emotions as the soul of being" with the goal being "authentic" feelings in the here and now.
>
> (p. 79)

As time went on, the rivalry in the seminars reached new levels, and the four "Horsemen" (English, 2010, p. 206) closest allies of Berne, challenged each other more and more. Steve Karpman, one of the Seminar attendees, described himself this way: "Mostly I would just hold a position and challenge Berne—or rather I would challenge the ideas. I got D's in deportment all through grammar school, acted up dreadfully in medical school. I pride myself on this" (Jorgensen & Jorgensen, 1984, p. 193).

Pat Crossman, in Cornell's (2008) paper, spoke of the unkind atmosphere:

> In 1964 Eric was "small time." In 1969 he was "big time" and famous. And this is what killed him. He was like Sisyphus, always rolling the stone up the mountain but never quite making it. But what happens if he makes it! *Games People Play* [1964] was a runaway best-seller and Eric was on top. That spoils the game. Eric became depressed and very unhappy and some of his disciples were less than kind. I remember in 1967 Jack Dusay and Claude Steiner standing up stating that there was no such thing as the "unconscious." I remember Eric commenting quietly, "Then what about the defenses?"
>
> (p. 94)

Indeed, the *Transactional Analysis Bulletin* reports that Steiner "reviewed the usual meanings of the term unconscious, and concluded that nowadays the term is often used vaguely" (Steiner, 1967b, p. 63). He proposed "a transactional as well as dynamic (repression) explanation is able to account for the phenomena observed by Freud as follows: so-called 'unconscious material' is conscious to the Child and capable of being reported at any time" (p. 63). Repression, as Steiner saw it, was an unwillingness on the part of the Child to report to a Parent. From this position, it was clear that the transactional analyst's job was to "cathect the Adult and have an Adult to Adult conversation about the Child's conscious phantasies or acts" (p. 63).

In his article "What Do You Say If You Don't Say 'Unconscious'? Dilemmas Created for Transactional Analysts by Berne's Shift Away from the Language of Unconscious Experience," Cornell (2008) suggested that Berne was making "an important theoretical challenge" (p. 96) to the way that the unconscious was considered in classical Freudian theory. The Freudian approach saw the unconscious as "the location of regression, irrationality, infantile transference fantasies, and psychopathology" (p. 96). Berne's earlier writings on intuition, as indicated in Chapter 1 of this book, accounted for an unconscious that was not only repressed, that is, one with a capacity for creativity, in line with Bucci's (2011) subsymbolic processes and Stern's (2003) unformulated experience.

The shift from the language of unconscious experience heralded a move in transactional analysis to becoming a decisional theory. This tied in with Berne's emphasis on cure and change. In some ways, this was a refreshing move away from a long-drawn-out psychoanalysis. In other ways, it oversimplified the depth, breadth, and complexity that has been developed and appreciated by transactional analysts in more recent times.

The San Francisco Social Psychiatry Seminars, although marred in some ways by the competition and rivalry, were a rich breeding ground in which Berne's foundational thinking could be expanded. Seminar attendees were encouraged in their own thinking and development of the theory. We still appreciate today some of the classical transactional analysis ideas that were honed in the seminars, including such building blocks of transactional analysis as ego states, life positions, transactions, script theory, strokes, rackets, and games. These were expanded in those early days by many seminar participants, such as Dusay, Ernst, Steiner, English, and Karpman.

The October 1967, the *Transactional Analysis Bulletin*, published the proceedings of the Fifth Summer Conference, which included a lively discussion of a paper produced by Thomas Harris with Jack Dusay as the discussant. The paper was entitled "What Is OK?" (Harris, 1967). Harris challenged the orthodox view that "each infant starts as a prince, with the 'OK-OK' position." He proposed instead that "every infant takes an 'I'm not-OK' position early in life" (p. 94).

With discussion from Dusay and from the floor, there was a possible synthesis of these two views proposing:

> There is at some time or other the basic human feeling of "OK-ness." Whether this is in the womb, or while experiencing stroking with mother, or in the common experience of human growth, all of us feel OK sometimes. No matter how much Parental ambiguity there is, we also know that OK is the way to feel. All decisions settling for less than OK, whenever taken, are revisible [sic]. Regardless of when or how a prince's career was interrupted, he can pick it up again when his Adult chooses to do so.
>
> (p. 96)

As described earlier, there was a fervent emphasis on change and the assumption that the client had the capacity to choose different options. Even with the expansion of the theory throughout these years, the emphasis on successful therapy outcomes indicated by behavioral change in the most expedient way has remained the cornerstone of transactional analysis. Through Berne's (1966, pp. 233–247) therapeutic operations, the therapist's job was to provide insight such that clients' pre-conscious motivations became known, and they were subsequently freed from their defenses.

To understand the therapeutic stance at this time and put it into context today, it is helpful to consider Stark (1999), who differentiated three modes of therapeutic action. These are as follows:

1 The interpretive perspective of classical psychoanalytic theory;
2 The corrective-provision (or deficiency-compensation) perspective of self-psychology and those object relations theories emphasizing the "absence of good";
3 The relational (or interactive) perspective of contemporary psychoanalytic theory and those object relations theories emphasizing the "presence of bad." (p. 6)

Up to the 1969 issues of the *TAB*, the primary mode of therapeutic action was interpretive. In the mid- and late 1960s, we begin to see a shift in emphasis with the introduction of redecision therapy and reparenting and a move toward the corrective-provision mode of psychology. These two approaches will be covered in more depth in subsequent chapters.

The redecision model, developed in the mid-1960s by Robert and Mary Goulding, became very popular. They offered intense psychotherapy groups, which ran over several days. Graham Barnes (1995), who had become weary of the popularization of TA after the publication of *Games People Play*, arrived at the Goulding's institute two weeks after Eric Berne died:

> We were changing how we listened, and we were learning to listen and to see. Bob and Mary insisted on following and not leading the client. They demonstrated how to ask questions and how to keep the therapist's interpretations tentative with "I have a hunch" statements. They showed and taught effective psychotherapy procedures such as how to change suicide ideation.
>
> (p. 10)

Redecision therapy emphasized the revisiting of earlier childhood scenes to empower the Child against injunctions from their parent or parent figures. The Gouldings referred to Berne's (1961, p. 54) image of a pile of coins, which acted as a metaphor for wounds in childhood. Once the pile is skewed, it can no longer straighten itself but goes on being skewed. "As therapists, we are interested in the Child decisions that still 'skew the pile' for our patients, and our therapy is based on creating a therapeutic environment in which patients may redecide from the Child ego state" (Goulding & Goulding, 1976, p. 41).

In the July 1969 *Transactional Analysis Bulletin*, there was the beginning of a discussion of the treatment of schizophrenic patients. Berne proudly introduced Jacqui Schiff as guest editor of the July 1969 *TAB*:

> Freud said that for all conditions other than the transference neuroses, psychoanalysis was more or less unsuitable, and I, being a good Freudian, besides having tried it for other conditions, take his word for it. Hence transactional analysis, which is designed for "other conditions" and has shown some effectiveness in this respect. One of the other conditions is schizophrenia.
>
> (Berne, 1969, p. 45)

Berne referenced his own analyst, Paul Federn, who, Berne suggested, like the Schiffs, had invited a schizophrenic patient to live at his house. In actuality, Federn's treatment of his patient was quite different to the work that Schiff was doing. Federn (1952) wrote that there were periods of time in his own home when "We tolerated her emotional outbreaks, refusal of food when she feared poison, endless walking in her room during the nights, excessive smoking and recounting of her hallucinatory woes. She was unrestricted, although we knew this meant risking her suicide" (p. 123). And although Federn disallowed his patient from returning home, he influenced her mother and her brothers to "permit her to live by herself" (p. 124).

In that same issue of the *TAB*, Berne (1969, p. 47) described Schiff as a "sound transactional analyst," with his pride in her work evident. The *Bulletin* consisted of an outline of the theory and methodology of this new form of treatment, several patient autobiographies, and a summary report from Aaron Schiff, who was described as a layman with an intimate knowledge of the reparenting technique.

What was evident in the expansion of transactional analysis theory to that point was the vehement commitment to the client being able to revise their script with the help of the well-meaning analyst, either through interpretation or by providing corrective interventions. What stands out again is the apparent lack of curiosity about the client's internal experience.

Cornell (2022) made an important point that Berne, in his commitment to the idea that a cure for schizophrenia was to be found through transactional analysis, may have gone too far:

> Reading Federn's work suggests how Berne may have been so rapidly and rather unquestioningly enthusiastic about Schiff's work at his first encounter with it. The Schiffian model, however, did not breathe and listen with the phenomenological regard and subtly that Federn appears to have brought to his schizophrenic patients.
>
> (p. 43)

Throughout her attendance at the seminars, Fanita English frequently challenged Berne's views and was able to maintain curiosity regarding clients' and, indeed, her own subjective experience. English's curiosity and openness to examining her own processes is refreshing to read as far back as 1969. Her first publication was "Episcript and the 'Hot Potato' Game" (English, 1969). Her addendum to that article, entitled, "I'll Show You Yet (ISYY) or They'll Be Sorry They Kicked Me" (English, 1970) demonstrated English's lively curiosity and capacity for inquiry in her taking seriously a young man who said he was "not consciously aware of manipulating" and remembered "terror about the reality situation, guilt and penitence" (p. 14). He reported these experiences alongside "'inappropriate' feelings of triumph" (p. 15), which English also took seriously in the spirit of inquiry. She understood the feeling of triumph to be in the second-order structure of the ego states whereby the Adult in the Child acted in a "life-preserving" way "in the face of terrible survival odds" (p. 15). This example indicates a shift toward honoring the complexity of unconscious motivations in game analysis and a move away from a more simplistic assumption that conscious awareness in games is easily attained.

English died in 2022, aged 105. She left the TA community with a remarkable body of work in which she continued to expand TA theory, challenge assumptions, and pioneer ways forward for us to continue to develop. English's ideas were fresh, innovative, and forerunners of many theories being developed today.

English credited Berne with curing her of her writing phobia, and many of her writings were self-revelatory in a way that educates readers to normalize and depathologize their own and others' defensive patterns. Her "Episcript and the 'Hot Potato' Game" article was published after a series of stand-offs between her and Berne, who insisted that everyone presenting at conferences should offer a written paper. Fanita first presented the workshop and then sent him the paper:

> I had written on extra thin copy paper to annoy him, because I knew he hated it when articles were typed "on toilet paper," as he called such paper. I added a note to my text: "Here's what I still owe you." I expected him to throw the sheets away or call me angrily. Instead, he had his secretary copy the text neatly, on thick paper, and added helpful comments in red in the margins.
>
> (Röhl, 2021, p. 118)

The proceedings of the Seventh Annual Conference held in August 1969 show how TA was expanding as well as the beginnings of conference participants questioning each other. A panel was held on the subject of touching, with Joseph Cassius, a former boxer and judo teacher, advocating that postural, structural changes in the body often led to personality changes. In the *TAB*, it is evident that others were grappling with this and advocating that as long as the decision to touch was made through the Adult, then it was justified. Solon Samuels stated in a reproving tone, "The Adult in a therapist always finds a way to justify what he is doing. This is a game called Kosher: if you can prove it's Kosher, anything goes" (Cassius et al., 1969, p. 89). Berne concluded the panel with the statement "TA is a talking treatment and the basic question is, 'Is the contract for treatment or a trip? If it can be proven that touching is going to cure someone of something, fine; otherwise, it's a 'trip'" (p. 91). We are starting to see here the questioning of the psychotherapist's motivation.

Prior to Berne's death in July 1970, English had arranged to talk with him about another paper she was writing expanding on his theory of rackets. Unfortunately, Berne died before they could talk. However, English was invited by Franklin Ernst to submit the paper, which was split into two due to its length and published in the newly formed *Transactional Analysis Journal* (*TAJ*) (English, 1971, 1972). The creation of the *Transactional Analysis Journal* had been planned by Berne before his death because the editors of the *Transactional Analysis Bulletin* had agreed that a journal would be taken more seriously.

The first issue of the *Transactional Analysis Journal* was a memorial issue to Berne, with many touching articles from people who had known him and appreciated his impact on their lives and work. In the fourth issue, English's article on rackets was published. It is clear from it that English, who had challenged Berne about his theory on many occasions, had been developing a theory that was much less devoted to finding out what was wrong with clients that needed to be fixed than to understanding the unconscious motivations that led clients to hold on to their rackets or scripts. There was still an emphasis on behavioral change but increasingly a much more subtle approach to appreciating the formation of the defenses. Over the decades following

Berne's death, English consistently and persistently modified her ideas and shared them through articles and her wide travels to run workshops.

As more and more people became interested in training as transactional analysts, an elaborate procedure was established for certification. There was an extensive curriculum, that required candidates to have adequate knowledge of gross anatomy, general biology, physiology, pharmacology, somatic treatment, child development, and psychology, including perception, which affects conditioning, mental testing, experimental and statistical methods, psychopathology, psychoanalysis, somatic illnesses, prognosis, and referral procedures ("Minimal Basic Science Curriculum," 1969, pp. 108–110).

The schools of TA that were evolving included the classical school, in which the treatment focus centered on the use of the power in the Adult ego state; the redecision school, in which the focus was on empowering the Child ego state; and the Cathexis school, in which the focus was on remodeling the Parent ego state. As the rivalry in the seminars continued, so it did between these approaches and the institutes where people were trained. In the early 1970s, trainees were expected to have a person from each primary TA school endorse their journey to Clinical Membership certification. This meant that the oral examination was often fraught with members of the examination board representing their favored approach and competing with others whose views differed.

From then on, transactional analysis theory has continued to be reshaped, re-modeled, and expanded, and although competition and rivalry still exist, new developments that have a whole separate methodology are now considered to be approaches rather than schools.

Having set the scene with the history of TA so far, subsequent chapters of this book will consider the original schools of transactional analysis as well as new approaches that have emerged and offer appreciation and critique of each.

References

Barnes, G. (1995). You can always do TA. *Transactional Analysis Journal*. 25:1, 9–13. https://doi.org/10.1177/036215379502500104

Berne, E. (1961). *Transactional analysis in psychotherapy: A systemic individual and social psychiatry*. Grove Press.

Berne, E. (1963). Organizational history of the SFSPS [editorial]. *Transactional Analysis Bulletin*. 2:5, 45.

Berne, E. (1966). *Principles of group treatment*. Oxford University Press.

Berne, E. (1969). Introduction. *Transactional Analysis Bulletin*. 8:31, 45–47.

Berne, E. (1972). *What do you say after you say hello? The psychology of human destiny*. Grove Press.

Bucci, W. (2011). The interplay of subsymbolic and symbolic processes in psychoanalytic treatment: It takes two to tango—But who knows the steps, who's the leader? The choreography of the psychoanalytic interchange. *Psychoanalytic Dialogues*. 21:1, 45–54. https://doi.org/10.1080/10481885.2011.545326

Cassius, J., Karpman, S., Samuels, S., & Zechnich, R. (1969). On touching. *Transactional Analysis Bulletin*. 8:32, 89–91. https://doi.org/10.1080/03621537.2021.2011035

"Contributors." (1962). *Transactional Analysis Bulletin*. 1:1, 2.

Cornell, W. F. (2008). What do you say if you don't say "unconscious"?: Dilemmas created for transactional analysts by Berne's shift away from the language of unconscious experience. *Transactional Analysis Journal*. 38:2, 93–100. https://doi.org/10.1177/036215370803800202

Cornell, W. F. (2022). Schiffian reparenting theory reexamined through contemporary lenses: Comprehending the meanings of psychotic experience. *Transactional Analysis Journal*. 52:1, 40–58. https://doi.org/10.1080/03621537.2021.2011035

English, F. (1969). Episcript and the "hot potato" game. *Transactional Analysis Bulletin*. 8:32, 77–82. https://doi.org/10.1177/036215377100100408

English, F. (1970). I'll show you yet (ISYY) or they'll be sorry they kicked me. *Transactional Analysis Bulletin*. 9:33, 13–15.

English, F. (1971). The substitution factor: Rackets and real feelings. *Transactional Analysis Journal*. 1:4, 27–32. https://doi.org/10.1177/036215377100100408

English, F. (1972). Rackets and real feelings. *Transactional Analysis Journal*. 2:1, 23–25. https://doi.org/10.1177/036215377200200108

English, F. (2010). Personal encounters with a flawed genius: Eric Berne. *Transactional Analysis Journal*. 40:3–4, 205–211. https://doi.org/10.1177/036215371004000305

Federn, P. (1952). *Ego psychology and the psychoses*. Basic Books.

"George." (1962). *Transactional Analysis Bulletin*. 1:1, 3.

Gordon, H. S. (1972, 1 October). [Review of the book *What do you say after you say hello? The psychology of human destiny*, by Eric Berne]. *New York Times Book Review*, Section BR, p. 44.

Goulding, R., & Goulding, M. (1976). Injunctions, decisions, and redecisions. *Transactional Analysis Journal*. 6:1, 41–48. https://doi.org/10.1177/036215377600600110

Harding, D. E. (1967). The face game: Transactional analysis applied to Zen *Transactional Analysis Bulletin*. 6:22, 40–52.

Harris, T. (with Dusay, J.). (1967). What is "OK"? *Transactional Analysis Bulletin*. 6:24, 94–96.

Jorgensen, E. W., & Jorgensen, H. I. (1984). *Eric Berne: Master gamesman. A transactional biography*. Grove Press.

Kupfer, D. (1971). In the beginning .... *Transactional Analysis Journal*. 1:1, 62. https://doi.org/10.1177/036215377100100112

Matson, V. (1968). Pay back—an asthma game. *Transactional Analysis Bulletin*. 7:27, 64–65.

Minimal basic science curriculum for clinical membership in the ITAA. (1969). *Transactional Analysis Bulletin*. 8(32), 108–110.

"Research Terminology." (1962). *Transactional Analysis Bulletin*. 1:3, 24.

Röhl, S. (2021). *Fanita English: A therapist's life and work. From psychoanalysis to transactional analysis and Gestalt therapy*. Herstellung und Verlag. BoD.

Stark, M. (1999). *Modes of therapeutic action: Enhancement of knowledge, provision of experience and engagement in relationship*. Jason Aronson.

St. Cyr, C. (1965). A living problem: "Looking at grass." *Transactional Analysis Bulletin*. 4:16, 80.

Steiner, C. (1967a). The counter-script. *Transactional Analysis Bulletin*. 6:23, 66–67.

Steiner, C. (1967b). Training of professionals and the unconscious.. *Transactional Analysis Bulletin*. 6:23, 63.

Stern, D. B. (2003). *Unformulated experience: From dissociation to imagination in psychoanalysis*. Routledge.

TA and Gestalt therapy. (1968). *Transactional Analysis Bulletin*. 7:28, 79.

"Volume 1." (1962). *Transactional Analysis Bulletin*. 1:1, 2.

Wax, G., & Knapp, W. B. (1985). [Book review: *Eric Berne: Master gamesman*]. *Transactional Analysis Journal*. 15:3, 236–237. https://doi.org/10.1177/036215378501500310

Young, D. (1965). Family therapy. *Transactional Analysis Bulletin*. 65:15, 48.

Chapter 3

Bringing Transactional Analysis Theory into Practice

Complexities Generated by the Emergence of Special Fields of Application

The History and Development of Special Fields of Application

In this chapter, in addition to charting the history and development of the different designated fields of transactional analysis (TA), we wish to recognize the significant contributions to TA theory and development from specialists in counseling, education, and organizational approaches. The theory has benefited significantly from the breadth and depth of what practitioners bring from the fields outside our own field of psychotherapy.

The differentiation between the fields and the potential hierarchy that we see and hear of today originates in a meeting of the San Francisco Social Psychiatry Seminars in 1965 when the new International Transactional Analysis Association was formed and new bylaws and categories of membership were defined.

The differentiation of fields reflects several tensions that we think Berne, in particular, was holding. First, his approach as a psychiatrist, exemplified in his staff-patient staff conferences (1968) showed his clear commitment to a humanistic sensibility and patients' empowerment while, at the same time, he wanted to offer a serious alternative to psychoanalysis.

> The staff–patient staff conference first attacks the comfortable and well-established sociological roles of the "therapist" and "patient" and substitutes a "bilateral contract" with rational exceptions. Everyone is treated as a "person" with equal rights on his own merits.
>
> (Berne, 1968, pp. 11–12)

Yet, with its resounding sales success, the publication of *Games People Play* in 1964 also brought some reviews suggesting that it was oversimplified and superficial. Comments in the *Transactional Analysis Bulletin* (*TAB*) reflected this:

> **Games People Play** is receiving rather favorable reviews in the lay press, and has been on one or two bestseller lists. One result of this has been its treatment

by an Eastern bookseller in advertisements as a "Do-it-yourself" manual in popular psychiatry, something which was not intended, but which the author has no control over.

("Publications," 1964, p. 161)

Soon after this, in 1965, Clinical Membership was described as "a special distinction reserved for those with adequate clinical experience in transactional analysis and an intimate knowledge of its therapeutic application" ("Certificates of Attendance," 1965, p. 42). In addition, a new category of Research Membership was suggested if enough people came forward who could demonstrate an ability to use TA in research projects. It is interesting to note that the timing of these discussions followed so soon after the publication of *Games People Play*. Given this context, we wonder if the formulation of these categories was an expression of the tension described earlier.

Berne made explicit his intention to describe complex psychological phenomena in simple, accessible language, yet his model of training was based on the training models of psychoanalytic institutes and their hierarchical structure.

In July 1966, there were proposals for new bylaws to be considered at the forthcoming summer conference, where Research Membership was given the acronym SM and was

> open to those who have completed an Introductory Course and have in addition 100 hours of authorized advanced training in transactional analysis and have met such other requirement as are set up by the Executive Council and/or the Membership Committee ... They are also entitled to practice transactional analysis in their own specialized fields and to teach authorized courses in transactional analysis to members of their specialized fields.
>
> ("Revised Constitution and By-Laws," 1966, p. 158)

A further tension was outlined by Cornell (2013), who suggested that it was Berne's anxieties and biases that led to transactional analysis psychotherapy being promoted "at the expense of other modes of learning and growth" (p. 8) and that these led to other applications of transactional analysis being viewed as having lower standing. Cornell (2013) described how permission classes that were set up in 1967 by Claude and Ursula Steiner ostensibly conducted what was, in fact, psychotherapy while focusing on the ideas developed by Pat Crossman (1966) of permission and protection. Cornell argued that Berne, due to his own sexual anxiety (p. 8), imposed rules about clients being prescribed these classes if they needed interventions of touch or movement. Cornell questioned what this actually did to the psychotherapists' potency. Others were also asking this question:

> Asked why the techniques used in the permission classes were not used in the orthodox group sessions, the Steiners responded that the classes were designed to be "something special," that at this point the techniques were still being

tested, and that those techniques that show consistent therapeutic effectiveness can be applied more generally.

(Steiner & Steiner, 1968, p. 2)

As efficacious as the permission classes were, they remained as an adjunct to psychotherapy practice and were run by permission specialists who, while having expertise and qualifications of their own, did not have the precise academic credentials required for clinical transactional analysis status.

In just over a year after Berne's death, we started to see more published regarding applications of TA beyond psychotherapy. The October 1971 issue of the *Transactional Analysis Journal* (*TAJ*) began with an editorial by Franklin Ernst highlighting the place of transactional analysis in the field of education. In the same issue, Frazier (1971) wrote:

> Transactional Analysis is not a therapeutic island to be visited only once or twice a week in the small therapy group. Whether teaching or treating, setting limits or giving permission, confronting the student with a problem or helping him make a closure, the principles of Transactional Analysis can serve as useful tools in the classroom setting. TA, in teaching, recreation, and discipline, becomes effective when it is related to those other variables in the present moment, in the here-and-now.
>
> (p. 20)

In 1975, Martin Groder opened his *TAJ* editorial with an enlightened comment:

> This issue is dedicated by the Editorial Board to that soon-to-be-upwardly-mobile group of "second-class" citizens in the ITAA—the Special Fields Members, especially the business, management and organizational development types.
>
> (p. 344)

In a 1978 article in the ITAA newsletter, *The Script*, Joanne Moses argued that as the needs of the world were changing, the ITAA needed to adapt. She focused on the emphasis that the medical and psychological models placed on sickness and cure and advocated that

> a broader view focuses on vitality and the full enjoyment of one's being. Special Fields contracts this kind of life enrichment. It is in this area that I believe where yet unknown careers will develop in the mental health professions. And ITAA with its rapidly growing interest in Special Fields is already there with its training models.
>
> (Moses, 1978, p. 2)

The same acknowledgment of a changing world comes through in a paper written by Otto Altorfer (1977). The point he made is that there was a growing emphasis on linking people's productivity in the workplace with their emotional balance and involvement, aspects that are related to what he called Emotional Job Fitness: "People often succumb to the pressures of organization life. The concept of Emotional Job Fitness investigates these pressures and develops learning models which are designed to support people in staying emotionally balanced" (p. 339).

Again, what comes through in these writings is the idea that the world of emotion, affectivity, and internal balance is no longer the territory of the clinician alone, but that these psychological realities also need to be approached by practitioners active in the organizational domain.

During this era, many practitioners would qualify as certified transactional analysts and then choose to specialize in other areas. Joanne Moses, who had a Ph.D. in education, was the first educator to become a Teaching and Supervising Transactional Analyst.

It is clear from a special Training Standards Committee (TSC) insert in the April 1980 issue of *The Script* that there was a fear that the special fields members (SFM) were actually "wanna-be-therapists" alongside a suspicion that they might conduct clinical work clearly reserved for clinical members. Clear guidelines for oral exams stated that SFM candidates "are not to engage in the clinical practice of psychotherapy" ("Special Training Standards Insert," 1980, p. 5).

This was felt among the special field members as highlighted in a personal communication between Cornell and Clarke (Cornell, 2013) in which Clarke highlighted:

> I wrote the article you mentioned (Clarke, 1981) in an effort to point out that we educators are not unskilled wanna-be-therapists but a parallel set of professionals who use TA principles with a different professional toolbox of methods and with different goals. We believe a build-on-the-health goal is as valuable as the go-for-the-illness one and that both are necessary if TA is to be adequately used in the population at large.
>
> (p. 9)

Servaas van Beekuum, whose help we sought in writing this chapter, emphasized the importance of differentiating between applications of TA and the certifying process.

> The so-called special fields (SF in early literature) were originally meant as fields of application, different from Berne's original application of transactional analysis for psychotherapy. Transactional analysis turned out to be also applicable elsewhere. In kindergartens, high schools, in hospitals, in jails, in lawyer's and GP's practices, etc. In practice, someone can apply transactional analysis in their role as a lawyer. When this person wants to do a certification, s/he can only choose from four options.
>
> (van Beekuum, personal communication, 3 March 2023)

Credentialing Dilemma

In January 1983, it was decided that there would be a new nomenclature for certified transactional analysts in special fields and that people certifying with a specialization in education or organizational work would be certified as a transactional analyst with a clinical, educational, or organizational specialty. It was not until 1987 that the counseling specialty was added by the European Association for Transactional Analysis (EATA).

Soon after, another potential tension arose as the ITAA considered the credentialing advice from the National Commission of Health Certifying Agencies (NCHCA), which emphasized psychotherapy credentials. This was a US organization, whereas the ITAA was international. The then president, Ellyn Bader, saw this as a helpful way for the ITAA to gain a valid international credentialing system. The ITAA sought recognition and certification through the NCHCA and completed the first round of the process. However, the ITAA Board of Trustees (BOT) withdrew from the final round of evaluation and recognition by the NCHCA because the trustees could not justify the expense of the process, which would only serve US members at a time when nearly half the membership was outside of the United States (international).

By 1984, the number of national organizations that were members of EATA was increasing while the ITAA remained an individual member organization. Other organizations' membership was also growing, and at the joint EATA/ITAA conference held in 1984 in Villars, Switzerland, the ITAA posed questions for national organizations.

These broadly asked how the ITAA could work with other countries and cultures and how they could work effectively together.

In 1985, there was an agreement between EATA and ITAA that EATA's Council of Certification (COC) would adopt the ITAA's Board of Certification (BOC) exam procedures without any modifications and that there would be mutual recognition of the examinations by each organization. What became apparent, however, was that different countries had different laws regarding the desired qualifications of those who wished to take on certain titles. For example, in the United Kingdom, no law requires a psychotherapist to have a medical qualification or even a psychology degree. That was not the case for many other European countries in which a clear hierarchy exists, supporting the hierarchy and potential elitism that was apparent in ITAA at that time.

In June 1987, EATA's COC agreed that "the time has come to work out specific rules for the examination in Counselling and, at the same time, to adapt existing provisions for educational and organizational applications to European conditions" (Rautenberg, 1987, p. 1).

In November of that year, the German TA association held a meeting for trainers and provisional trainers to discuss the examination process. They had worked out a different structure for the written examination, which prior to this, had been a series of questions covering all aspects of TA theory and monitored by an assigned invigilator. This system had been established much earlier by ITAA.

EATA and ITAA were moving forward alongside each other, with EATA placing significant importance on the credentialing processes. EATA's responsibilities were and are different from those of the ITAA in that they represent national organizations in Europe who, in turn, represent training organizations that are part of their own national organization. This means EATA is an organization of organizations and carries the complex task of accommodating each different culture's requirements while still maintaining a cohesive credentialing system. The identity of the ITAA was, and still is, based on its individual membership structure. Although they were and still are different, both organizations agreed to recognize each other's exam processes as being equivalent. The ITAA and EATA had officially become affiliated by then, and the ITAA was in the process of drawing up affiliations with other countries, such as Canada.

Although EATA had decided in 1987 that they needed to work out specific rules for examining in counseling, it was not until 2000 that Jean Illsley Clarke wrote to ITAA's Training and Certification Council with a chart that defined the competencies of the psychotherapy, educational, and organizational fields so that trainers and trainees alike could be sufficiently informed. It was clear from her letter that the defined counseling criteria were still being worked out.

Regrettably, the ITAA, EATA, and other TA organizations around the world have yet to see the vision that Joanne Moses had described. As noted by Alan Jacobs (1996):

> [Berne] had the vision, seeing the relationship between psychiatry, social psychiatry, and social psychology. Too often his theories have been fragmented into clinical on the one hand, and special fields on the other, with no small amount of misunderstanding of each for the other.
>
> (p. 6)

Who Is In and Who Is Out? Tensions Arising Between the Special Fields and Forces Operating at the Periphery of the TA Community

In the paragraph just cited, Jacobs highlighted Berne's aspiration to provide a complex understanding of the human mind and a comprehensive theory of personality. In this aspiration, we may sense the presence of yet another tension: How do we find a robust framework that accounts for both the individuality of each human being and the fact that any form of psychological life is also a form of group life and is therefore intrinsically embedded in various group dynamics?

Berne (1963/2005) articulated this dilemma when he wrote about group structure:

> First there should be a model of the group as a whole and then one of the individual human personality. This makes it possible to consider the interplay between them: What such an ideal group does to the personality, and what such ideal personalities do in and to the group.
>
> (p. 53)

To understand this tension in more depth, we return again to aspects that represented significant influencing forces in the historical, social, and political arena of the time.

The "golden age" of American psychoanalysis that had run from roughly 1949 to 1969 was about to be brought to an end by the combined impact of:

> The feminist and gay rights movements with their numerous, highly valid complaints about the misogyny and homophobia endemic in postwar analysis; the rise of shorter-term and more behaviorally oriented therapies, but above all the explosion of pop self-help, much of which would expressly style itself in opposition to the expense and purported futility of years on the couch; the antiauthoritarian climate in general. The turn inward and the emphasis on the intrapsychic, or at most on intrafamilial, dynamics that had been so remarkably successful in the first two postwar decades had, in short, run aground.
> (Herzog, 2017, p. 5)

The experience of world wars, violence, and atrocities arising in community life seemed to call for some form of reflection regarding the level of destructiveness that emerges in groups at times. The articulation of such understandings was accompanied by the hope that some healing of the trauma caused by war would eventually take place. Cornell (2016) wrote that in this context various theories and models of group treatment began to take shape; authors looked for ways to address social conflict and engaged with various aspects of communal life.

In Chapter 1, we described some of the challenges that Berne faced in the social and political arenas, as well as the way in which they shaped his writings and some of his theoretical elaborations. This was also the case with group structures and group dynamics. He invested a good deal of energy in keeping transactional analysis apolitical, meaning separated from the complicated, potentially threatening, web of power relationships, and protected from a state of dependency on other structures. We wonder whether this rather defensive stance might have reflected itself in his models about group work that did not account for some of the more uncomfortable aspects of social and political interaction. This approach did not provide transactional analysts with a paradigm robust enough to address emerging unrest. Stability was prioritized over encountering uncertainty and turbulence. Therefore, aspects related to otherness, differentness, mistrust, anxiety, and aggression would remain operating outside the practitioner's focus of interest (Cornell, 2016).

In our reading of Berne (1963/2005), the tension between the individual and the collective was sometimes clearly formulated. For example, he compared organizational structures with individual structures and analyzed their mutual effects on each other (pp. 62–63). He also described the delicate balance between individual proclivities and group cohesion (p. 75). Moreover, he even began to formulate an understanding of internal processes in terms of the various functions that occurred in a group (pp. 100–102) in a manner that echoed Bion's approach (1961) to group life.

Paradoxically, however, in his accounts of practicing group work, Berne tended to privilege an individualistic lens over a more group-centered perspective. The leader's position remained that of an outside observer concerned with game analysis, script analysis, and the chain of transactions exchanged between members. Leadership and membership were mostly addressed from the point of view of the individuals attending the group; their meaning as group functions remained underdeveloped in practice. Hence, the tension between the group and the individual was kept mostly in the realm of theoretical reflections, without becoming an embodied principle of practicing group psychotherapy.

The same difficulty in making space for the lived experience of this particular tension can, in our view, be noticed elsewhere also. It becomes visible when we look for ways to understand the processes and dynamics activated within the community of transactional analysts, both inside the boundaries of this professional group and beyond its margins, namely, in its relationships with other professional factions. This time the needs of the group seemed to have been privileged to the detriment of individual particularities.

In previous chapters, we highlighted the fact that Berne faced significant pressure to differentiate transactional analysis from psychoanalysis. Earlier in this chapter, we pointed out that the historical context at the time was urging practitioners to work effectively and to step more closely to various social realities with which people were confronted. Moreover, we brought into discussion the fact that Berne felt strongly about keeping TA outside the sphere of political movements as well as outside the world of academia. Some (Cornell, 2004; Steiner, 2010) have considered that this was primarily due to his painful experiences of being brought before the US government House of Representatives Select Committee on Un-American Activities. These elements reveal a landscape of complex forces, each pushing and pulling in various directions, generating opportunities as well as establishing constraints. We imagine that forging an identity under the influence of such forces must have been a challenging though still necessary endeavor. We may understand how, under these conditions, there must have been a good deal of focus on strengthening the external boundary (Berne, 2005, p. 56) of the group formed by transactional analysts.

For Berne and his colleagues at that time, finding a place that was recognized and legitimized on the wider map of contemporary approaches to human development must have been considered a priority as it directly involved the group's survival. In Berne's (2005) view, the existence of any group rested on three pillars: the group's ideology, its physical continuity, and its effectiveness (p. 68). This perhaps accounts for the amount of energy involved in the development of the theory and in the drive to be effective at all costs in various fields of practice. It perhaps also accounts, in part, for the founding of the international association as a structure that would provide a form of continuity.

Consequently, we hypothesize that there was little energy left for the community to work out and establish flexible, healthy internal boundaries (Berne, 2005, p. 58) that would foster meaningful demarcations between the leadership and the membership as well as between various categories of membership, such as the distinct fields of application that were gradually emerging. The voice of the collective was louder than that of differentness or otherness emerging inside the group. We imagine the struggle to affirm oneself as a transactional analyst overshadowed the aspiration of articulating distinctions between individual fields of application.

What happens when the tension between the individual and the group can no longer be held? Landaiche (2016) argued that such collapse leads to various forms of violence that are manifested toward those who are not alike. Aspects of difference no longer foster collaboration but competition and polarization. Dalal (2016) wrote of a similar process, addressing it from a slightly different angle, namely, that of power relations. His stance was that power dynamics and politics are necessarily part of the fabric of all social relations. They bring tension, unpredictability, and instability in the group. When the space for reflection breaks down there is the danger of experiencing various degrees of domination, control, and subjugation. The ones "in power" impose their reality on all those who are not "in power":

> Tyrants decree how the world is and brook no alternative. Voice something that goes against the ruling paradigm, and the tyrant's response is likely to be punitive. One of the most feared of punitive gestures is being made an outcast and being cast out beyond the pale, no longer allowed to belong.
>
> (p. 98)

A question then arises, namely, were these power struggles active inside the TA community between practitioners from different fields of application? Was there a particular specialization that was considered to impose its own discourse on others?

We had multiple conversations with transactional analysts practicing in each of the four fields. Most of them described their experience of a hierarchical relationship operating between the psychotherapy field, on the one hand, and the organizational, educational, or the counseling field, on the other. In this hierarchical arrangement, the felt sense of the practitioners we spoke to recently (regardless of their field of specialization) was that the psychotherapy field dominates in terms of the number of practitioners and psychologically appears to hold the upper hand: The implicit discourse seems to be that this is where the "deeper" work takes place, where structural change becomes possible, and where the intrapsychic domain is available for exploration (Grégoire, 1998). We might ask if this stance leads to an assumption that the psychotherapy field has a more privileged position in relation to the counseling, educational, and organizational fields of TA and whether this creates a strong feeling of belonging among TA psychotherapists as well as one of exclusion for transactional analysts practicing in other fields. Many people noted that there are still some people in transactional analysis psychotherapy training who appear to remain unaware that four fields of application and certification exist among those who use TA.

In our view, complementing the focus on what was going on at the periphery of the TA community with attention on various subgroups that were emerging may have offered an alternative to the experience of power struggles and a potential for more collaboration. We imagine that the encouragement of healthy differentiation within the wider group of transactional analysts would have contributed to the creation of permeable internal boundaries that could tolerate exchanges and constructive interdependence between fields.

We believe an additional comment is important at this point. When we write of encouraging differentiation and collaboration, we do not envisage an unnecessarily liberal, easy-going attitude. What we wish to advocate for, instead, is the creation of a vigorous space in which there is room for processing conflict, aggression, and anxiety alongside other less comfortable experiences. From this point of view, we agree with Cornell (2016) that "as we face the disorder and alarm of living in groups, we can discover places of extraordinary generativity" (p. 145).

The idea of a fruitful collaboration between fields of TA practice is not a new one. It was formulated as early as 1984 in an article by Joanne Moses (1984). Her stance was that special fields could step in to address economic as well as social gaps in the system and could provide help in areas where the clinical field (i.e., mental health services) was overwhelmed. She further argued in favor of the benefits that educational transactional analysts could bring in offering support to people who, for example, lived in elderly nursing homes:

If staff can be taught to help residents through stroking, permission, positive suggestion, and staying clear of their games, quality of life for both staff and residents will be improved. Another service that can improve the quality of life for residents is offering educational programs for families. Adult children often carry heavy burdens of guilt, regret, and inadequacy. Learning about family systems, role reversal in old age, and communication with confused parents can greatly assuage their pain. Group learning opportunities usually function like support groups allowing people to ventilate their feelings. The thrust suggested in this article, then, is educational, not clinical. Yet that educational effort can reach some of the most psychologically handicapped people in our society in ways that offer some relief at nominal cost (p. 197).

More recently, some transactional analysts have shifted the prevailing perspective on the issue of boundaries between the four fields of application. In an article written in 1998, Grégoire argued that there was value in giving up the metaphor of boundary as a demarcation between territories because it unnecessarily encouraged the contrasting elements pertaining to each field without honoring the aspects that they shared. Moreover, it invited people to define the four fields *vis-à-vis* one another (i.e., regression is reserved for the realm of psychotherapy and not counseling), which reinforces nothing but a symbiotic relationship between them. Instead, Grégoire suggested the possibility of understanding boundaries as "envelopes of coherence" (p. 316). Hence, within this framework the emphasis lay on what was common between the fields as well as on the necessity of building internal consistency and coherence inside each of them. Consequently, the specific goal of each field and the contract needed to be congruent with the methods of intervention and the protection that these specific methods could provide. If this was the case, then they each field could become an effective agent of change:

> There is a place to welcome and validate all positive change. It is indisputable that profound personal change, including script change, takes place in supervision, education, counseling, and organizational development as well as in daily life. The supervisor, the teacher, or the change agent can validate and welcome what he or she sees as the beneficial results of his or her own behavior, congratulate the client for the results achieved, and congratulate himself or herself on it. This is one more way of respecting others and oneself.
>
> (p. 320)

Interestingly, we return to the theme of effectiveness that we mentioned at the beginning of this chapter, but this time from quite a different angle. The kind of effectiveness described here is a direct consequence of a more robust form of group functioning, one in which there is room for diversity between members and differentness is regarded as a source of growth. Moreover, questions and reflections coming from practitioners specializing in different fields but sharing a common philosophy foster new developments. In this case, effectiveness comes from within the group and is a powerful indicator of its maturation.

References

Altorfer, O. (1977). Authentic courtesy and personal power: Two aims of emotional job fitness. *Transactional Analysis Journal*. 7:3, 339–341. https://doi.org/10.1177/036215377700700416

Berne, E. (1968). *Staff-Patient Staff Conferences*, UC San Francisco, Library, Special Collections, Berne (Eric L.) Collections. https://calisphere.org/item/8cf14477-194b-45fb-b993-69daded52f94/

Berne, E. (2005). *The structure and dynamics of organizations and groups*. Lippincott. (Originally published 1963)

Berne, E. (2010). *A Montreal childhood* (T. Berne, Ed.). Editorial Jeder.

Bion, W. (1961). *Experiences in groups and other papers*. Basic Books.

Certificates of attendance. (1965). *Transactional Analysis Bulletin*. 4:14, 42.

Cornell, W. F. (2004). Remembering Eric Berne: A conversation with Terry Berne. *The Script*. 34:8, 6–7.

Cornell, W. F. (2013). "Special fields": A brief history of an anxious dilemma and its lingering consequences for transactional analysis counselors. *Transactional Analysis Journal*. 43:1, 7–13. https://doi.org/10.1177/0362153713483274

Cornell, W. F. (2016). In conflict and community: A century of turbulence, living and w-orking in groups. *Transactional Analysis Journal*. 46:2, 136–148. https://doi.org/10.1177/0362153716632494

Crossman, P. (1966). Permission and protection. *Transactional Analysis Bulletin*. 5:19, 152.

Dalal, F. (2016). The individual and the group: The twin tyrannies of internalism and individualism. *Transactional Analysis Journal*. 46:2, 88–100. https://doi.org/10.1177/0362153716631517

Frazier, T. L. (1971). The application of transactional analysis principles in the classroom of a correctional school. *Transactional Analysis Journal*. 1:4, 16–20. https://doi.org/10.1177/036215377100100405

Grégoire, J. (1998). Criteria for defining the boundaries of transactional analysis fields of application. *Transactional Analysis Journal*. 28:4, 311–320. https://doi.org/10.1177/036215379802800405

Groder, G. (Ed.). (1975). Editorial. *Transactional Analysis Journal*. 5:4, 344. https://doi.org/10.1177/036215377500500403

Herzog, D. (2017). *Cold war Freud: Psychoanalysis in an age of catastrophes*. Cambridge University Press.

Jacobs, A. (1996). Letter from the guest editor. *Transactional Analysis Journal*. 26:1, 6–7. https://doi.org/10.1177/036215379602600103

Landaiche, N. M. III (2016). Maturing as a community effort: A discussion of Dalal's and Samuels's perspectives on groups and individuals. *Transactional Analysis Journal*. 46:2, 116–120. https://doi.org/10.1177/0362153716628803

Moses, J. (1978). Special fields: What and whither? *The Script*. 8:10, 2.

Moses, J. (1984). Part-time mental health technicians: A special fields study in an intermediate care facility. *Transactional Analysis Journal*. 14:3, 199–204. https://doi.org/10.1177/036215378401400306

Publications (1964). *Transactional Analysis Bulletin*. 3:12, 161.

Rautenberg, W. (1987). Defining the special fields. *European Transactional Analysis Newsletter*. 29. 1

"Revised constitution and by-laws (1966). *Transactional Analysis Bulletin*. 5:19, 157–160.

"Special training standards insert." (1980). *The Script*. 10:3, 5–9.

Steiner, C., & Steiner, U. (1968). Permission classes. *Transactional Analysis Bulletin*. 7:25, 2.

Steiner, C. M. (2010). Eric Berne's politics: "The great pyramid. *Transactional Analysis Journal*. 40:3–4, 212–216. https://doi.org/10.1177/036215371004000306

Chapter 4

Development of the Cathexis and Redecision Schools

Traces of the Early Imprint

As articulated in previous chapters, our aspiration with this book is to contribute to an exploration of transactional analysis as a living organism, one that is open to transformation rather than a closed system with the mission of enunciating absolute truth or unquestionable wisdom.

To step into this territory, we invite you to allow some space in your minds where it becomes possible to get a sense of the life of this organism, of its flesh and bones. In other words, we invite you to participate in the creation of a primal image (Berne, 1977) of transactional analysis theory.

What may stand out, perhaps, are traces of the life and thinking of Eric Berne. His explorative mind can be seen in his writings:

> When you read Berne, just as with Freud, you are taken on a revolutionary journey. It is his journey, for sure, but you become part of it, a journey of his creative and innovative mind in which you are invited to participate. In Berne's case, it was often also a humoristic journey.
>
> (van Beekum, 2016, p. 11)

Berne's complex relationship with psychoanalysis also comes through. Psychoanalysis represented both the bedrock for Berne's emergent ideas regarding the human psyche and a world from which he needed to differentiate himself. This shaped some rather sharp edges at the interface between TA and psychoanalysis. In an attempt to describe the relationship between the two, Berne (n.d.) wrote in *Principles of Transactional Analysis* that

> transactional analysis is more general than psychoanalysis. Hence attempts to fit the former into the latter will give rise to skepticism, difficulties, and unfair criticism on both sides, just as any attempt to fit the general into the particular. On the other hand, psychoanalysis fits quite smoothly and snugly into the framework of transactional analysis, to the mutual satisfaction of both parties.
>
> (pp. 5–6)

As we deepen our perceptions, we may also become poignantly aware of Eric Berne's fragility. Sometimes, this has been crystallized in the views articulated by his colleagues:

> While increasingly impressed and grateful for his remarkable achievements, I must also say, with pain, that over the course of the years, I became more and more aware of Eric's sad, wounded Child along with the perky, difficult Child I had seen early on. Regrettably, perhaps because he never overcame the fear of feeling "one down," I also got to witness how he overcompensated with a certain kind of grandiosity and imperviousness to social circumstances, whereby he sometimes sabotaged his own goals.
>
> (English, 2010, p. 209)

At other times, in pieces of writing by Berne himself, his aches and tenderness made themselves known. Here is a fragment from a letter written to his deceased father, which may well shake and move the reader to the deepest corners of his psyche:

> Father, my dear father, in heaven perhaps, more surely non-existent, except in the picture which I have before me of your kind face bent over a book, a book explaining to good men how best to do good: I say to you this: life has become intolerable. It is impossible to live ... My kind father, in truth there is no heaven, and I will join you, rotting in the damp earth, food for hungry worms who know no good and no evil, only the law that one must receive to live. I give myself to them, and after my body is gone, they, who were born only to eat me, will die.
>
> (Berne, ca. 1935)

As we begin to play with these traces, we may organize them into a more structured understanding of how the bones of TA theory form a skeleton, meaning a comprehensive system of basic principles.

First, there is a strong emphasis on "getting well" as an alternative to "making progress." Time seems to be of the essence, and cure becomes paramount. This may be an indicator of a difficulty in conceptualizing loss and developing appropriate methodologies for treatment (Heathcote, 2016). It may also signal an impetuous desire for making a significant impact, an insatiable hunger for recognition. Six months after Berne's death, Warren Cheney (1971) wrote a biographical sketch commemorating Berne's life and work. It ends with what seems to reflect an ambitious aspiration as well as a rather strong imperative to achieve grand outcomes:

> It is safe to predict, by the year 2000, no new psychotherapy will have been created that is more powerful, more successful than transactional analysis unless built upon the basic principles Eric discovered, defined, illustrated, tested, and made practical. It is safe to predict increasing numbers of mentally disturbed patients each year will get well faster and stay well longer thanks to being treated

by TA. It is safe to predict that transactional analysis will become the preferred treatment of choice for clinicians the world over, thanks to Eric Berne and the professionals he trained.

(p. 22)

Second, transactional analysis puts forward an emergent understanding of the unconscious that is different from the repressed unconscious already articulated by Freudian psychoanalysis. Berne began to conceptualize aspects related to non-conscious functioning and organization. This was understood to contain elements that remained traumatic or undigested, but it was not limited to such psychological content. The Bernean notions of ulterior transactions (Berne, 1961), protocol (Berne, 1963/1975), and intuition (Berne, 1955) represent the pillars of this architecture of the unconscious.

Third, in the early years of TA, there was little room for integrating the dynamics of transference more robustly with the rest of transactional analysis theory. Initially, transference was mainly considered to be the working tool of psychoanalytic methodology, hence a laborious, time-consuming process that would also contribute to an undesired, potentially perilous power imbalance between patient and therapist. Rather, the aim was to achieve social control and autonomy. In *Principles of Transactional Analysis* Berne (n.d.) wrote:

> They [patients] can then proceed to the more advanced phases of game analysis and script analysis with the therapeutic goal of attaining social control. They are then able to conduct their relationships with others in an autonomous way at their own options and are no longer victims of unconscious uncontrolled impulses to exploit or be exploited.
>
> (p. 14)

Lastly, transactional analysis set out to mark a departure from the medical model, aspiring to provide people with a more humanistic approach to treatment. This is the reason why it defined itself as a social psychiatry, a method that remains anchored in the clinical realities faced by the therapist and is based on equality between patient and therapist. As Berne (1968) wrote:

> Everyone is treated as a person with equal rights on his own merits. Thus the patients have as much right to hear what the staff has to say as the staff has to hear what the patients have to say.
>
> (p. 158)

The aspects just described as pertaining to the core structure of transactional analysis remain significant and reflect themselves in subsequent developments of TA theory and practice.

We will continue with a more in-depth reflection on two major psychotherapy approaches that have left their mark in the history of TA in the community of transactional analysts: the Schiffian reparenting approach and the Goulding redecision approach. We will look into how Bernean thinking was ingrained in these two approaches and consider what their aspirations and dilemmas may have been as well as some of their potential blind spots.

The Schiffian Reparenting Approach: Waging War Against Pathology

Schiffian reparenting is a method of treatment founded by Jacqui Schiff, a transactional analyst with a background in social work, and Morris Schiff, who was a psychiatric social worker. They established The Psychiatric Rehabilitation Project in Virginia, a facility that aimed to find a cure for schizophrenia.

The dimensions of experimentation and the aim to cure psychiatric conditions are key in understanding the Schiffian approach, as they clearly respect the ethos of TA at the time. In his introduction to the first writings in the TA literature to mention the use of reparenting with schizophrenia, Berne (1969) wrote the following:

> Freud said that for all conditions other than transfer neuroses, psychoanalysis was more or less unsuitable, and I, being a good Freudian, besides having tried it for other conditions, take his word for it. Hence, transactional analysis, which is designed for "other conditions" and has shown some effectiveness in this respect. One of the other conditions is schizophrenia.
>
> (p. 45)

He credited Jacqui and Morris Schiff as practitioners endowed with "boldness, theoretical clarity, and devotion" (Berne, 1969, p. 46) and recounted with a sense of pride that when invited on a television program and asked how she would respond to those who criticized her work as encouraging dependency, Jacqui Schiff's answer was that patients got better. The space for dialogue around the theory collapsed as achieving cure became imperative. Uncertainty needed to be sacrificed in the service of effectiveness. Controversies with other theoreticians in the community were gradually silenced, and this was taken as proof validating the approach (Schiff et al., 1975, p. 3) or as an indicator of a radical perspective, one that was soundly grounded in the practitioners' total commitment.

The Schiffian method rested on the creation of a highly structured residential environment where patients Were treated (Schiff et al., 1975, p. 4). Essentially, it was a facility where patients were received and integrated into a proper family that operated on the assumption of healthy psychological functioning, with "healthy standards" being defined by the Schiffs. There was a strong emphasis on undefended relating, an expectation of intimacy between those living there, and a clear sharing of responsibilities between therapists and patients alike. The actual roles of therapist and client underwent significant alterations because patients ceased to be patients and were adopted by the Schiffs as their children instead. They were required to give up their families of origin and take on—contractually—a different pair of parents: Jacqui and Morris. This arrangement was considered a viable alternative to hospitalization in the psychiatric facilities of the time, and structure became a substitute for medication.

Here is what one of Schiff's patients wrote:

> While I was in the hospital I was blamed for not getting well enough although nothing was done to meet my needs. Therapy was just talk ... Dependency was defined as bad.
>
> ...
>
> In the hospital my relationships with other patients were without intimacy and were frequently based on mutual dissatisfaction with the staff. I developed a big investment in being sick and being hospitalized. This was because my relationship with my doctor depended upon my being sick; if I got well, no relationship.
>
> ("Being a Member of My Family," 1969, pp. 67–68)

The issue of transference–countertransference was not considered worthy of too much reflection by the Schiffs. Rather, it was viewed as something that was managed by psychiatrists "from opposite sides of a desk" (Schiff et al., 1975, p. 3) and, implicitly, as a defense against the use of touch stroking to address early developmental needs. As a reaction to this, practitioners at Cathexis Institute chose to accept patients' transference as an "investment of power," which was considered "useful in developing capacity for relating and trusting and accepting nurturing, that can certainly be considered desirable" (Schiff et al., 1975, p. 102).

As a reaction to this medical model, the Schiffian perspective was one in which dependency needs were encouraged and addressed using regression as a methodological framework. More in-depth understanding and conceptualization of transferential dynamics was therefore replaced with the notion of regression as a reenactment of childhood, the main methodological compass being a mapping of early infantile needs. Being held, stroked, fed, bathed, loved, and part of a healthy family with two responsible parents (Schiff & Day, 1972) were the ingredients that guaranteed the pathway to cure. Some of those elements were also explicitly encouraged by Berne (1969), who wrote that what had been missing in treating schizophrenia was addressing aspects related to early oral development, which he considered "an integral part of transactional analysis theory, known colloquially through such terms as stroking, the feeling of Okayness, time structuring, the spinal cord shriveling up, etc." (p. 46).

What becomes palpable at this point in our exploration is perhaps a somewhat missionary-like zeal in the hope of stroking patients out of their schizophrenic state. This was done in the name of effectiveness and came to be considered a revolutionary alternative to other methods of treatment. In the next section, we will reflect on the way in which this attitude both called for the development of new ways of working and entailed a high cost.

A Journey Through Heaven and Hell: Where Aspiration Meets Clinical Failure

Eric Berne focused on a particular understanding of regression in his writings (Landaiche, 2022), one that was mostly related to the idea of the patient going back in time to the problematic developmental age and experiencing, in therapy, a situation that was different from the original one and that remained phenomenologically embodied from there on. The hope was that this experience would correct the old one and would therefore lead to cure.

This understanding is rather different from that of regression conceptualized as a loss of the capacity to function in the here and now according to the person's age and capabilities.

In the Schiffian approach, the first of these meanings of regression is used when designing intervention techniques. This particular meaning was analyzed further by Landaiche, and he distinguished between psychotic and nonpsychotic regression. Psychotic regression is defined as a process whereby the person functions from a very young Child ego state and has no access to older states. In cases of nonpsychotic regression, the person is able to cathect other states—either ego states from a later age or the Parent and Adult ego states of the same age as the Child at the regressed moment—or responds to a currently traumatic situation, in which case it is an adaptive regression. Those processes occur as reactions to (internal or environmental) stimuli that are experienced as stressful.

In their writing about regression as a therapeutic technique, it was mainly the psychotic regression that received attention in Schiffian theory. That generated a context in which cure became possible. When we consider the difficulty of treating schizophrenia at that time, this is all the more a question of rendering something that was viewed as unimaginable into a palpable reality. However, the fervent aspiration of curing schizophrenia took on a somewhat omnipotent approach in actual practice.

From a Schiffian perspective, the therapist functions both to correct and confront behavior as well as to provide a nurturing experience.

> Crazy behavior (different from regressive behavior) is not permitted and children learn quickly what they can and cannot get away with. Inappropriate behavior is punished. Flat affect results from stroke-hunger and disappears quickly when touch stroking is available. Withdrawal serves two functions: it is a defense against regressive needs which no one will meet and is often in conformity to script (frequently derived from hospital experiences with seclusion utilized to control inappropriate behavior). All of these problems can be corrected within days.
>
> (Schiff, 1969, p. 52)

Consequently, it rests in the mind of the therapist to make a judgment about what is adaptive or healthy and what is not.

In clinical practice, however, the therapist's mind needs to tolerate and reflect in conditions of ambiguity and uncertainty. Unfortunately, this was something that failed to happen consistently in the case of those practicing from a Schiffian framework. Here is what J. Schiff wrote about the experience with Dennis, one of the residential patients:

> There was so much we didn't know. It was difficult to distinguish pathology from regressive needs and we guessed at which behavior to support and which to discourage. Much of the time we simply reacted on the basis of how we would have reacted to a normal child if he had behaved as Dennis did, but that was difficult, too, because of his size and the maturity of his thinking.
> (Schiff & Day, 1972, pp. 75–76)

It appears that failures in the treatment did not necessarily foster learning and were not managed by the staff taking responsibility. This would have been unbearable given the cost of the investment they had made in their work. Instead, it was considered that love was the magic ingredient that made patients get well.

> The child in me believes there is some kind of magic in loving—that if I had only loved Rosita enough, I could have found a way to help her get well. Sometimes I could feel the wish for health and happiness—only to have it slip out of both our grasps.
> (Schiff & Day, 1972, p. 179)

All My Children (Schiff & Day, 1972) is an account of the work with several patients who came to receive treatment at the Psychiatric Rehabilitation Program in Virginia. According to the program, patients were required to give up their family of origin and become part of a new family. In this new system, they were the children, Moe and Jacqui were their parents, and the rest of the patients were their siblings. As treatment progressed and regression was conducted, what occurred in several cases was an increase in what was considered "crazy" behavior, namely, outbursts of anger and hostility. In the absence of a clinical understanding of the meaning of this behavior, the intervention was behavioral correction accompanied at times by punishment, which could also involve physical punishment. Albeit extreme in some cases, such interventions were labeled as a radical departure from traditional treatment and, therefore, something to be welcomed and pursued further (Schiff & Day, 1972).

In the absence of such drastic measures, the Schiffs would have probably experienced distressing levels of uncertainty and not knowing. Unfortunately, there was little space for acknowledgment of either of these vulnerabilities to the point that clinical reflection was replaced by a sense of being right, all in the name of their commitment to those who had become their "children" (Schiff & Day, 1972).

The Schiffs recruited patients whom they considered had become well to be part of the staff and work with new patients. With such an unquestioning attitude on the part of those in charge, what resulted was an escalation of patients' violent behavior and a corresponding increase in violence inflicted by staff members. This was a clear indication of clinical failure in some cases, eventually leading to a series of charges of assault and battery against Jacqui (Mountain, 2022). Soon, she lost her license to run the Rehabilitation Center and had to move to California where she set up the Cathexis Institute (Crossman, 2004). Unfortunately, there, too, things took a tragic turn, as reparenting treatment resulted in the serious injury and hospitalization of a residential patient, whose life could not be saved. (For a more detailed account of this episode, please see Crossman, 2004.)

Looking back, what we believe failed to happen was an acknowledgment of the fact that the clinical terrain provided the context for a phenomenological experience of both aspects of regression that we described at the beginning of this section: one containing the seeds of hope and potential growth, the other more intimately linked with the unbearable echoes of horror and anguish embedded in the patient's psyche. The second was sacrificed in favor of the first and was, therefore, never addressed therapeutically. We believe that Berne (1969) may have had an incipient understanding of this phenomenon, since he made the following comment in the closing of an article written by Jacqui Schiff in the *Transactional Analysis Bulletin* on reparenting in schizophrenia:

> Here we learn not only how to set up the proper attitude and environment for curing schizophrenics, but also new things that are revealed as the pathology falls away. These new points are of considerable interest. But beyond that, they can be used right now to indicate special points of therapeutic attack in the process of reparenting.
>
> (p. 84)

Our understanding is that what needed to be conceptualized in more depth were the intricate transferential dynamics that occur between patient and therapist. Transference was essentially considered to be a vehicle for replacing an "unhealthy" frame of reference with one that should have granted "sanity" because it was provided by the therapist. Transference was not so much a therapeutic tool designed to make space for the meaning of what goes on in the patient's mind but rather an instrument of correction. We believe that this is where we witness both the aspiration toward something different and the collapse of developing a robust method of treatment.

Where Is My Mind? An Exploration of Schiffian Theory

The essence of the later Schiffian reparenting approach, as articulated by practitioners working at Cathexis Institute, presented in a book entitled *The Cathexis Reader*. In its preface, Schiff et al. (1975) wrote that "although this material was developed over several years, it was mostly written in an intensive write-in weekend" (p. vii), which again seems to us to be a reflection of the same emphasis on effectiveness and the necessity for clear-cut formulations that are not subject to doubt.

Defining Pathology

The Schiffian framework postulates that the source of pathology, including schizophrenia, can be found in the dysfunctional symbiotic relationships between infant and caregiver. These may generate competitive relationships, in which there is rivalry for the same position in the symbiosis, or complementary relationships, in which there is an agreement regarding the position each person occupies in the symbiotic arrangement. Such configurations are kept in place by the complex intrapsychic processes of discounting, grandiosity, and thinking disorders. They manifest externally through four passive behaviors:

- Doing nothing, characterized by non-responsiveness
- Over-adaptation, involving an adhesion to someone else's goals as if they were one's own
- Agitation, representing repetitive activity that lacks purpose
- Incapacitation/violence, which is a discharge of energy accumulated over prolonged periods of passivity

Underlying these manifestations are various mechanisms. One of them is discounting, which is defined as a minimization or ignoring of various aspects of self, other, or the surrounding reality. Another mechanism is grandiosity, which is an exaggeration of those aspects of self, other, or the external reality. Thinking disorders are yet another mechanism that is involved in the maintenance of unhealthy symbiotic relationships.

> Disorders occur when people operate primarily from either an internal frame of reference, or try to adapt totally to external situations without reference to internal frame of reference, or when interpretation of data is atypical, making difficult an alliance between what is internal and what is external.
> (Schiff et al., 1975, p. 19)

From a Schiffian perspective, those mechanisms come together to generate the process of redefinition, which is used to maintain an already existing view of self, other, and the world. This view is further conceptualized as a pattern of responses to stimuli that has the role of integrating the individual's ego states. Schiffian theory refers to it as a frame of reference and "can be thought of as the skin that surrounds the ego states binding them together and acting as a 'filter' on reality" (Schiff et al., 1975, p. 50). It plays a major role in how treatment decisions are made, an aspect that we will discuss later.

It is important to note that pathology was explained by Schiff and her colleagues in terms of dysfunctional frames of reference that the child incorporates from the parent and that are afterward preserved in the unhealthy symbiotic relationship between them. The dysfunction was understood to be a result of the parent feeling in a constant state of comparison and competition with others in the world and trying to achieve success in terms of those standards defined by society, instead of formulating autonomous and realistic goals for themselves. This process was then perpetuated in the dynamic with the child.

In this context, schizophrenia is explained as a situation in which there is "a locked system of messages in the Parent, corresponding adaptations in the Child, and an Adult which is misinformed" (Schiff et al., 1975, p. 74). The key element is that those adaptations involve survival decisions related to stroking and feeling. It is further stated that

> with a Child who perceives the pathology as necessary for survival, a Parent who confirms this, and an Adult unable to contradict it, the person has no exit from the system without external intervention.
>
> (p. 74)

Again it is important to note this stance because it is intimately related to treatment considerations that Schiffian theory considers appropriate in cases of schizophrenia.

Designing Treatment Intervention

If we immerse ourselves in the Schiffian perspective, it becomes quite clear that the source of disturbance lies in a distorted frame of reference that is rather rigidly maintained in the Parent ego state. What is required for healing, therefore, is a change in the frame of reference. Schiff (1975) and her colleagues postulated three ways in which this can be achieved:

> (1) The Child becoming uncomfortable with the present frame of reference and seeking Adult information and new permission, (2) the Child becoming uncomfortable with the present frame of reference and seeking new permissions, or (3) a Parent (external) structure "imposing" a new frame of reference.
>
> (p. 51)

What seems to be common in all three cases is that the person needs to receive permissions, thereby taking on some kind of "reconstruction" work at the level of the Parent ego state. To J. Schiff, this seemed like a task that could be tackled. Her approach was received with skepticism by her colleagues in the San Francisco Social Psychiatry Seminars, who supported the idea that the Parent part of the personality was "permanent and inflexible" (Schiff & Day, 1972, p. 42), considering that "the closest anyone had ever come to restructuring a personality was through psychoanalysis" (p. 42).

Instead, Schiff believed that what needed to take place was a process of reparenting, meaning replacing already existing aspects of the Parent (or the Parent in its entirety) with something new. The new represented the therapist's own mind, which needed to be injected "in a forceful and caring way" (Schiff et al., 1975, p. 103) into the patient's psyche. The aim was to support an autonomous development and expression of the Child ego state, which was viewed as the "real self" heavily distorted by a broken society, a view which does not depart much from Berne's reflections regarding humankind and that places the person in a strong opposition with society: "Somewhere in primitive man, if only we can clear out a lot of the cultural garbage that intercedes between who he is and who we are, lie the resources for solving all the important problems that confront people" (Schiff & Day,1972, p. 24). At this point, we may wonder whether this opposition does not, paradoxically heighten the sense of operating from competitive frames of reference, rather than decrease it as was considered to be effective (Schiff et al., 1975, p. 74).

Given these premises articulated by the Schiffian treatment philosophy, the question that emerges quite organically is how to get rid of what is defined as unhealthy or even toxic but that which resides in the person's mind, possibly inhabiting it from a very early age. The answer to this question was regression used as a therapeutic tool.

As in the case of transference, regression had a bad reputation in the psychiatric world at the time because it was considered to be risky and limited in what it had to offer (Schiff & Day, 1972): "Regression, known to be a reenactment of childhood, is considered 'crazy' or pathological and discouraged in conventional treatment because neither therapists nor mental hospitals are prepared to handle infants" (pp. 42–43).

Again, the Schiffian approach took quite an opposite stance and held the view that this intervention could be used effectively and that if the environment was supportive enough, treatment could be successful.

Nevertheless, more recent developments in transactional analysis theory have started to address the fallacies in the Schiffian reparenting theory and to articulate new ways of working with psychiatric conditions such as schizophrenia (Cornell, 2022; Mellacqua, 2014, 2020).

The Goulding Redecision Approach: Keeping the Cowboy Spirit Alive

Robert (Bob) Goulding and his wife Mary Goulding were part of the group of practitioners who trained and worked with Eric Berne. The two developed their own approach to treatment in the mid-1960s through the early 1970s, which they called redecision therapy, and that was grounded in the principles of transactional analysis and Gestalt therapy. Bob had a background in psychiatry and Mary was a social worker. Together the Gouldings founded the Western Institute for Group and Family Treatment (WIGFT). Their way of practicing and conceptualizing treatment has had a significant influence on the TA community.

Although they put forward a theoretical system and a methodology that departed from Berne's views quite significantly at times, the Gouldings seemed to articulate similar principles in their philosophy of treatment. For example, the same emphasis on effectiveness and cost-effective therapy is clear throughout their writings.

Long-term work was discouraged, and it was considered that change needed to happen quickly, starting from the moment the client[1] walked through the door. Their message was a loud call to action where the challenge was to give up old patterns of feeling and behavior in order to break free from archaic demands and celebrate the present. Growth and health were the states that the Gouldings promoted strongly and rather fervently at times. This is what Mary Goulding wrote to her clients in the opening of one of the books she co-authored with Bob entitled *The Power is in the Patient* (Goulding & Goulding, 1978):

> I am bored with pathology. I am excited by health. And growth ... I am not interested in your sucking in my protection, permission, or potency. My potency is: I give me to be with you in health, in growth, so that you, too, will discard in boredom your pathology and celebrate yourself in health.
>
> (p. 15)

The overall sense seems to be that time should not be wasted. As we let ourselves be moved by this idea, we may perhaps hear that it conveys a delicate edge between empowerment and a yearning that threatens to weigh heavily on the person's psyche.

The work of the Gouldings acknowledges those processes that belong to the realm of the unconscious in the broader sense that Berne wrote about. As we will discuss in more detail later in this chapter, the redecision approach promoted a strong focus on the Child ego state and the autonomy that each person has when making decisions, both at young ages as part of the script and also in adulthood as part of the individual's process of change. In the Gouldings' view, the latter ones—called redecisions—rely rather significantly on intuition and the person's capacity for spontaneity. As one becomes familiar with the clinical illustrations presented by the Gouldings, one may notice how these aspects were something to which they used to lend an attentive ear in a way that Bob Goulding considered consistent with Berne's teachings. He wrote this of Berne's influence: "He taught me to listen in a way that nobody could—not even Fritz Perls. I am still listening" (Goulding & Goulding, 1978, p. 11). We believe that the "way" Bob mentioned is intimately related to intuition and the part it plays in remaining receptive to the ulterior level of communication.

Interestingly, this view led to a demystification of the unconscious, which was no longer a realm of darkness inhabited by witches or monsters as it had been in the traditional psychoanalytic perspective of that time. Instead, unconscious processes were considered to be part of being human and very much in the service of the person's capacity to change and decide freely.

This shift found a match in taking on a more "realistic" or "down to earth" outlook on life and the world, one where magic would be replaced by the power residing in the individual. Such a perspective was quite influential in the humanistic *geist* of that era. It therefore made sense that the Gouldings' approach to transference dynamics was to discourage them or place them outside of the therapeutic relationship, questioning both their value as a therapeutic tool but also the level of training transactional analysts needed to have in order to be able to work them through (Goulding, 1981). Removing the therapist as a transferential figure from the clinical landscape was something meant to facilitate the autonomy of the client, the "power ... in the patient" (p. 50).

We believe this is an aspect that is worth noting and wondering about. The rather unbending refusal to study transference and consider it a matter of clinical research seems to be quite at odds with the Gouldings' more general stance, which was one of curiosity and an appetite for discovery. Identifying himself with the cowboy spirit, even after Berne's death, Bob Goulding (1981) wrote the following: "I know that there is no way in which the Cowboys and Cowgirls won't continue to ride off in all directions" (p. 53). So what could have potentially been so disturbing about transference that eventually determined redecision practitioners to shut down this area of clinical interest? Might such dynamics, unfolding especially in long-term work, bring about longings and yearnings of dependency that may have been particularly frightening or painful?

Finding a sound anchor in the humanistic philosophy and, above all, Gestalt theory, the redecision approach places a strong emphasis on contracting as a tool meant to balance out power dynamics between client and therapist. The practitioner is someone who learns about the client at the same time that the client learns about him/herself (Goulding & Goulding, 1978). The focus is always on health and personal choice instead of pathology. This view is in stark contrast with the medical tradition at the time, in which the doctor would be highly invested with the power of having access to absolute truths. The doctor's job would be to treat illness rather than being curious about the intrapsychic blocks that get in the way of the person's potential for intimacy, autonomy, creativity, spontaneity, and growth.

Those aspects just highlighted are traces of Bernean thinking and philosophy that remain engrained in the spirit of redecision theory. In a way that remained loyal to Berne's legacy, the Gouldings also demonstrated a passion for discovery, a keen interest in the client's welfare, and an intense engagement in achieving fast, permanent cure.

Getting in My Own Way: Reflections on Redecision Theory

Rough Edges

From his writings, we get a fair sense of the value Bob Goulding placed on challenging teachings and beliefs that proved limiting in relation to change and growth, one of his main supporting arguments being that this spirit of continuously challenging the status quo was something deeply embedded in the birth story of transactional analysis (Goulding, 1981). Therefore, he did not shy away from expressing uncomfortable disagreements with Berne's views on script formation and script cure. Berne's main thesis was that the parent's Child ego state was inserted like an electrode into the child's ego state structure. This electrode contained powerful messages called injunctions that "scripted" the person's life, becoming part of the Parent in their Child ego state and having vigorous influences on the individual and thereby limiting their capacity for autonomy. For change to take place, the therapist's power was considered to be the appropriate antidote in the sense that the therapist would have to work with the person's Adult in order to free the Child from parental programming. In this endeavor, script analysis and Adult decontamination from transference dynamics operating within the Child ego state proved to be essential.

The framework brought forward by the Gouldings relied heavily on a fundamentally opposing premise: They advocated for the person's free will and their capacity to make decisions both in childhood, in order to ensure survival at a physical and psychological level, and in adulthood, when redecisions could be made so that the person became free from a life-constraining functioning that was strongly influenced by script mechanisms. This capacity was translated into a sense of empowerment that resided in the patient and that lay at the heart of their understanding of treatment. Therefore, the role of the therapist was to support that power instead of offering permission, protection, potency and thereby encouraging transference dynamics: "THE POWER IS IN THE PATIENT. The patient must also protect himself, and give himself permission to change. I can't do it for him" (Goulding, 1981, pp. 50–51).

When aspects of transference, especially negative transference, emerged in redecision work, they were "*immediately* worked through" and put where they belonged (Goulding & Goulding, 1978, p. 186). This meant that the client was invited to use chair work, a technique whereby a client would envisage someone (possibly a parent) on an empty chair and converse with them in order to address any transferential needs, feelings, and longings. They were not analyzed or made part of a meaning-making process between client and therapist. Rather, they were confronted and handled outside the therapeutic relationship. This conceptualization of treatment gains depth as we consider it in conjunction with the stance that the Gouldings took toward Schiffian reparenting. They considered that this approach inappropriately encouraged dependency on the therapist—treatment often occurring from the therapist's Parent ego state—so they questioned its long-term therapeutic value (Goulding & Goulding, 1978). Bob Goulding explicitly voiced disagreement and concern regarding the ways in which transactional analysts worked with transference. His view was that it was one of "the analysts' tools of trade" and that TA practitioners did not have the required training to facilitate transference resolution (Goulding, 1981).

As we sit longer with what comes through in the writings of Bob and Mary Goulding, we begin to get a clearer sense of how their approach was also vigorously influenced by opposition and contradiction with other views and treatment directions. We hear a restlessness in challenging previous theories in an attempt to not repeat errors from the past but to remain faithful to the aspiration of always growing and pushing beyond limitations. Remaining true to a particular theory out of loyalty to its author was something they passionately fought against. We also wonder, however, how much of this fighting spirit paradoxically became yet another norm for practitioners to take in and (over)adapt to.

As we step away from the rough contours embedded in the foundation of the redecision approach, we discover an innovative apparatus of theory and practice, one that tries to address important clinical dilemmas and that at times remains vulnerable to particular aspects that were avoided or overlooked.

The Intricate Architecture of the Child Ego State

One of the major contributions made by redecision theory is related to the development of a more in-depth understanding of the Child ego state. What is acknowledged is the fact that it develops from a young age at the interface between several complex psychological forces. One such force is the child's dependency on obtaining strokes from significant others so that they feel loved, recognized, and welcomed into the world. The second force is the impact generated by particular parental messages called "injunctions" (Goulding & Goulding, 1978), which are "given to the child by the parent's Child, usually (but not always) without the awareness of the parent's Adult" (p. 19). These describe how the child can achieve recognition. They are considered to be the force behind a person's script and the games played in order to support that particular script. Based on observations made in their clinical practice, Bob and Mary Goulding identified the following injunctions: Don't Be, Don't Be You, Don't Be a Child, Don't Be Grown Up, Don't Be Close, Don't, Don't Make It, Don't Be Sane, Don't Be Important, Don't Belong.

The Gouldings argued that the impact elicited by injunctive messages is an individual experience that carries the trace of both personal characteristics (such as the child's emotional strength, resourcefulness, or capacity to design coping mechanisms) and environmental aspects (such as the availability of alternative messages from other significant adults that the child can rely on). Therefore, two children who received the same parental message will most probably react differently, something that will translate into the script they choose to live by as well as the capacity to change in adulthood. More specifically, the stance taken by the Gouldings is that the Child ego state is the source of life decisions, thereby accommodating archaic needs and longings. And those decisions may be revisited at a later stage if the person so chooses. This fundamental principle had quite a strong influence on treatment methodology, as we will examine in a bit.

The intrapsychic function of life decisions is to keep at bay potential tensions emerging between the person's needs and the injunctions received from significant adults. Those tensions were called "impasses," a term borrowed from Gestalt psychotherapy. Phenomenologically, impasses describe situations in which the person would be facing the threat of losing the caregiver's love, nurturing, and recognition should they consider giving up early decisions and no longer living by the injunctions received. From an intrapsychic point of view, impasses refer to a state of conflict between ego states. There are three kinds: The first-degree[2] impasse between the Adult in the Child ego state (A_1) and the Parent ego state (P_2);

the second-degree impasse between the Adult in the Child ego state (A_1) and the Parent in the Child ego state (P_1), and the third-degree impasse between the Adapted Child and the Free Child.

Along with deconstructing the Child ego state and its underlying dynamics, redecision theory also puts forward a relevant perspective in understanding the Parent ego state. In 1968, Mary Goulding (then Mary Edwards) wrote about the existence of two Parent ego states coexisting in each individual: the "influencing" Parent and the "active" Parent. The influencing Parent addresses the Child in an internal dialogue that establishes acceptable patterns of feeling and behavior and is usually associated with the person's primary caretaker. Phenomenologically, this is a private experience in the sense that others can only infer the presence of the influencing Parent based on observing the person's reactions. The active Parent does not entertain an internal dialogue but is adamant in giving people instructions about how to think, feel, or behave; it defines reality, norms, or what things should be like in the world and is formed at a later stage of development. Making an appropriate diagnostic assessment thus becomes essential because it informs the therapist with regard to necessary treatment interventions. Within a redecision framework, interventions are directed toward the Child ego state; clinical data about the Parent is used to gain insight into how to best treat the Child.

Based on this astute mapping of the Child ego state, Mary Goulding, Bob Goulding, and Robert Drye (a psychiatrist and colleague/associate at the Western Institute) (1973) elaborated a clinical tool for assessing and monitoring suicidal risk. The issue of suicide or staying alive is conceptualized in terms of decisional processes that the person makes in the Child ego state. These are fundamentally different from promises or agreements made in relation to someone else because they account for the individual's autonomy and capacity to make choices.

There is, by now, no doubt that for redecision practitioners the Child ego state was what lay at the heart of treatment. Aided by our imagination, we may begin to distinguish textures in this aspect of the person's psyche that would then become engaged in redecision work: immersed in emotions of various intensities, carrying echoes and bruises of archaic rejections from significant others, holding on to the idea that the present comes with the possibility of choosing freely and generating change, and weighing whether to forever trade old yearnings for the exhilarating taste of autonomy and individual power. This would be quite a complex territory that one would have to navigate and work through. What should be the framework for accommodating such therapeutic endeavor?

An Environment Conducive to Change: From Magic to Personal Power

The framework designed by the Gouldings had to follow particular requirements, namely, to ensure a brief, rapid process and to remain transference-free. Their solution was to move the focus away from the person of the therapist onto the environment and the techniques that would help the person reach a redecision.

Most of the Gouldings' redecision work was carried out in a group format. After experimenting with several options, they opted for weekend marathons as the structure "truly conducive to change" (Goulding & Goulding, 1978, p. 19). The experience was described by most participants as intense. Group members were such keen supporters of new decisions that one may wonder if they functioned as a form of peer pressure in relation to archaic decisions that needed to change in order for cure to take place. It is equally imaginable that such pressure might have had its roots in group etiquette (Berne, 1963/1975, p. 110) and in the firm rules that were established during therapy marathons:

Once we had gathered, they went over the rules. They were few and simple. No alcohol was to be consumed except for the wine that would be served with dinner. If you brought grass with you, take it off the property and bury it somewhere immediately as it was an illegal substance. There was to be no violence or threats of violence. If someone needed to express his rage by breaking a piece of furniture, that would be OK as long as the person paid for it first. There was to be no sexual contact or sexual flirtation with anyone except the partner who came with you. If you couldn't agree to the rules, leave.

(McNeel, 2022b, p. 4)

Another element that was part of the group culture was the use of confrontation as a therapeutic tool. The use of expressions such as "I'll try," "I hope," "I wish," or "I can't" was consistently met with disapproval because it was viewed as a way of sabotaging the therapeutic process. Cure was the goal, and making progress was understood to be a strong antithesis to it, a direction that could eventually prove to be antitherapeutic from a redecision perspective.

Contracting was an essential part of the working frame, both with its administrative as well as psychological implications. For instance, working slots could not exceed 20 minutes because anything beyond that was thought to encourage dependency in the therapeutic relationship. Any piece of work would begin with the question "What do you want to change today?" which was believed to stimulate the person's autonomy and to diminish resistance.

As we became increasingly acquainted with the atmosphere of redecision group marathons, we began to sense a particular kind of energy, one that frantically voices the fact that change is possible and that it is actually a course of action that needs to be taken. It becomes a synonym for freedom and personal power. Goulding (1981) wrote that the therapist is the one who facilitates impasse resolution rather than the one who treats transferential entanglements. The Gouldings steered away from seeing themselves as providing a facilitating environment in favor of assuming that change was the natural progression for everyone. We wonder whether this perspective paradoxically supports the idea that the client should necessarily choose freedom and autonomy and bypass internal feelings of doubt, helplessness, or vulnerability. McNeel (2021), a transactional analyst who worked and trained closely with the Gouldings, reflected on how this philosophy became quite rigid, leading people to make defiant decisions, thereby going against their script, yet not necessarily succeeding in making lasting transformative changes:

> The Gouldings' work was impactful. In the progression from feeling despair, hopelessness, and disempowerment, they tapped into a person's energy for change even if from a defiant place. But although the intent of the decision might reside with the person for some time, the absence of active support in transitioning to new ways of thinking and behaving could leave a person confused and vulnerable. It is unrealistic for that state to be the final destination. Living from a defiant position is exhausting and makes the person more vulnerable to the despair when it reappears. On the other hand, living from a defiant position feels better than living from despair.
>
> (p. 220)

The role of the therapist was to accompany clients back to early childhood scenes where archaic decisions had been made and to help them work through impasses so that they could redecide. There was a lot of emphasis on the fact that the process needed to address not only the cognitive layer of the individual's psyche but also the affective one. This was achieved with the use of various Gestalt techniques, such as imagery and chair work. Bob and Mary Goulding stepped into this intrapsychic territory of childhood yearnings, hurts, and disappointments determined to remain entirely untouched by them and outside of the process so as to avoid evoking feelings of dependency in the client and to keep their own Parent ego state removed from the encounter with the client. Here, we notice certain similarities with Berne's own positioning as the outside observer, keeping a certain separateness and avoiding parental interventions. Some clients' lived experience stands proof of the fact that this intention proved to be a form of wishful thinking, given the complexities put forward by the terrain of clinical practice: "They did nurture me. Hell, they parented me! They stroked the dickens out me. They affirmed me every step of the way. They were outrageously kind and generous with me" (McNeel, 2022c, p. 10).

As we allow the echo of this testimony to move us, we may begin to grasp the level of faith and commitment that Bob and Mary Goulding put into their work. Their trust in the human potential to be free and empowered was ferocious, so much so that at some point it may have ceased to be solely a potential and may have become certainty, an unquestionable truth about being human. Such conviction may have fueled their aspiration of facilitating profound change in their clients, helping them become autonomous and giving up painful yearnings or longings to be in someone else's care. This same conviction may also have over-emphasized the feeling of personal power and potency to the point of failing to acknowledge vulnerability and the need for the presence of another mind, another body, who can carry with us what otherwise feels overwhelming or an experience that is sensed as too raw and fragile. Such endeavors often call for facing the challenging, murky territory of transference–countertransference dynamics. Otherwise, this journey of personal growth runs the risk of remaining deeply lonely and lifeless: "I think Bob and Mary subscribed more to the belief that suffering is optional. I think they saw it as a racket that could be banned from one's life. I feel sorry about that. It isolated them" (McNeel, 2022c, p. 9).

Similarly to Berne, Bob and Mary Goulding also had a deeply embedded desire for peace and justice: "*I believe that psychotherapy is the best way to end war over time. I believe that if people feel OK about themselves and see others as being OK people too, they won't kill them*" (Robert Goulding as cited in McNeel, 2022a, p. 1). Considering the lingering, destabilizing echoes of atrocities such as the Second World War and the Vietnam War, this desire was perhaps a rather complex web in which hope and the push to restore trust in humanity was intimately interwoven with despair and the pull to remain strong and self-sufficient when experiencing vulnerability. The aspiration of the theory and methodology of the redecision framework left the imprint of a "can do" attitude and failed, in our view, to maintain a reflective space, which is much needed in the ongoing struggle of humanity.

What we set out to explore in this chapter was precisely the humanness in both the Schiffian reparenting and the redecision approaches—hence, the aspirations, the flaws, and the vulnerability that we have seen while reflecting on the theoretical frameworks they provided and the context in which those frameworks were elaborated.

Both models claimed to be firmly grounded in Berne's work and transactional analysis, but they stressed opposite ego states as the source of trouble and the focus of treatment: Authors from the reparenting tradition emphasized the role of the Parent ego state, whereas those from the redecision school prioritized the necessity of addressing the Child ego state. Both approaches aspired to offer innovative methods of working therapeutically with severe forms of psychological trouble, including psychosis or trauma. In their particular ways, they both set out to facilitate access to treatment for a larger number of individuals than what was available at the time and considered that the role of a group or a community was significant in the process. These were all core values and passions partly absorbed from the social and historical context of the era and partly inherited from Berne's early writings.

Sadly, the legacy of both theories included agonizing feelings of loss, disillusionment, hopelessness, and lived experiences of atrocity. In the absence of finding meaning, we have come to think that these experiences remained dissociated, generating various forms of radical attitudes toward cure as well as a sense of urgency to be effective and a certainty with regard to theory and methodology. In our view, it then became the task of subsequent TA generations not only to further refine the concepts and their application in practice but also to wonder, process, and perhaps abide by the lingering emotional wounds of the past.

Notes

1 The term "patient" is used interchangeably with the term "client" in the writings of Bob and Mary Goulding. From here on, we will use the latter word given that it is consistent with contemporary TA vocabulary.
2 The term "degree" refers to the type of impasse, not to its severity.

References

"Being a member of my family" (1969). *Transactional Analysis Bulletin.* 8:3, 66–68.
Berne, E. (n.d.). [*Principles of transactional analysis*] UC San Francisco, Library, Special Collections, Berne (Eric L.) Collections. https://calisphere.org/item/7b28ef43-297b-4c8d-9782-5abb80567625
Berne, E. (ca. 1935). [Eric Berne letter to Father (David Hillel Bernstein)]. UC San Francisco, Library, Special Collections, Berne (Eric L.) Collections, https://calisphere.org/item/efd3c521-e2ed-4bc8-9138-27c28de1a811
Berne, E. (1955). Intuition IV: Primal images and primal judgment. *Psychiatric Quarterly.* 29, 634–658.
Berne, E. (1961). *Transactional analysis in psychotherapy: A systematic individual and social psychiatry.* Grove Press & Evergreen Books.
Berne, E. (1963/1975). *The structure and dynamics of organizations and groups.* Grove Press. (Original work published 1963)
Berne, E. (1968). Staff-patient staff conferences. *The American Journal of Psychiatry.* 125:3, 286–293. https://doi.org/10.1176/ajp.125.3.286
Berne, E. (1969). Introduction. *The Transactional Analysis Bulletin.* 8:31, 45–46.
Berne, E. (1977). Primal images and primal judgment. In E. Berne, *Intuition and ego states: The origins of transactional analysis* (P. McCormick, Ed.). TA Press. (Original work published 1955 as Intuition IV Primal images and primal judgment)
Cheney, W. D. (1971). Eric Berne: Biographical sketch. *Transactional Analysis Journal.* 1:1, 14–22. https://doi.org/10.1177/036215377100100104
Cornell, W. F. (2022). Schiffian reparenting theory reexamined through contemporary lenses: Comprehending the meanings of psychotic experience. *Transactional Analysis Journal.* 52:1, 40–58. https://doi.org/10.1080/03621537.2021.2011035
Crossman, P. (2004). The etiology of a social epidemic. *The Skeptic.* www.astraeasweb.net/politics/crossman.html
Drye, R., Goulding, R. L., & Goulding, M. E. (1973). No-suicide decisions: Patient monitoring of suicidal risk. *American Journal of Psychiatry.* 130:2, 171–174. https://doi.org/10.1176/ajp.130.2.171
Edwards, M. (1968). The two parents. *Transactional Analysis Bulletin.* 7:26, 37–38.
English, F. (2010). Personal encounters with a flawed genius: Eric Berne. *Transactional Analysis Journal.* 40:3–4, 205–211. https://doi.org/10.1177/036215371004000305
Goulding, R. L. (1981). Challenging the faith. *Transactional Analysis Journal.* 11:1, 50–53. https://doi.org/10.1177/036215378101100111
Goulding, R. L., & Goulding, M. M. (1978). *The power is the patient: A TA/Gestalt approach to therapy* (P. McCormick, Ed.). TA Press.
Heathcote, A. (2016). Eric Berne and loss. *Transactional Analysis Journal*, 46:3, 232–243. https://doi.org/10.1177/0362153716648979
Landaiche, N. M. III (2022). Schiffian reparenting: 15 years in the early TA literature (1961–1975). *Transactional Analysis Journal.* 52:1, 8–23. https://doi.org/10.1080/03621537.2021.2011025
McNeel, J. (2021). From cure to healing: Rethinking the nature of cure within a redecision perspective. *Transactional Analysis Journal.* 51:3, 216–225. https://doi.org/10.1080/03621537.2021.1951469
McNeel, J. (2022a, March 23). Chapter one: I meet Bob. In J. McNeel, *Redecision therapy.* www.aspiringtokindness.com/redecision-therapy
McNeel, J. (2022b, March 23). Chapter two: My training begins. In J. McNeel, *Redecision therapy.* https://static1.squarespace.com/static/5b5a2d76b40b9d0ca1148654/t/5c7c7f18f9619a8f90672a64/1551662873436/BOB+AND+MARY-+Chapter+Two.pdf
McNeel, J. (2022c, March 23). Chapter five: They did what they said and they said what they did. In J. McNeel, *Redecision therapy.* https://static1.squarespace.com/static/

5b5a2d76b40b9d0ca1148654/t/5c89aba0ec212dca0a29f8c1/1552526341275/ BOB+AND+MARY+%23+5.pdf

Mellacqua, Z. (2014). Beyond symbiosis. The role of primal exclusions in schizophrenic psychosis. *Transactional Analysis Journal*. 44:1, 8–30. https://doi.org/10.1177/0362153714529410

Mellacqua, Z. (2020). When a mind breaks down: A brief history of efforts to understand schizophrenia. *Transactional Analysis Journal*. 50:2, 117–129. https://doi.org/10.1080/03621537.2020.1726657

Mountain, C. (2022). Schiffian reparenting: A critical evaluation. *Transactional Analysis Journal*. 52:1, 74–88. https://doi.org/10.1080/03621537.2021.2011041

Schiff, J. L. (1969). Reparenting schizophrenics. *Transactional Analysis Bulletin*. 8:31, 47–63.

Schiff, J. L., & Day, B. (1972). *All my children*. Pyramid Books. (Original work published 1970)

Schiff, J. L., Schiff, A. W., Mellor, K., Schiff, E., Schiff, S., Richman, D., Fishman, F., Wolz, L., Fishman, C., & Momb, D. (1975). *Cathexis reader: Transactional analysis treatment of psychosis*. Harper & Row.

van Beekum, S. (2016). Beyond the concepts: Celebrating Eric Berne's legacy. *Transactional Analysis Journal*. 46:1, 8–12. https://doi.org/10.1177/0362153715611687

Chapter 5

Room for a Diversity of Thinking and Approach

The Development of Constructivist, Constructionist, and Co-Creative Approaches in Transactional Analysis

As we reviewed the questions, reflections, and shared philosophy from our colleagues in fields different from ours and the ensuing maturation of ideas, we began to think more generally about how and when some transactional analysis (TA) practitioners had begun to move away from the certainty we highlighted in earlier chapters and adopt a more questioning approach.

The 1980s and 1990s were a time of much research, particularly in the areas of developmental psychology and cognitive science research. Alongside this were important feminist contributions such as those of Carol Gilligan (1993), who worked alongside Erik Erikson and Lawrence Kohlberg. Gilligan argued that research by Kohlberg on moral development held a bias because his conclusions and development of a scale of moral maturity valued logical deduction more often found in answers from boys more highly than the uncertainty more often found in girls' answers. Gilligan argued that the girls' answers did not show a failure in logic but, rather, a difference in approach to the problem, one based on wondering about other possibilities and with more emphasis on mutuality and reciprocity. The feminist critique on scientific objectivity was making its way into the world of transactional analysis opening the door for questions about how meaning is made.

In addition, findings in the cognitive sciences also advocate for the importance of how we construct narratives to give meaning to our experience, emphasizing that the clinician should focus on the individual's idiosyncratic way of creating a (life) story. From this perspective, some TA authors wrote about script as a narrative in its own right, one that would ensure coherence and that could be subjected to change. This view is also compatible with an understanding of the person more as an author of interpretations rather than a depository/"container" of lived experience.

What Can Be Relied Upon?

James and Barbara Allen had for some time been developing ideas that disturbed some in the TA community. In 1989, James wrote to the *Transactional Analysis Journal* (*TAJ*) editor hoping to reduce confusion about the ideas they had been considering. His reason for doing this was that they had received many letters, some expressing excitement and others confusion and "even horror," and he wished to clarify some of their thinking.

> First, our basic position is that evidence is accumulating to suggest that each of us actually creates the self he or she considers himself or herself to be, his or her script, and the world he or she inhabits. We do this constantly and "in the now," reviewing, creating, and recreating our pasts and our futures. Thus, in some cases, we may actually be creating in the present the injunctions we believe we received, the experiences we believe we had.
> (Allen, 1989, p. 118)

Allen continued by expressing that their intention was not to destroy the basic tenet of script analysis by suggesting that a person's ideas of their script are not real and that TA interventions to help a person redecide were not valid. Their emphasis was more that there may be multiple ways of understanding these premises, which can change and shift over time.

We imagine that the editors of the *TAJ* in the late 1980s and early 1990s were continually sharpening their pencils in editing and holding space for the many debates that were ensuing with regard to what constituted truth. What could be relied upon? How could the transactional analysis community keep moving on from the potential reification of Berne's ideas? In a letter to the editor published in January 1990, Edward Zerin wrote, "Neither observation nor reason are authorities. Their most important function—and even of intuition and imagination—is to help us in the critical examination of those bold hypotheses which are the means by which we probe into the unknown" (Zerin, 1990).

Zerin's letter was in response to an article by William F. Cornell entitled "Life Script Theory: A Critical Review from a Developmental Perspective" (1988). There ensued a lively exchange. Cornell, who appreciated Zerin's questions, wrote:

> It was my intention in that article to educate and provoke, not to declare a new theory, a new truth, or a more absolute reality! I wanted to introduce another perspective and body of literature to TA practitioners. I do believe it presents important information and challenges to theoretical deductions based on clinical work with adults. TA theory has been overly deductive and "reductive" in its development. I wanted to poke hard at that aspect of TA theory. I hope it won't be the last poke.
> (Cornell, 1990, p. 85)

While Cornell had no desire "to declare a new theory, truth or reality," his "poking" and thorough research on script theory to date did offer a decidedly new lens. He acknowledged that as far back as 1972, Allen and Allen had proposed influential factors outside the family sphere that determined script development. Cornell also introduced the idea of mutual influence with the developing child influencing as well as being influenced by their environment.

Constructivism and Constructionism

In 1991, a joint conference sponsored by the International Transactional Analysis Association (ITAA) and the USA Transactional Analysis Association (USATAA) was held in Stamford, Connecticut, and was entitled "Creating Future Realities: Choice, Chance, Change?" James Allen gave the keynote speech, the stated intention of which was "to explore the construction of reality in terms of Transactional Analysis" (Allen, 1991, p. 3).

In 1997, a theme issue of the *TAJ* was devoted to constructivism, a theory that suggests that understanding and meaning-making is an active process of integration of new information gained through social discourse with prior lived experience. In that issue, there were seven articles and two guest editors, James Allen and Bruce Loria; one of the authors, Graham Barnes, introduced a speech given in 1977 by Gregory Bateson, one of the fathers of cybernetics, a study of systems of communications. In 1997, Bateson had been somewhat critical of TA and its leanings toward creating a science based on energy theory. In his *TAJ* article, Barnes (1997) wrote:

> It seems appropriate to include Bateson's lecture in the first issue of this journal on constructivism and transactional analysis. Our theory created hypotheses out of the metaphors of the culture and time in which it was put together. Berne and his colleagues did not seem to acknowledge that they knew they were constructing a theory that was limited by the premises of its culture and that was specific to its time and place.
>
> (p. 136)

In their article in that *TAJ*, James and Barbara Allen (1997) proposed a new type of transactional analysis, constructive transactional analysis, and offered ideas on script work with a constructivist sensibility. Allen and Allen questioned the emphasis in transactional analysis on pathology, believing that "strength can be forged in the fires of trauma and abuse" (p. 94).

In his letter as guest editor of that same edition, Allen (1997) reminded readers of the importance of context. The constructivist sensibility keeps in mind that each individual constructs their world of experience, while the social constructionist is "interested in the narratives or discourses that have taken on a normative standard against which people measure and judge themselves. In other words, it deconstructs the Grand Narratives by focusing on how the prevailing norms have evolved over time" (Doan, 1997, p. 129).

One challenge that the Allens offered to the normative standard was related to the TA slogan of "I'm OK, You're OK," which had become so established.

> Many years ago, Virginia Satir's version of existential positions embraced the contexts in which one lives as well as the self and the other. "I count, you count, and the context(s) count(s)" was her formulation. Somehow, the context got lost

in transactional analysis, and we adopted the truncated form: "I'm OK, You're OK." It now seems the time to reintroduce the context(s).

(Allen, 1997, p. 88)

It is quite feasible that "I count, you count, and the context(s) count(s)" was not quite as catchy as "I'm OK, You're OK" in the global capitalism that reigned in the 1960s and 1970s and may not have served many in the more individually focused transactional analysis community at that time.

Loria (1997), in his guest editor letter in the same issue, believed transactional analysis in the United States was steeped in the "temptation of certitude" (p. 84) and that Berne's early death brought about "transactional analysis fiefdoms" whereby trainers separated themselves from the roots of psychoanalysis and believed that transactional analysis provided a "complete theory of psychotherapy and personality" (p. 84).

With hindsight, such isolation, although perhaps serving a legitimate defensive purpose, might have deprived transactional analysts of the possibility of entertaining more vigorous conversations with colleagues from non-TA modalities that were emerging and developing at the time. We may, perhaps, understand this as a cutting off from the multiple contexts generated by these other paradigms or approaches. To some degree, certainty might have been preferable to ambiguity, and continuity (i.e., remaining loyal to the already existing theory) must have been prioritized over coherence (i.e., revising those models that lacked clarity or integrating findings from other fields).

New Questions and New Creations From Old Roots?

As TA practitioners moved into the new millennium, along with the work of the constructivists and constructionists, there was the emergence of further questioning and critique of the pathologizing and reductionist attitude of transactional analysis. Summers and Tudor (2000), who particularly acknowledged the influence of Allen and Allen (1997), Cornell (1988), and Stern (1985, 2004), among others, embarked on a comprehensive "postmodernist project of retelling transactional analysis" (Summers & Tudor, 2000, p. 35).

Their ideas were an invitation for people to develop critical thinking. Their experiences of being trained and the development of their ideas as TA trainers led to them have concerns regarding the overemphasis on pathology in TA and that in the process of transactional analysis psychotherapy, adult clients were often infantilized.

Their ideas developed alongside those of Hargaden and Sills as they all met as colleagues regularly over seven years in peer consultation. In true constructivist fashion, they, who had shared training experiences and continued to meet as their careers developed, constructed different approaches and some different meanings from their concerns about the reductionist views held in traditional TA theory. (An outline of the relational approach developed by Hargaden and Sills will be developed in the next chapter.)

Summers and Tudor (2000, 2014) bemoaned that TA had lost some of the radical roots developed by Claude Steiner and Hogie Wycroff in the 1970s and 1980s and outlined their intention of returning to some basic concepts in TA while "discovering new meanings or reaffirming old ones, and applying these to a changing and postmodern world" (2000, p. 23). Their approach is based on a "positive health perspective" (p. 23). This approach, which was never meant to be a new school or tradition in TA (Summers & Tudor, 2014, p. 184), was clearly influenced not only by their TA experiences but by their experience and training in other approaches, namely, Gestalt and person-centered therapies. They took what they considered to be the building blocks of TA—ego states, transactions, scripts, and games—and offered a deconstruction and reconstruction of the elements of TA theory and application. They did this by positing three basic principles: we-ness, shared responsibility, and present-centered development.

In proposing the principle of we-ness, Summers and Tudor wished to make a major shift from the assumption that many supervisors made in the 1990s whereby a reference to *We* in the therapeutic relationship was interpreted to mean that the therapist had colluded in an unhealthy symbiosis with their client. Summers and Tudor considered that this was an assumption of Parent/Child relating that they deem as unhelpful. They also built on the ideas of Parlett (1991) to bring forward the importance of relationship and community: "Members of the American Gestalt therapy movement have overstressed 'I'-ness because they are unaware of their cultural predisposition toward individualism with its corollary, aversion or avoidance of lasting intimacy or committed 'we'-ness" (Saner, 1989, p. 59, quoted in Parlett, 1991).

For Summers and Tudor, their concept of we-ness emphasized the importance of the therapeutic relationship, and their ideas are consistent with other research findings (Benjamin, 1974; Strupp, 2001) that a valued therapeutic relationship contributes more to successful outcomes than any specific treatment approach.

The importance of shared responsibility in co-creative theory and application is, in Summers and Tudor's view, a rebalancing of the swings in therapeutic attitude in terms of who holds responsibility. They believed that in the early days of transactional analysis, there was an overemphasis on the clients' responsibility. Conversely, in the 1980s and 1990s, with the emergence of integrative psychotherapy, Summers and Tudor suggested that there began to be an overemphasis on the therapist's responsibility.

Summers and Tudor credited the influence of Daniel Stern (1985, 2004) with their focus on present-centered development. Believing that much of transactional analysis was too focused on the past, they stressed the importance of present-centered human development as opposed to past-centered child development. They suggested that psychotherapy, or, indeed, any human development work, is better focused on Adult–Adult relating, which in their view minimizes the danger of adults being infantilized in the process of psychotherapy.

Summers & Tudor (2000), article introduced some new terms, the first being cocreative reality (p. 25). This describes how the therapeutic relationship is cocreated through transactions whereby a shared reality is established. Following this, there is a discussion of the three other pillars of TA theory: ego states, which Summers and Tudor termed "co-creative personality"; scripts, which they termed "co-creative identity"; and games, which they termed "co-creative confirmation."

Co-Creative Reality (Transactions)

Summers and Tudors centered their work regarding transactions on what happens in the therapeutic relationship. In the spirits of the positive psychology approach, their emphasis was on the co-creation of a new reality: "A transactional analysis model of therapeutic relationships needs to be based on the analysis of transactions in the therapeutic relationship: a co-creative transactional relationship" (Summers & Tudor, 2000, p. 26).

They considered that the new reality is found through the co-transferential matrix, in which there are four ways of relating: present-centered relating with both I and You in the present, which Summers and Tudor called Adult–Adult transactional relating; past-centered relating with I and You relating from the past, which they termed co-transferential relating; and partial transferential relating with either I or You in the past and one of us in the present.

In co-creative TA, Summers and Tudor adopted an approach whereby there is agreement between client and therapist that familiar ways and fresh ways of relating are cocreated within the therapeutic relationship. The contractual process is one in which the original transferential meanings are explored, clarified, and brought to new understandings within the present-centered Adult-to-Adult relationship through a framework of intersubjective phenomenology. Similarly, Summers and Tudor's position on impasses or stuck places within clients was that they originated in relationship, are potentially co-maintained through transferential relating, and can be co-resolved through Adult-to-Adult exploration and meaning-making.

Co-Creative Personality and Debate Over Ego State Models

In 1988, a theme issue of the *TAJ* on ego state models provided articles showing the lively debate that was being held in the TA community. One article was based on part of a 1987 conference roundtable discussion that centered on "Transactional Analysis Theory: Past, Present, and Future." The discussants were Richard Erskine, Petrūska Clarkson, Robert Goulding, Martin Groder, and Carlo Moiso (1988). The article presented only the discussion on ego states and offered a wide range of views on who defines reality and the ongoing debate about ego state and pathology. An excerpt is shown below. Bob Goulding had just proposed a question to Richard Erskine regarding in which ego state would he play yesterday's experiences. Carlo Moiso answered followed by Richard Erskine and then Bob Goulding.

CM: I have a comment on where we put yesterday. I think it is very difficult to put together time extension and psychic functioning. I think some of yesterday went in the Parent, some in the Child, and some in the Adult. I say that to be consistent with one of the properties of ego states defined by Berne, biological fluidity. Each ego state grows with time.

RE: I hope your Parent is not growing, but is really shrinking. And I hope your Child is not growing, and that it's also shrinking to the point where it's integrated within the Adult.

BG: I don't understand that at all. What's wrong with my Parent changing? I do an awful lot of my nurturing from my Parent ego state. You may think it's Adult! (Erskine et al., 1988, p. 9)

In the same issue, Richard Erskine's article "Ego Structure, Intrapsychic Function, and Defense Mechanisms: A Commentary on Eric Berne's Original Theoretical Concepts" engendered some intrepid exploration of different ego state models. Erskine proposed that

> the healthy ego is one in which the Adult ego state, with full neopsychic functioning, is in charge and has integrated (assimilated) archeopsychic and exteropsychic content and experiences. When earlier defense mechanisms remain fixated, as evidenced by the Adult ego state remaining syntonic with or contaminated by Parent and/or Child ego state experiences, or when the boundaries between ego states are too permeable or loosely defined, the Adult ego state cannot serve this healthy, integrative function.
>
> (Erskine et al., 1988, p. 19)

By 1994, a request was published in the *TAJ* from the then editor Theodore Novey asking writers to clearly specify which ego state model they were referring to in their writings. Novey (1994) summarized that the three ego state model

> is made up of three types of ego states—Parent, Adult, and Child—all of which can be updated or changed at any point during a person's life, all of which can be in contact and utilized in the here-and-now, and all of which can contain memories and learning that result in what we identify as healthy or pathological internal experience and external behavior.
>
> (p. 156)

The integrated Adult ego state model he described as assuming that:

> the human personality is made up of three types of ego states—Parent, Adult, and Child—but only Adult ego states can be in contact with the here-and-now, healthy internal experience and external behavior is associated only with Adult

ego states, and pathological internal experience and external behavior is associated only with Parent and Child types of ego states.

(p. 156)

The debate continues to this day, with proponents of both models citing inconsistency in Berne's original writing as the main point of confusion and confirming that he wrote from both points of view.

We believe it is worth noting that this debate often runs the risk of becoming a competition in which the right to define reality is at stake. The space for holding multiple meanings and realities collapses, and what seems to matter is establishing the truth with regard to the ego state model. Engaging in this kind of dynamic has been, in our view, one of the hindrances that prevented TA theory from gaining more robustness and coherence. This is a point we will develop further in Chapter 9.

From the stance of Summers and Tudor, their development of co-creative TA, and their subsequent coining of ego states as personality creation, it follows that they would prefer the integrated Adult model with its emphasis on present-centered Adult relating.

Ten years after the first article on co-creative TA was published in the *TAJ*, Tudor (2010) presented a thoroughly researched article entitled "The State of the Ego: Then and Now" in which he advocated for an appreciation of difference between the two models and his wish to not argue for the primacy of one model or set of models over another.

Co-Creative Identity (Script)

With the inherent emphasis on dynamic possibilities in the co-creative model, Summers and Tudor advanced the script model proposed by Cornell in 1988 to develop a script matrix showing mutually influencing vectors between child and parent or parent figures. They were at pains to emphasize that they did not wish to imply that there was a mutuality of power between parents and children. Consequently, they later modified this matrix after discussions with Steiner in 2008 to show more of a power imbalance with regard to "one polarity of influence" (Summers & Tudor, 2014, p. 211).

In the continuing spirit of "discovering new meanings or reaffirming old ones, and applying these to a changing and postmodern world" (Summers & Tudor, 2000, p. 23), Summers and Tudor developed a script helix to account for their belief that the script is co-constructed. They offered a helix as "a cocreated series of matrices, rather like a constantly changing helix of relational atoms, spinning around us, by which we tell, retell, and reformulate the stories of different influences on our continuing development" (Summers & Tudor, 2000, p. 34). The helix incorporates influences from the ever-increasing plethora of possibilities in an ever-changing world.

Co-Creative Confirmation (Games)

Consistent with the co-creative orientation toward health psychology, Summers and Tudor re-visioned game theory as being able to describe healthy and pathological processes and believed that Berne's (1964/1968) definition of a game as "an ongoing series of complementary ulterior transactions progressing to a well-defined, predictable outcome" (p. 44) is consistent with this.

They referred to Berne's (1964) much less quoted work on good games, where "the social contribution outweighs the complexity of its motivations" (p. 143). They also made reference to Satir (1978), who had taken game theory and developed four distinct categories of games. She named these rescue games, coalition games, lethal games, and growth vitality games. The growth vitality games feature freedom of expression by oneself and others such that each can agree or disagree and maintain flexibility from moment to moment.

Summers and Tudor (2000) viewed games as patterns and as the mechanism through which we "co-create confirmation of versions of reality" (p. 37).

> These versions of reality may be past- or present-centered and can incorporate either discounting or, importantly, accounting and, therefore, nonexploitative ulterior transactions. In many ways, game theory is the aspect of transactional analysis in which Berne particularly emphasized the cocreated nature of relationship patterns.
> (pp. 37–38)

In 2014, Summers and Tudor published a book entitled *Co-Creative Transactional Analysis: Papers, Responses, Dialogues, and Developments*. The book consisted of ongoing co-creative discussions between Summers and Tudor and contributions from other colleagues. Since their 2000 *TAJ* paper, they had each further developed aspects of the theory, so they offered each other questions and critique about their individual developments.

One development that Tudor had written about in a 2003 chapter in a book entitled *Ego States* (Tudor, 2003 in Sills & Hargaden, 2003) was the integrating Adult. By that, he meant integrating as a process rather than a state. Tudor developed a new diagram of an Adult ego state with overlapping circles to emphasize the dynamic nature and the idea of an expanding Adult ego state (p. 217). In later years, Summers and Tudor (2021, p. 12) have preferred to refer to the integrating Adult as the Neopsyche (Figure 5.1).

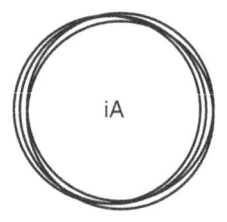

Figure 5.1 The Neopsyche/integrating Adult

Diagram of the Adult Ego State

In 2011, Summers wrote a chapter entitled "Dynamic Ego States in Relational Transactional Analysis: Principles in Practice" (Summers, 2011). In it, he referenced the work of Daniel Stern (2004) and proposed a dynamic ego state model whereby Parent and Child ego states comprise conscious, pre-conscious, and unconscious processes and that the Adult ego state comprises conscious, pre-conscious, and *nonconscious* processes. Summers's differentiation between unconscious and nonconscious was to highlight that there is implicit knowing in the Adult ego state that may not yet be able to be put into words but is not repressed as in the unconscious processes of the Parent and Child ego states.

> The heart of the transformational process, however, takes place within implicit nonconscious inter-relations through the co-creative (but not necessarily conscious, verbal, or explicit) Adult–Adult "moments of meeting" (Stern, 2004, p. 165) and new ways of being with another that develop in parallel with co-transferential replays The additional significance of acknowledging a nonconscious implicit realm of experience and relating is that it supports the conceptualization of the expanded/expanding Adult ego state.
>
> (pp. 61–62)

Making this distinction between unconscious and nonconscious processes also reflects the strong emphasis placed on health, instead of pathology. In this context, the first term is used mainly to refer to traumatic experiences that linger unprocessed in the person's psyche, whereas the latter aims to describe normal, healthy occurrences throughout life.

Further work by Tudor as described in his 2011 *TAJ* article "Empathy, A Co-creative Perspective" clearly situated co-creative TA as part of the relational tradition. He clarified the differences in approach both between co-creative TA and integrative TA, and co-creative TA and relational TA in terms of the way they consider empathy.

> While both approaches view empathy as the principle method, the integrative approach tends to rely on the potency of the therapist and the therapist's empathy, whereas in the co-creative model, the therapist's empathic resonance and responsiveness is a stimulus for both client and therapist to engage in a search for further understanding of the client's experiencing process and internal frame of reference … It is more accurate to say that the power or potency of the therapeutic encounter lies in the cocreated relational field, which is why co-creative transactional analysis reflects and represents a two-person psychology if not, or as well as, a two-person-plus psychology.
>
> (Tudor, 2011, p. 330)

The difference between co-creative TA and relational TA is to be found in three specific areas. The first is in their differing analysis of the self. For example, in

2001 and 2002, Hargaden and Sills situated the self in the Child ego state and showed a preference for the three ego state model of health, whereas co-creative TA promotes the integrating Adult. In the co-creative model, the self is expanded through a process of abstraction, that is, through the expansive experience of new relational possibilities.

> The client, in effect, integrates this experiential knowledge into responses that are increasingly acceptant and empathic of herself or himself and others, including the therapist. This is the intrapsychic aspect of the integrating and expanding Adult process ... This integration *is* the therapy.
> (Summers & Tudor, 2014, p. 130, emphasis added)

The second is in their differing approach to empathic transactions, which in Hargaden and Sills are directed toward the Child ego state, whereas co-creative TA promotes moment-to-moment, present-centered transactions. The third difference is in their approaches to relating and working. Hargaden and Sills advocated working through varying transferential understandings and co-creative TA emphasizes the creation of new relational possibilities in the present-centered relationship.

We are aware that co-creative TA has not defined itself as a school, a paradigm, or even as an approach to clinical treatment. It is within these premises that there is an emphasis on working in the present while using the parameters of the therapeutic relationship to create new possibilities. These possibilities, it is argued, will eventually serve as alternative constructions of meaning that the client can use more effectively.

Although Summers and Tudor are clear that co-creativity is not defined as a way to work, we are aware that the hunger for structure means that those inspired by the model can take on a more concrete application and miss the subtleties of the respectful inquiry into phenomenology that the originators value.

It is in this respectful inquiry that we emphasize the thorough attention that needs to be paid to the potential of clients' traumatic histories and possible different ways of processing. This is where lived experience is received and honored in the clinical encounter.

In our view, it is paramount that the clinician who practices from a co-creative sensibility is also well equipped with a sound understanding of the more disturbing aspects of the human psyche, such as the impact of trauma on the mind or psychotic processes. Similarly, there may be clients for whom expectations of relating may actually be the trauma. It is here that the importance of Summers's term "respectful speculation" (personal communication, April 4, 2023) into a client's phenomenology cannot, in our view, be overemphasized.

To conclude this chapter, to loop back to our consideration of the special fields and forward to our consideration of the relational TA. We acknowledge that a major advantage in the evolutionary nature of co-creative theory is its ever-expanding application. The emphasis away from pathology and toward positive psychology inclines the application of the ideas to all fields in transactional analysis and fits with the ideas of Grégoire (1998):

> There is a place to welcome and validate all positive change. It is indisputable that profound personal change, including script change, takes place in supervision, education, counseling, and organizational development as well as in daily life. The supervisor, the teacher, or the change agent can validate and welcome what he or she sees as the beneficial result of his or her own behavior, congratulate the client for the results achieved, and congratulate himself or herself on it. This is one more way of respecting others and oneself.
>
> (p. 320)

References

Allen, J. R. (1989). Letter to the editor. *Transactional Analysis Journal.* 19:2, 118–119. https://doi.org/10.1177/036215378901900210

Allen, J. R. (1991). Constructivist TA: The exploration of TA reality. *The Script.* 23:2, 3.

Allen, J. R. (1997). Letter from the guest editor. *Transactional Analysis Journal.* 27:2, 87–88. https://doi.org/10.1177/036215379702700203

Allen, J. R., & Allen, B. A. (1997). A new type of transactional analysis and one version of script work with a constructionist sensibility. *Transactional Analysis Journal.* 27:2, 89–98. https://doi.org.10.1177/036215379702700204

Barnes, G. (1997). A story about telling stories: Introducing Bateson's "epistemology of organization. *Transactional Analysis Journal.* 27:2, 134–137. https://doi.org/10.1177/036215379702700209

Bateson, G. (1997). Epistemology of organization. *Transactional Analysis Journal.* 27:2, 138–145. https://doi.org/10.1177/036215379702700210

Benjamin, L. S. (1974). Structural analysis of social behavior. *Psychological Review.* 81:5, 392–425.

Berne, E. (1964). *Games people play: The psychology of human relationships*. Penguin.

Cornell, W. F. (1988). Life script theory: A critical review from a developmental perspective. *Transactional Analysis Journal.* 18:4, 270–282. https://doi.org/10.1177/036215378801800402

Cornell, W. F. (1990). Letters to the editor. *Transactional Analysis Journal.* 20:1, 83–85. https://doi.org/10.1177/036215379002000113

Doan, R. E. (1997). Narrative therapy, postmodernism, social constructionism, and constructivism: Discussion and distinctions. *Transactional Analysis Journal.* 27:2, 128–133. https://doi.org/10.1177/036215379702700208

Erskine, R. G., Clarkson, P., Goulding, R. L., Groder, M., & Moiso, C. (1988). Ego state theory: Definitions, descriptions, and points of view. *Transactional Analysis Journal.* 18:1, 6–14. https://doi.org/10.1177/036215378801800103

Gilligan, C. (1993). *In a different voice, psychological theory and women's development.* Harvard University Press. (Original work published 1982)

Grégoire, J. (1998). Criteria for defining the boundaries of transactional analysis fields of application. *Transactional Analysis Journal.* 28:4, 311–320. https://doi.org/10.1177/036215379802800405

Loria, B. (1997). Letter from the guest editor. *Transactional Analysis Journal.* 27:2, 83–86. https://doi.org/10.1177/036215379702700202

Novey, T. B. (1994). Letter from the editor. *Transactional Analysis Journal.* 24:3, 154–157. https://doi.org/10.1177/036215379402400301

Parlett, M. (1991). Reflections on field theory. *The British Gestalt Journal*. 1, 69–81.
Saner, R. (1989). Culture bias of Gestalt therapy: Made-in-U.S.A. *The Gestalt Journal*. XII:2, 57–73.
Satir, V. (1978). *Conjoint family therapy*. Souvenir Press. (Original work published 1967)
Sills, C., & Hargaden, H. (Eds.) (2003). *Ego states* (pp. 201–231). Worth Publishing.
Stern, D. (1985). *The interpersonal world of the infant: A view from psychoanalysis and developmental psychology*. Basic Books.
Stern, D. N. (2004). *The present moment: In psychotherapy and everyday life*. Norton.
Strupp, H. H. (2001). Implications of the empirically supported treatment movement for psychoanalysis. *Psychoanalytic Dialogues*. 11, 605–619.
Summers, G. (2011). Dynamic ego states. In H. Fowlie, & C. Sills (Eds.), *Relational transactional analysis: Principles in practice* (pp. 59–67). Karnac.
Summers, G., & Tudor, K. (2000). Cocreative transactional analysis. *Transactional Analysis Journal*. 30:1, 23–40. https://doi.org/10.1177/036215370003000104
Summers, G., & Tudor, K. (2014). *Co-creative transactional analysis: Papers, responses, dialogues and developments*. Karnac.
Summers, G., & Tudor, K. (2021). Reflections on co-creative transactional analysis: Acceptance speech for the 2020 Eric Berne Memorial Award. *Transactional Analysis Journal*. 51:1, 7–18. https://doi.org/10.1080/03621537.2020.1853345
Tudor, K. (2003). The neopsyche: The integrating adult ego state. In C. Sills, & H. Hargaden (Eds.), *Ego states* (pp. 201–231). Worth Publishing.
Tudor, K. (2010). The state of the ego: Then and now. *Transactional Analysis Journal*. 40: 3–4, 261–277. https://doi.org/10.1177/036215371004000311
Tudor, K. (2011). Empathy: A cocreative perspective. *Transactional Analysis Journal*. 41:4, 322–335. https://doi.org/10.1177/036215371104100409
Zerin, E. (1990). Letters to the editor. *Transactional Analysis Journal*. 20:1, 83–85. https://doi.org/10.1177/036215379002000113

Chapter 6

The Development of Relational Transactional Analysis

Collective Efforts Toward Restoring Reflective Space

In writing this book, we have searched for ways to articulate our phenomenological understanding regarding the various theories and models that have found their way into the transactional analysis framework over time. We have looked for ways to "listen" to the clinical challenges that they were trying to conceptualize, the aspects that were overemphasized, underemphasized, or completely overlooked, as well as threads of the wider socio-historical contexts in which they emerged. Often, we have come to experience a sense of feeling disconcerted when coming up against what seemed to us a rigid focus of defining the right way to attain a cure, or on normalizing a particular vision regarding mental health (such as the longed-for status of an autonomous person that was promoted within the redecision approach). Such focus, in our view, inevitably led to a loss of subjectivity and a diminishing of vitality, both in the client, as well as the therapist.

In the history of transaction analysis (TA), perhaps the most extreme and tragic version of such loss of subjectivity happened within the Schiffian approach to diagnosis and treatment. It is not our intention in this chapter to examine this model, as we have offered our understanding of it in Chapter 3. Also, another in-depth theoretical and methodological analysis of Schiffian reparenting is available to the reader in the articles published in the special issue of the *Transactional Analysis Journal*, "Schiffian Reparenting Theory and Practice Reexamined." What we wish to bring forward at this point is the fact that transactional analysts' relationship to theory began to gain increasingly more attention and weight in the TA literature, perhaps also as a consequence of the fact that the community came to experience the painful consequences of theoretical rigidity, as well as of some forceful (or even violent at times) attempts to substitute theory for reality.

For instance, in his article about theory as ideology, Jacobs (1994) wrote that: "Theory becomes ideology when it is granted more than limited significance, that is, when it is held to be universal and pure. Totalist systems create overgeneralized ideology because they seek wide application and acceptance" (Jacobs, 1994, p. 51).

In order to address this risk and preempt the potentially harmful consequences that may result from the perpetuation of such systems, Jacobs' plea was for the TA practitioner to examine various epistemological aspects, to question the methods and premises that our clinical knowledge rested on. He specifically drew attention to the transactional analyst's relationship to theory, stating that theory itself could become a transference object, to the point where the person could remain rigidly and defensively attached to it, instead of maintaining a curious and reflective stance.

A few years later, the *Transactional Analysis Journal* published a "Letter to the Editor" written by Mitch Rouzie and Ann Arbor (1999). This contained not only a phenomenological account of the authors' experience at the Cathexis Institute, but also their reflection regarding reparenting and regressive techniques. Their stance was that such techniques and the way in which they were applied led to submission rather than reflection, to over-adaptation rather than structural change and that the Cathexis Institute eventually became a psychotherapy cult with destructive implications for those who joined it. Rouzie and Arbour ended their letter with a call to keep an open mind toward other prominent theories when examining transactional analysis models and concepts. Again, the emphasis seemed to be on not prioritizing theory at all costs. Nancy Porter-Steele (1999), the editor of the same issue, responded to this letter by pointing out once more that the theories we use may have the potential to cause harm and that, therefore, they need to be treated as "… a limited thing. Theory is concepts, and concepts have no inherent reality. Concepts point to some aspect of experience, but they are not the experience" (p. 90).

When theory is taken and used literally, when it becomes a frame of reference that should define reality, what follows is a profound loss of subjectivity (Barnes, 1999), a collapse of plurality, and an impossibility of allowing dialogue between multiple perspectives. Difference is either erased or painfully turned into a standardized, approved version of psychological reality. As a consequence, character and identity need to "be reshaped, not in accordance with one's special nature or potential, but rather to fit the rigid contours" (Jacobs, 1994, p. 50) of the doctrine.

Both therapist and client become merely objects, dehumanized entities who perform a ritualized action, rather than two human beings risking an encounter with the unknown, or the unpredictable in an attempt to make meaning (Rowland, 2016).

Intimately linked to the topic of objectification, there was another important theme which emerged in the transactional analysis literature as part of what we consider to be a collective effort to find more meaningful ways of relating to theory: the theme of power. We have come upon a persistent interest regarding the matter of power dynamics between therapist and client. Transactional analysts began to ask themselves questions about what would happen when the notion of power was applied in psychotherapy. Most importantly, perhaps, was it not an inherent logical flaw to assume that one (in this case, the client) could give power to someone else (the therapist) who would then take it and return it at some subsequent stage (Barnes, 1999)?

A special issue of the *Transactional Analysis Journal* (1994) that focused on ethical concerns included articles written by Petruska Clarkson (1994) and William Cornell (1994), which addressed the complexities of dual relationships in TA practice. The theme of power and its misuse came to the foreground: Would engaging in such dynamics inevitably lead to abuse, or on the contrary, would it make room for a more balanced perception of the other, thereby discouraging mystification or idolization? Clarkson was quite passionate in describing how important it was to also account for the therapist's particularities, life circumstances in specific situations, being explicit about the fact that it was not only the client who could be subjected to abuse in the psychotherapeutic relationship, but also the therapist. Cornell's stance was that an ethical and responsible approach consisted of making space to openly live through, discuss, and negotiate "the potential for dissonance and conflict in relation to factors such as role expectations, obligations, and power" (p. 29).

Later, Ken Woods (1998) wrote an article in which he reviewed reparenting techniques in the treatment of psychosis. His perspective was that, in some cases, methodologies ended up giving way to an abuse of power and the establishment of sadomasochistic dynamics in the psychotherapeutic relationship.

We have allowed our minds to wander and discover some aspects that were starting to preoccupy the wider TA community. It is our understanding that these concerns were of an ethical nature, but also of a theoretical and clinical one. Particular models were being put into question and the centrality of theory itself was challenged in a way that seemed to call for a shift in the already existing paradigm. Finding out "the truth" about the origin of psychological trouble seemed to lose its magic; yet, articulating a coherent framework that could help the practitioner navigate through the complex, unsettling processes occurring in the clinical encounter was still missing. Fanita English (1994) beautifully described this tension between the human desire for certainty and the impulse to grow a curious and free mind:

> This is the blessing of our species, though perhaps it is a curse for us as individuals, because there is no way to avoid the anxiety that accompanies uncertainty. However, when all is said and done, I would not want to relinquish my curiosity and my ability to doubt and disobey established authority. So I remain a proud daughter of Eve, who felt driven to bite into the apple in the Garden of Eden and to take the consequences, rather than to live eternally like a contented cow in its pasture. Was she right to do what she did?
>
> (p. 292)

In our view, these struggles and tensions would form the background and early seedlings of the relational approach in transactional analysis. Before moving further into discussing its conceptual framework and understanding of treatment, we will briefly mention some specific theoretical advancements which we consider to have been significant in the development of this approach to treatment.

Forerunners of the Relational Approach

Anchoring in the Roots that Grow Close to Home

The cornerstone of the relational approach was represented by the original structural model of ego states as elaborated by Berne (1961) and described in Chapter 1. The essence of that theoretical conceptualization of the human psyche that seems relevant to point out in this context is related to what Federn (1952) argued, namely, that the ego may be experienced as subject and object simultaneously. In his article "A Retrospective on States of the Ego," Ken Woods (1999) wrote that holding this view in mind was significant in order not to objectify internal experience, meaning the client's "observable states of the ego" (p. 268). Reflecting on how the model evolved over time, Woods noticed that sometimes TA theory provided the tools for both therapist and client to collude and defensively move away from a painful experience. To ensure this type of defense, the ego came to be treated only as an object; its quality as subject would disappear. Hence, by placing the trauma "out there" and treating it as external to the person through analysis and interpretation, the client would become objectified, something to be examined, rather than somebody with a complex internal architecture. Woods' emphasis and call toward practitioners was on finding methods of intervention (p. 271) that addressed the trauma while at the same time accounting for the person's subjectivity.

Another strong emphasis on the importance of subjectivity in psychotherapy can also be found in the writings of Petruska Clarkson (Clarkson, 1993; Clarkson & Gilbert, 1988). She traced valuable links between this idea and the value that Berne (1961) placed on transactional analysis as a "systematic phenomenology" (p. 244), thereby acknowledging the client's internal experience as a legitimate reality. Clarkson wrote that "Phenomenology as a philosophical approach values the importance of the person's subjective experience above any interpretation, prejudgment, or preconceived theory or idea" (p. 37).

We consider that these ideas were followed up and further developed by Helena Hargaden and Charlotte Sills, as founding authors of the relational perspective in transactional analysis. Their way to approach these issues theoretically and to maintain a clinically effective balance between the ego as object and the ego as subject was by integrating Berne's structural model with aspects related to the development of the self (we will elaborate on this further later in the chapter). In the introduction to their book, *Transactional Analysis. A Relational Perspective*, Hargaden and Sills (2002) argued that the self and the ego are not two distinct aspects of a person, but that "the self is intrinsically central to the ego. It is the core of identity and the foundation for the formation of the personality" (p. 4). Furthermore, the two authors located the self in the Child ego state and designed a methodological apparatus based on this understanding, which is something that we will examine in another section of this chapter.

At this point, we find it important to wonder about what might have been the challenge that transactional analysts had begun to grapple with. One way of thinking about this would be that they were faced with the question of how to access and address psychological trouble or disturbance without resorting to an objectification of the client, but with lending an ear to the phenomenological experience instead. The answer of theorists in the relational approach was that such work would entail the deconfusion of the Child ego state, meaning a working through of unintegrated archaic experiences. They support the idea that deconfusion could be attained most effectively by using the transferential dynamics that took place in the psychotherapeutic relationship as the main tool for intervention:

> A central premise of the model is that elements of an undeveloped or disturbed early self emerge in the transference within the client–therapist relationship and that the transferential relationship is the major vehicle for deconfusion. Essentially, we see the therapeutic relationship as a real relationship, but one which has the potential to involve therapist and client in many dimensions and many realities. An imaginative exploration of these multiple realities is made possible by an examination of the transferential relationship.
> (Hargaden & Sills, 2002, p. 4)

Several transactional analysis authors had already voiced the necessity to articulate a comprehensive theoretical understanding of transference and its centrality in working out the intricacies of unconscious communication.

For example, Michele Novellino (1987) wrote about protocol aspects which occurred in the psychotherapeutic work with borderline and narcissistic personality disorders. His view was that these primitive, archaic aspects manifested themselves in the transference and that, therefore, it became paramount for the therapists to analyze their countertransference. This would enable them to understand their unconscious identification with various dimensions of the patient's unconscious (p. 274). Resting on a psychodynamic background, the author further developed and refined methodologies to work with transferential and countertransferential phenomena in the service of deconfusing the Child ego state (Novellino, 1990; Novellino & Moiso, 1990).

Peg Blackstone (1993) undertook an in-depth analysis of the architecture of the Child ego state, considering it a dynamic part of the personality, that is continuously permeable to change. Her perspective was a developmental one which focused on integrating Bernean thinking with notions from object relations theory and self-psychology. In the context of this chapter, it is important to note that she also stressed the role played by the therapeutic relationship: She considered it to be the ingredient capable of bringing about change within the internal structure of the Child.

> Therapists who share this view understand the therapeutic relationship as one among many authentic, here-and-now relationships that provide the opportunity for the client to attach and benefit from that attachment. What kind of environment,

then, is needed to invite the Child to open up to new influences and to resolve internal conflicts by using the therapist as a self-object and guide?

(p. 230)

Diana Shmukler (1991) took a similar stance, namely, that intrapsychic change could become possible through the use of the therapeutic relationship. She was more specific in stating that this would be the case only for certain personality organizations, where "structural repair" was the treatment goal. Anchoring her thinking in Bernean theory, as well as object relations theory, she conceptualized transference as the appropriate vehicle that could effectively address early relational deficit experienced by the client.

As we trace the struggles and dilemmas of those involved in the development of TA theory, we notice how some turned not only to incipient Bernean thinking, but also to psychoanalytic models, such as object relations theory (Klein, 1975; Winnicott, 1958), or theories of the self (Kohut, 1977; Stern, 1985). In our understanding, this was a response to two significant aspects. One was the fact that there was an increasing acknowledgment of transactional analysis being originally rooted in psychoanalytic thinking; the energy invested in differentiating TA from Freudian theory and methodology was no longer so forceful, which allowed the space for more curiosity toward bridging some theoretical gaps and clarifying elements in Berne's models that had remained somewhat muddled or contradictory. The second significant aspect was that there was some awareness among transactional analysts that TA had become a rather self-referential system (Barnes, 1999), so a generative opening toward other approaches was vital for its development.

To further understand the philosophy and existential stance of relational transactional analysis, we also need to turn to some other interesting and relevant movements that were impregnating the world of psychotherapy and its wider social context in the late 1990s and early 2000s.

Riding the Wave of Worldwide Contemporary Thinking

Times were changing and theories were undergoing profound transformations in other psychotherapeutic orientations, also. Such was the psychoanalytic world which was buzzing with challenging ideas and innovative approaches to treatment, all articulated together in what came to be known as the relational turn (Mitchell & Aron, 1999, p. xiii). Relational psychoanalysis emerged as a paradigm that offered alternative understandings of similar issues as those tackled by classical (Freudian) theory, only with a different sensibility in the foreground. The analyst could no longer be considered as removed from the analytic endeavor, given that the image of a monadic mind functioning in isolation defied most scientific findings and philosophical thinking of the time: "One mind presumes other minds" (Mitchell, 2000, p. xii).

Rather, it was the interaction between the properties of the therapeutic dyad and the subjectivity of both analyst and patient that was viewed as essential (Mitchell & Aron, 1999).

Originally, relational theorists searched for coherent ways to bridge the gap between perspectives offered by interpersonal relations theories and object relations theories; gradually, they were influenced by other approaches, such as self-psychology, intersubjectivism, or social constructivism (Mitchell & Aron, 1999). Moreover, they acknowledged and integrated findings coming from infant research and attachment theories, relying to some degree on the writings of Daniel N. Stern, Peter Fonagy, and John Bowlby, as analyzed by Mitchell (2000). Similarly to what was going on in the TA community, their endeavor also stemmed from a necessity to revisit past models in order to revise current practice and to imagine future possibilities.

This shift in psychoanalysis, in our view, would find an echo in transactional analysis theory and methodology. The first element of resonance would be one about the nature of the mind, namely the fact that it grows in interaction with significant others and that it creates an individual phenomenological experience. A second concordant idea would be that the analyst's subjectivity was not only undeniably present in the clinical process, but that his or her participation was required for facilitating deep characterological change in the patient and for experiencing intimacy and mutuality. Powerful feelings, including love and hate, were no longer something in the patient's psyche to be interpreted and solely attributed to past relational experiences, but they were fostered by the relational context emerging from the analytic dyad. Therefore, a third aspect that both frameworks came to acknowledge was the fact that contemporary theory and methodology were no longer explaining transference and countertransference dynamics as going on "out there," but rather "in here," meaning in the therapy room. Developing ways to attend to them was going to become the main task of the therapeutic couple. Consequently, the work would have to be placed in the transference, instead of the analyst mainly resorting to interpretations of transferential processes. This would be accompanied by an acknowledgment of both the mutuality and the asymmetry characteristic of the therapeutic relationship (Mitchell, 2000; Mitchell & Aron, 1999).

Lastly, we find it important to articulate another significant aspect of compatibility between the relational turn in psychoanalysis and the relational approach to transactional analysis. This aspect transcended methodology and technique and had to do with a level of involvement and immersion in the work that lend itself to being conceptualized only with difficulty. Mitchell (2000) wrote about it and referred to it as a form of "caring":

> As we become more deeply involved with a person, as we become fond of him and identify increasingly with him, we care more and more about what happens to that person, we take pleasure in his successes and suffer pain at his defeats. The same processes take place with patients; "caring," a banal word for a complex affective involvement, is centrally important. I don't find myself

caring, in the same way, for all my patients; some move me more than others. I think that the way I care or don't care for each one is probably a unique product of the interpersonal chemistry between us.

(p. 134)

This form of "caring" would provide fertile soil for the practitioner's grounding in a philosophy that valued the analyst's participation as a witness to the patient's struggles and profound existential dilemmas. Within such a frame of reference, there would be little space left for a discourse based on power dynamics, or for exchanges where someone (in the traditional sense, the analyst) would be designated as the rightful owner of knowledge and meaning. The complex humane experience of being in the world would gain weight in the face of finding out "the truth" or working out a "correct" theoretical model.

Once this premise of "right" and "wrong" faded into the background, ideas related to difference and plurality became more influential. Another arena which supported this change of perspective and contributed to the creation of a new sociopolitical paradigm was the feminist movement, more specifically writers affiliated with postmodern and third-wave feminism (Tong, 2009). They were adamant about rejecting single explanations that should be taken as absolute truths and passionate about women proudly asserting themselves in their differences.

For example, Hélène Cixous wrote about the importance of liberating our minds from the constraints imposed by binary thinking which shaped the world in terms of activity/passivity, day/night, man/woman, and so on. She argued that beyond these dichotomies lay a very rich and complex territory, that of the unthinkable, or the unthought. Once arrived there, one could experience oneself as a being fluid instead of fixated, a self in continuous change (Tong, 2009). This perspective bears similarities to how Hargaden and Sills (2001) emphasized the importance of two subjectivities being involved in the psychotherapeutic process that of the client alongside that of the therapist. They are explicit about the fact that the therapist "is required to use herself imaginatively, allowing time for reflection and being prepared to share her understanding of the patient as a type of offering for consideration rather than as a fact or a theoretical certainty" (p. 60).

The therapist's job no longer seems to be that of accompanying clients to find their way outside their script (as opposed to being in their script), but rather to generate their own personal meanings.

Judith Butler was another feminist writer who grappled with the issue of society defining gender and sex and the way in which this may sometimes find itself in strong tension with the individual's subjective experience relative to those aspects (Tong, 2009). She pointed out that the person could not elude socio-cultural determinations, but that there was an alternative to engaging in a power struggle with such norms either by submitting to them, or by refuting them. In Butler's view, this alternative consisted of choosing to interpret norms in a way that would organize them anew. Making this choice would be an act of freedom and imagination, whereby the individual relished in his own agency, as well as the capacity to create meaning.

As we navigate through the various philosophical discourses or theories which were contemporary with the emergence of the Relational TA school, we begin to notice themes that are intimately woven into the fabric of this particular approach. Among these themes are the nature of the therapeutic relationship, the importance of transference as a tool in designing treatment, the necessity of accounting for both the client's and the therapist's subjective experience, as well as the replacement of hierarchies and patriarchal dynamics with an attitude that values difference and the co-existence of multiple truths.

Once Upon a Time, There Was a Self ...

... and its place within the architecture of the human personality was a rather controversial topic among transactional analysts. The roots of the controversy departed from Berne's ambiguous use of the notion of ego states, which he came to use interchangeably, to describe both a theoretical construct and a phenomenological experience (Allen & Allen, 1989). He wrote about "the real Self," which some authors understood as the ego state that an individual perceived to be his or her "I" or an equivalent of the Adult ego state (Goulding, 1988, as cited by Allen & Allen, 1989), opposed or different from a "false Self," designating "the introjected Parental contents and other contents from previous experiences in the Child ego state" (p. 6).

Other authors elaborated on Berne's model and theorized the self and the ego as two different and interdependent dimensions of the personality, the first eluding the possibilities of intervention provided by structural analysis (Cox, 2001).

Hargaden and Sills (2002) took their own turn in contributing to the writing of this story, proposing a different perspective that theorized various aspects regarding the development of the self and methodologies of addressing the self in the psychotherapeutic process. Theirs was a view that considered the self to be central to the ego, representing the foundation for the formation of the personality and for the elaboration of identity.

In proposing our theory of self, we recognize that our thinking is, of course, simply a story. We find it useful, however, for making sense of some of the complex processes involved in psychotherapy of the Child ego state. We propose that C_2 is the whole "self" and that the internal organization of the "self" is comprised of C_1, A_1, and P_1. We link the internal organization of the self in C_2 with Stern's (1985) domains of the self (Hargaden & Sills, 2001, p. 55).

Pursuing the story as narrated by Hargaden and Sills, we acknowledge the self as being the central character of the psychotherapeutic endeavor. The necessity of working with the self was observed by these authors in their work with schizoid processes, where it was essential to access primary processes and complex mental states. (A struggle that was not foreign from the dilemmas and impasses encountered by transactional analysts at the time when the Schiffian reparenting model emerged; for further details, please see Chapter 3.) We also acknowledge the fact that this central character in the story was called "the Child."

As we allow the narrative to unfold, we are able to discover more about the authors' understanding regarding the nature and the internal organization of the Child. This part of the personality encompassed three parts: C_1, A_1, and P_1, each having a correspondence with Stern's theory about the domains of the self (Hargaden & Sills, 2001). C_1 was equivalent to the core self, A_1 was equivalent to the verbal and intersubjective self, and P_1 was equivalent to the internal object representation. Furthermore, C_1 was the siege of C_0, or the emergent self, of P_0, or the environment where the emergent self came into being, and of A_0, or the repository of experiences resulting from various complex interactions between the emergent self and its environment. Below is a Figure 6.1 that illustrates this internal architecture of the Child (Hargaden & Sills, 2001, p. 56).

The authors wrote of how the baby came into the world as a bundle of bodily-affective states (C_0), yearning to be held and in contact with a good-enough environment facilitated by an effective self-regulating other (P_0). From this interaction, a sense of integration and internal cohesiveness would emerge (A_0). On the contrary, in the absence of an attuned P_0, the baby would have to deal with the consequences of harboring a sense of internal fragmentation. To do so, he would have to resort to splitting off intolerable internal experiences and function from a structure that relied on a coherent, but limited, sense of self. The split-off part of self, the intolerable aspects or experience, according to Hargaden and Sills, would either be walled off in C_0 or stored in P_1 along with representations of significant others.

Further on, Hargaden and Sills explained that in the course of development, the child attempted to make meaning of the world and relationships with others. The results of these learning experiences would be organized in A_1, or the verbal and intersubjective self. These experiences would either be accompanied by satisfaction and joy (A_1+), or disappointment and rejection (A_1-). In a good-enough relationship with a significant other, the child managed to integrate the aspects stored in A_1+ and A_1-, respectively. Otherwise, various aspects of the personality related to self-worth and self-esteem would be considerably scarred, or damaged.

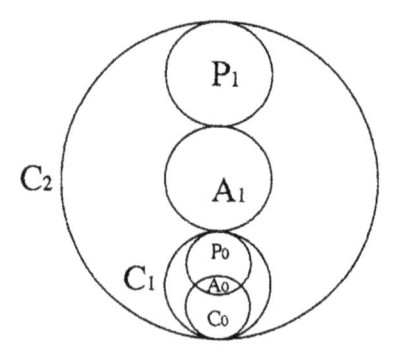

Figure 6.1 The self: Child ego state

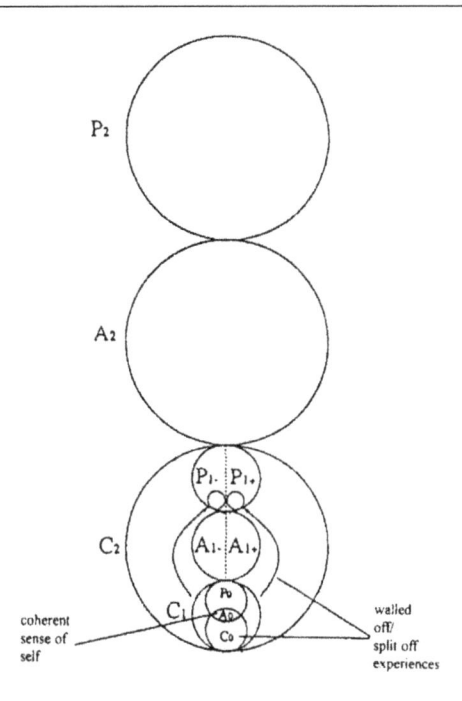

Figure 6.2 The development of the self

As the child is not fully equipped to face the world from the beginning, he comes up against situations and internal experiences that could be described as unbearable. In the authors' view, these would be organized in P_1, along with the child's representation of significant others who could either be idealized (P_1+), or demonized (P_1−).

Figure 6.2 illustrates the development of the self, as conceptualized by Hargaden and Sills (2001, p. 57).

The model stipulated that a healthy enough childhood resulted in an organization of the self (C_2) that facilitated growth. Despite potential imperfections or misalignments, the person would be capable of functioning well in the world and engage with it from a place of a consistent and coherent sense of self. In the case where such healthy development failed to take place, fragmentation would ensue.

More recently, other authors concentrating on the development of transactional analysis theory with a relational tilt elaborated alternative models of the self. For example, Peter Keller van Leer (in Fowlie & Sills, 2011) wrote about aspects of selfhood. His perspective supported the idea that the self of the child emerged for the first time in the symbiotic relationship with the "(m)other" (p. 71) and was subsequently restructured after the acquisition of language. Keller suggested that there were several layers (or aspects) of the self, each containing distinct psychological contents. He labeled one of them the conscious aspect of the self, involved with making meaning mainly through language; this could either be fluid, evoking a realm of multiple possibilities, or it could be rigid, defensive, or a mere quest for certainty. Keller continued to expand on the architecture of the self, as he wrote about the pre-conscious which

> comprises the distillations of interactions that have been integrated within a coherent-enough sense of selfhood, manifest as an enduring sense of identity, or personal narrative, which gives rise to the sense of a core "me" that transcends temporally situated relational contexts.
>
> (p. 73)

In the author's view, the pre-conscious corresponded to the person's life script and to what Hargaden and Sills (2001) called walled-off elements of experience in C_0. Furthermore, another aspect of selfhood was the subconscious enclave that contained those relational aspects experienced by the individual, aspects which he could not comprehend, and which would become reactivated within a present life context in an attempt to create meaning. If that was possible, then the sense of a coherent self would be strengthened, but in case the process failed, then the subconscious enclave would harbor unintegrated, fragmented elements of the self. In his model, Keller also made space for another significant aspect of selfhood, which was the unconscious. He wrote about the fact that it had a language of its own, which was unique for each individual, and which needed the presence of an attuned ear in order to coalesce and gain robustness. This particular mode of listening would have to account for the existence of ambiguity and the sometimes difficult-to-bear lack of certainty.

Once again, we may remark that what relational TA authors maintained in the center of their attention was the fragmented individual, who was in need of a particular type of psychological "glue" (Hargaden & Sills, 2002, p. 3) that would help him find his own place in a postmodern world where uncertainty dwelled uninvited. Dealing with various aspects of not knowing "the truth" and learning to tolerate doubt represented a major preoccupation in relational TA psychotherapy, so much so that it was subsequently coined as a methodological principle (Stuthridge & Sills, in Fowlie & Sills, 2011).

When a Self Is in Trouble

Conceptualizing the self as described above became crucial in the understanding of psychological disturbance and in the elaboration of appropriate psychotherapeutic interventions.

This model offered a framework to reflect about complex mental states and primary processes (such as the schizoid process, for example, which Hargaden and Sills (2001) mention as something that was in the foreground of their clinical interest). They were incipient events of a mind that would come into being as a result of intricate interactions with the environment. From our reading of the theory, relational authors referred to this environment as one that was exclusively human and entirely relational. Therefore, they rather unquestioningly placed the origin of psychological disturbance in the early attachment between the infant and the mother. The source of the trouble was something that they generically named "parenting deficit" (Hargaden & Sills, 2002, p. 21) and which had the force to determine the extent of damage produced in the self.

Clearly, the greater the extent of the deficit in parenting (and this could include intrusive parenting) the greater will be the split within A_1 and the more excluded will be the C_1 (p. 22).

The splitting within A_1 referred to the individual's self-image, his overall sense of well-being that could be profoundly distorted, depending on the relationship with the significant other. The sense of well-being, they wrote, came from "retaining the attachment with the other" (p. 21), despite moments of misalignment, friction, or even rupture.

The self, as conceptualized in the relational TA framework, was considered equivalent to the Child ego state as defined by Berne (1961), "a set of feelings, attitudes and behavior patterns which are relics of the individual's own childhood" (p. 77). Thereby the nature of psychological suffering was powerfully impregnated with the scents of the past.

When we consider these premises, we acknowledge similarities with the Schiffian reparenting model which also attempted to address the clinical particularities of working with complex mental states, explaining the troubles of the mind through a series of failures in the archaic symbiotic relationship between mother and infant (Schiff et al., 1975). More specifically, both approaches described the failure as a "parenting deficit," a deficit which inevitably translated into unmet needs residing in the person's Child. Therefore, psychological treatment had to find ways to address these early losses. While sharing an emphasis on parental deficits, the Schiffian model defined the Parent ego state as the source of psychopathology, while the Relational model situates the trouble within the Child. As analyzed in Chapter 3, when designing methodological interventions the Schiffian approach resorted to reparenting techniques. Relational TA theorists raised serious criticism toward such forms of treatment.

In our view, these techniques can sometimes result in the client becoming infantilized and controlled within the therapeutic relationship, with a concomitant loss of her autonomy. We question how effective this way of working is in the long term, as an overuse of techniques that seek to gratify the client's needs could continually block the underlying depression, despair, and grief. On the contrary, true integration requires that the client access deep affective states where meaning exists and integration is possible (Hargaden & Sills, 2002, p. 36).

The therapist's dilemma was then how to engage in work with archaic or yet unformulated aspects of the client's psyche while respecting personal autonomy. Also, how could the psychotherapeutic process facilitate the deconfusion of the Child ego state without obliterating past experience, but offering instead a possibility to create new meanings?

Transference as the Knight of the Self in Trouble

The response offered by relational transactional analysts to the dilemma formulated above was to work within the transferential relationship emerging between client and therapist. Unlike regressive techniques which, in the view of Hargaden and Sills (2002), had the potential of challenging script patterns and which proved to be useful in the decontamination stage of psychotherapeutic treatment, transference was the key to accessing self-identity processes that operated beyond the realm of verbal phenomena. Therefore, working through transference dynamics was a way of addressing developmentally regressed aspects of the Child ego state without infantilizing the client.

When the internal organization of the Child ego state is fragile, integration can only take place within a relationship in which the therapist is willing to take part in the different psychological positions required of him or her. Such a need arises from the internal object world of the infant and materializes within the transferential relationship (Hargaden & Sills, 2001, p. 59).

Bringing transference at the heart of the work was equally a way of acknowledging and redressing an imbalance that characterized transactional analysis theory at the time. In the context of Berne's criticism of psychoanalysis, namely, that it focused too much on transference, thereby ignoring the person's phenomenological experience, TA models had become almost exclusively oriented on developing techniques which emphasized the latter to the detriment of an in-depth understanding of complex transference phenomena (Hargaden & Sills, 2001).

As we previously discussed in Chapter 3, Schiffian reparenting techniques fostered the enactment of transference processes which eventually brought serious damage to the therapeutic endeavor; as a counter-reaction, the redecision approach subsequently proposed a moving away from any manifestation of transference, the therapist being completely removed from such potentially threatening dynamics. Relational TA models addressed the issue of transference from a different angle, namely that it needed to be rooted in a coherent theoretical model and that it had to be considered in the context of the therapeutic relationship. Therefore, transference had to be understood as a form of communication and a tool toward understanding the client's unconscious. It was the therapist's job to be receptive to such communication and examine his or her subjective experience, meaning his or her countertransference, in order to gather significant data about the client. In the case where the therapist was willing to make space for such aspects, the transference relationship was going to be richly embedded in the phenomenology of the client's experience, therefore providing "reality" to the therapeutic relationship. In this context, "real" referred to the "here-and-now" exchange spontaneously emerging between therapist and client which had the potential to come to life unhindered by "there-and-then" echoes already rigidly fixated in the Child or the Parent ego state.

Transference came to be invested with the promise of bringing the real self to life. In some ways, it was the Knight in the story, whose undertaking was that of aiding the Self in trouble. Such a complex endeavor required a robust framework and methodology. Hargaden and Sills (2001) put together a theoretical model that offered a coherent understanding of transference; elaborating on the work of Carlo Moiso, they wrote about "domains" or types of transference (p. 61). Each type of transference conveyed a particular aspect of the needs, feelings, or fantasies in the Child ego state. The task of the therapist, therefore, was to listen for and distinguish between:

1 *Introjective transferences* informed the therapist of archaic longings in C_0 which belonged to early symbiotic processes occurring in the relationship between child and caretaker. In the case where these processes were not managed well enough so as to provide the Self a sense of continuity, the child's unmet needs would be communicated through:
   a *Mirror transferences*, where the client would unconsciously look for ways to create a first-order symbiotic mode of relating with the therapist, or to elicit approval and admiration in the therapist.
   b *Idealizing transferences*, where the client would try to recreate a state of illusion, in which absolute safety could be found, alongside the presence of a powerful, protective other.
   c *Twinship transferences*, where the client would make attempts to find sameness with the therapist, in order to reach validation and a sense of belonging.
2 *Projective transferences* informed the therapist of early splitting that the child needed to resort to in the absence of a sufficiently attuned other, so that the Self could form and maintain a sense of coherence. Those aspects of the Self which threatened coherence (conceptualized as P_1+ disclosed through idealization, or P_{1-} revealed in the negative transference) were understood to be disowned and further projected onto the therapist.
3 *Transformational transferences* allowed the therapist to be "injected" with feelings or fantasies that the client could not bear and which had to be split-off (such psychological content was conceptualized as part of C_0 and P_1). Therefore, the therapist's role would be to contain such aspects of experience in a way that could facilitate meaning-making and integration.

These pieces of significant unconscious communication could only be made available to the attuned ear of the psychotherapist on condition that he allowed himself to be used in the service of treatment and that he paid a particular kind of attention to countertranferential responses. Receptivity toward the client's affective world and the willingness to engage with subjective layers of experience would provide the psychotherapist with rich information. The ensuing clinical issue, then, would be related to discovering ways in which this lived experience could be organized and used for diagnostic and treatment purposes. And, equally important, would this paradigm alter the clinician's understanding of "cure" and "change"?

With regard to the latter, Hargaden and Sills (2002) offer a direct and clear response:

> Where the initial contract is well defined, the therapist should be ready to return to it and update it regularly, so that as the client discovers "more of himself" he is able to widen his choices, options and directions. Furthermore, the contract should relate to the client himself—that is, it is about understanding his contribution to the circumstances in which he finds himself and offering himself new options with which he might choose to experiment.
>
> (p. 32)

As we pointed out at the beginning of the chapter, the relational turn in transactional analysis marked a departure from working out "the truth" or achieving a particular state of health and well-being essentially pre-defined by theoretical models from the beginning of treatment. Relational authors highlighted the value found in forming a relationship with one's own subjective self which was something that a thorough psychotherapeutic process could facilitate.

In designing the appropriate clinical tools of interventions, Hargaden and Sills returned to early Bernean concepts, such as deconfusion and therapeutic operations, re-examining them through a relationally sensitive lens. Therefore, in their view, the deconfusion process no longer rested on the therapist functioning only from Adult, but also from Child. This internal connection between those two ego states would be considered a cornerstone: It would allow gathering relevant data from the relational field regarding the client's developmental history and his transferential needs without enacting the transference. Those aspects of the self that had been spilled off or disowned would have the chance of being brought into awareness and integrated in a meaningful, reflective way. In this context, deconfusion represented an intrinsic dimension of the therapeutic alliance and was not a specific, sequential stage of treatment that followed decontamination, as in the classical model.

Berne's therapeutic operations (1966)—inquiry, specification, confrontation, explanation, illustration, confirmation, interpretation, crystallization (p. 233)—were enriched by three additional interventions: holding, invitation, and the self-disclosure of countertransference. From a relational framework, all operations were designed to address and work through the various domains of transference described above.

Hargaden and Sills (2002) defined holding as "offering the steady containing presence of a nonjudgmental therapist who is perceived as having the potency to offer the protection and permission needed" (p. 67). The authors were explicit in clarifying the fact that this was a metaphorical holding which had to do with the energy field in the therapeutic relationship and it was not to be taken literally, as a physical gesture. Again, here one may notice the attention given to addressing the transference without enacting it, something that was considered possible due to the fact that, through introspection, the therapist had access to both Child and Adult, meaning to both archaic and here-and-now information.

The intervention named "invitation" referred to encouraging the client to voice feelings and thoughts about the therapist, as a way of working through the projective transferences which occurred in the relationship.

The self-disclosure of countertransference was a technique considered useful when wanting to highlight links between particular here-and-now dynamics and childhood, or when conveying an understanding of the client's protocol.

According to relational authors, it was essential that these operations respected the structure of "empathic transactions," so that they could facilitate access to deeper states of experience. When making an empathic intervention, the therapist's clinical intention would be

- to respond to the client's contaminated Adult, in order to communicate a sense of safety and foster an environment that allows a deepening of the experience.
- to bond with the client's Child through the imaginative use of his own Child ego state, in order to understand something about the architecture of the client's self without making a mission out of eliciting change.

Hargaden and Sills described (2002) empathy both as a cognitive and a feeling process which provided the necessary containment for the therapeutic relationship, where the emphasis was on non-verbal cues, rather than verbal ones. The authors were quite adamant in stating that empathic interventions were not about the therapist getting it right and about avoiding potential relational tensions, or even contact ruptures at times, but about providing the client with the experience of being seen, heard, and understood. This would, in turn, facilitate the integration of traumatic experiences, as well as the processing of primitive mental states, while at the same time acknowledging the fact that the therapeutic relationship was one established between two adults, two subjectivities, each bringing their own unconscious discourse to the encounter. This premise marked the beginning of a significant shift in transactional analysis theory and practice. It was a departure from the Bernean tradition where the therapist's subjectivity was not theorized; equally, it was a reflective way of holding such subjectivity into awareness so that it stayed relevant to treatment.

Living to Tell the Tale

We started off this chapter with something that could be imagined as a prequel to a story. Perhaps the choice to examine the TA Relational approach with the help of this metaphor was to honor one key idea of this framework, namely, that there needed to be space for the imaginative use of the self in the consulting room, so that the process could hold the possibility of a multitude of meanings, understandings and phenomenological experiences. Hence, what revealed itself in our reading of the texts written by relational authors was the existence of one main character, namely the Child ego state—or the self—who searched ways to communicate and bring itself into the world. Most of the time this endeavor would be largely unconscious, therefore needing considerable participation from others.

The Knight who would be capable of taking on such a significant task would be the transferential relationship established between client and therapist, considered to be the vehicle through which more of the Child ego state could come to be known and understood.

Like the majority of stories, this one also follows a set of guidelines or principles that support the coherence of the narrative. Therefore, it is important to include here the principles of Relational transactional analysis. They were put together in a book edited by Heather Fowlie and Charlotte Sills (2011), a volume to which several other authors contributed and offered their understanding of particular facets and meanings of working from a relational sensibility.

1. The centrality of the relationship is the principle that states that the relationship is both the arena where psychological trouble began, as well as the potential playground where new possibilities might emerge in a way that supports the growth of the individual.
2. The importance of engagement suggests that the subjectivities of both therapist and client are important in the therapeutic process and that, therefore, the clinician cannot remain equanimous or function as a provider of unmet needs that shaped the client's life in his/her historical past.
3. The significance of conscious and nonconscious relating is another clinical principle which emphasizes the ongoing influence processes occurring outside the individual's awareness which need to be accounted for in order to understand one's internal world.
4. The importance of experience is an idea that articulates how psychotherapeutic treatment needs to rely on what happens in the here-and-now, meaning in the clinical encounter, so that a particular form of reparation takes place.
5. The importance of subjectivity and self-subjectivity once more highlights the fact that the therapist's interventions need to be rooted in a close examination of countertransference responses, as they provide information about psychological realities in the client.
6. The importance of uncertainty advocates for the richness and complexity made available when we become open to considering multiple social and cultural meanings, instead of remaining stuck in the illusory comfort provided by ready-made explanations or frames of reference.
7. The importance of curiosity, criticism, and creativity is a guiding principle that speaks to the importance of each individual—client or therapist—having a mind that is free to explore, think, create meanings, and reflect on them critically.
8. The reality of functioning and changing adults is a principle that forcefully brings forward the intention of the Relational approach and differentiates itself from a "parental paradigm," where the client is at the receiving end and the therapist needs to step in and provide a corrective experience. On the contrary, the client is envisaged as an adult, capable of forming a reciprocal and mutual relationship with the therapist which can still respect the asymmetry coming from the fact that each person contributes to this encounter from a different role.

This perspective about the human psyche and the nature of the psychotherapeutic endeavor was initially considered by some practitioners in the TA community to be quite radical and a moving away from Berne's original writings (Haragaden & Sills, personal communication, 2022). Moreover, since the relational framework supported the centrality of transferential processes, it stirred doubt and defensive reactions in some members of the TA community, in the sense that it was considered to be an attempt to convert transactional analysis to psychoanalysis. In our view, if we consider theory to be more like a vehicle for creating meaning for what the clinician encounters in practice rather than "the truth," then other aspects are more likely to come to the foreground and transferential processes can be acknowledged as rich sources of information.

Therefore, we may wonder whether the relational approach, in the way it was articulated, may have favored particular clinical realities to the detriment of others, similarly to how the states we find ourselves in may sometimes obscure others which remain outside awareness. We may ask ourselves about potential blind spots or gaps in the model. This is what we would like to examine in the following section of this chapter.

Listening to the Voices of Secondary Characters

We have already outlined the fact that, in our reading of relational TA authors, the model they put forward advocated for the centrality of the relationship and emphasized the transferential aspects emerging in the clinical encounter. Such a lens may produce its own distortions:

> ... when our theories privilege and idealize mutuality or co-construction, we may risk missing the richness and disturbance of separateness, privacy, and personal encounter, and lose the opportunity to develop the capacity and responsibility to know, articulate, and keep one's own mind.
> (Cornell, in Fowlie & Sills, 2011, p. 148)

The importance of both the therapist and the client maintaining their own private mental spaces, separate from each other, is an idea supported by various authors (Corbett & Grossman, in Aron et al., 2018). Privacy is not to be taken as an equivalent of isolation, but rather as an essential ingredient in the development of the psyche, where reverie and dreaming should be allowed to dwell without obtrusions coming from the other.

We remain curious as to how the constant return to transference being the main key in addressing complex mental states may prove to have limitations. Here are some of them that we have come across when reading and reflecting on these aspects:

1 It may bias the therapist in the way that he may come to rely primarily on the examination of countertransference and may forget of other useful therapeutic tools, such as disciplined observation and quiet focus (Seligman, in Aron et al., 2018).

2   It may place a lot of pressure on the therapist to constantly use his self as a tool for making diagnostic judgments, or in choosing appropriate treatment interventions. Such pressure may implicitly feed into the phantasy that if the therapist was an astute enough examiner of his own subjectivity, then transformations should take place in the patient's psyche. When unacknowledged, such a stance could lead to grandiose expectations and an omnipotent view of what the relational space has to offer.
3   Also, it may involuntarily create the expectation in the therapist to make self-disclosures. Using self-disclosure as a treatment tool may become embedded in the culture of practicing relationally. It has been pointed out that issues such as what the practitioner discloses, how he finds the appropriate words for it and at what stage in the work he makes this intervention are delicate issues to weigh and consider (Shmukler, 1991, in Fowlie & Sills, 2011).
4   Considering that transferential processes are there to begin with in the case of every client may not fit with clinical reality. Some authors write about particular personality structures where the main characteristic is the person's lack of capacity to entertain a relationship with the unconscious. In this context, Robert Grossman (in Aron et al., 2018) writes about patients who suffer from psychic deadness and a complete absence of mentalization or symbolization. Also, Christopher Bollas (1987) describes the "normotic personality" (p. 136), that is someone who rarely engages in introspective activities and attempts to replace any sign of subjective life with descriptions about what is objective or normal; their universe as one mainly inhabited by a collection of facts, rather than meanings. In such cases, different avenues to treatment need to be considered.

We are aware of the fact that relational transactional analysis has been evolving and developing, and that authors have carried out ongoing dialogues in order to further inform and adjust their approach to treatment. We will continue to reflect on these more recent developments in subsequent chapters and to hopefully also contribute to the collective effort of thinking together about a theory that remains both alive and robust.

References

Allen, J. R., & Allen, B. A. (1989). Ego states, self, and script. *Transactional Analysis Journal.* 19:1, 4–13. https://doi.org/10.1177/036215378901900102

Aron, L., Grand, S., & Slochower, J. (Eds.) (2018). *De-idealizing relational theory. A critique from within*. Routledge.

Barnes, G. (1999). About energy metaphors III: Basic conceptual issues. *Transactional Analysis Journal.* 29:4, 237–249. https://doi.org/10.1177/036215379902900402

Berne, E. (1961). *TA in psychotherapy: A systematic individual and social psychiatry*. Grove Press & Evergreen Books.

Berne, E. (1966). *Principles of group treatment*. Oxford University Press.

Blackstone, P. (1993). The dynamic Child: Integration of second-order structure, object relations, and self psychology. *Transactional Analysis Journal.* 23:4, 216–234. https://doi.org/10.1177/036215379302300406

Bollas, C. (1987). *The shadow of the object: Psychoanalysis of the unthought known.* Free Association Books.

Clarkson, P. (1993). Transactional analysis as a humanistic therapy. *Transactional Analysis Journal.* 23:1, 36–41. https://doi.org/10.1177/036215379302300104

Clarkson, P. (1994). In recognition of dual relationships. *Transactional Analysis Journal.* 24:1, 32–38. https://doi.org/10.1177/036215379402400107

Clarkson, P., & Gilbert, M. (1988). Berne's original model of ego states: Some theoretical considerations. *Transactional Analysis Journal.* 18:1, 20–29. https://doi.org/10.1177/036215378801800105

Cornell, W. F. (1994). Dual relationships in transactional analysis: Training, supervision, and therapy. *Transactional Analysis Journal.* 24:1, 21–30. https://doi.org/10.1177/036215379402400105

Cox, M. (2001). Beyond ego states. *TA UK.* 60, 3–8.

English, E. (1994). The human quest for truth. *Transactional Analysis Journal.* 24:4, 291–292. https://doi.org/10.1177/036215379402400411

Federn, P. (1952). *Ego psychology and the psychosis.* Basic Books.

Fowlie, H., & Sills, C. (Eds.) (2011). *Relational transactional analysis. Principles in practice.* Karnac Books Ltd.

Hargaden, H., & Sills, C. (2001). Deconfusion of the Child ego state: A relational perspective. *Transactional Analysis Journal.* 31:1, 55–70. https://doi.org/10.1177/036215370103100107

Hargaden, H., & Sills, C. (2002). *Transactional analysis. A relational perspective.* Routledge.

Jacobs, A. (1994). Theory as ideology: Reparenting and thought reform. *Transactional Analysis Journal.* 24:1, 39–55. https://doi.org/10.1177/036215379402400108

Klein, M. (1975). *Envy and gratitude.* Dell Publishing. (Original work published 1957)

Kohut, H. (1977). *The restoration of the self.* International Universities Press.

Mitchell, S. A. (2000). *Relationality. From attachment to intersubjectivity.* The Analytic Press.

Mitchell, S. A., & Aron, L. (Eds.) (1999). *Relational psychoanalysis. The emergence of a tradition.* Routledge.

Novellino, M. (1987). Redecision analysis of transference: The unconscious dimension. *Transactional Analysis Journal.* 17:1, 271–276. https://doi.org/10.1177/036215378701700103

Novellino, M. (1990). Unconscious communication and interpretation in transactional analysis. *Transactional Analysis Journal.* 20:3, 168–172. https://doi.org/10.1177/036215379002000306

Novellino, M., & Moiso, C. (1990). The psychodynamic approach to transactional analysis. *Transactional Analysis Journal.* 20:3, 187–192. https://doi.org/10.1177/036215379002000308

Porter-Steele, N. (1999). Letter from the editor. *Transactional Analysis Journal.* 29:3, 162–163. https://doi.org/10.1177/036215379902900301

Rouzie, M., & Arbor, A. (1999). Letter to the editor. *Transactional Analysis Journal.* 29:2, 158–160. https://doi.org/10.1177/036215379902900213

Rowland, H. (2016). On vulnerability. *Transactional Analysis Journal.* 46:4, 277–287. https://doi.org/10.1177/0362153716662874

Schiff, J. L., Schiff, A. W., Mellor, K., Schiff, E., Schiff, S., Richman, D., Fishman, F., Wolz, L., Fishman, C., & Momb, D. (1975). *Cathexis reader column Transactional analysis treatment of psychosis.* Harper & Row.

Shmukler, D. (1991). Transference and transactions: Perspectives from developmental theory, object relations, and transformational processes. *Transactional Analysis Journal.* 21:3, 127–135. https://doi.org/10.1177/036215379102100303

Stern, D. N. (1985). *The interpersonal world of the infant: A view from psychoanalysis and developmental psychology*. Basic Books.
Tong, R. (2009). Postmodern and third-wave feminism. In *Feminist thought. A more comprehensive introduction* (pp. 270–291). Westview Press.
Winnicott, D. W. (1958). *Collected papers: Through pediatrics to psychoanalysis*. Tavistock Publications.
Woods, K. (1998). The danger of sadomasochism in the reparenting of psychotics. *Transactional Analysis Journal*. 28:1, 48–54. https://doi.org/10.1177/036215379802800111
Woods, K. (1999). A retrospective on states of the ego. *Transactional Analysis Journal*. 29:4, 266–272. https://doi.org/10.1177/036215379902900405

Chapter 7

Evolutions at the Intersections of Transactional Analysis

The Delicate Edge Between Theory and Mythology

In various places in this book, we brought into discussion the risk of treating transactional analysis (TA) theory as a framework used to define reality or to pinpoint what might be considered "true knowledge." When we referred to cathexis theory and the redecision model (in Chapter 3), we made a link between such an outcome and the unmourned loss of Eric Berne, which left the community in a state of grief and confusion.

However, it may be a useful inquiry to wonder about the tendency to regard theory as a powerful tool used to designate what is real and what is unreal (or false) in the context of Berne's writings. His aspiration, as we understand it, was to find a way of balancing scientific rigor with the phenomenological sensibility that was mostly missing from the clinical world at the time. Hence, his attempt to describe abstract concepts through the use of metaphor, in order to denote and evoke meanings that would otherwise remain unarticulated, unformulated. However, the "as if" quality of metaphorical expression got lost at times, and his writing style became less tentative and less figurative. What ensued was a process of reification (Loria, 1990), as the metaphorical meaning became a thing in itself; descriptive language was transformed into a language of nouns that designated specific entities. We agree with Loria's view that this took its toll on the internal consistency of the theory:

> A tradition is needed that will ask why Berne and others made their claims, how they substantiated them, and what their rationale was for proposing new theory or altering existing theory. Transactional analysis is in need of an in-depth attempt to understand its historical antecedents and the contexts of its theoreticians.
>
> (p. 153)

Moreover, the space for thinking became a space where mythological characters could come into being: Witches, ogres, and an entire panoply of fairy-tale-like characters became part of the habitual TA vocabulary, describing not so much a felt sense of the client or the practitioner, but entities with a concrete embodiment that would be dwelling in the dark corners of the person's psyche.

We believe that this process of reification diminished the space for reflection and for a more curious engagement with the theory. Instead, it magnified confusions and tensions, particularly with regard to those aspects of Bernean theory that were contradictory, or unclear. One such example refers to the two contrasting ways in which Berne wrote about ego states. In *Transactional Analysis in Psychotherapy* (1961), he presented ego states as discrete ways of organizing experience, the Parent and the Child ego states being entirely associated with fixated, archaic modes of existence, and the Adult ego state being responsible for integrating pieces of information from the present moment with information about the past and the psychological influences of the past over the present. Moreover, Berne formulated an understanding of the human psyche that was based on intrapsychic conflict; this was considered to be relational and developmental in origin.

In *What Do You Say After You Say Hello?* (1972), however, he began to focus more on the descriptive and behavioral aspects of ego states, equating them with roles or behaviors that corresponded to particular roles. Cornell (2010) hypothesized that in his ailing health, Berne had become more focused on destiny, holding, on the one hand, to an abiding view of overcoming script and, on the other, to a dilemma that this may not be possible. Cornell believes that Berne was moving toward the idea of aspiration rather than adaptation with a pessimistic outlook on what was truly possible and died before these reflections were articulated into something more robust. His premature death meant his work was unfinished. We might wonder about the apparent anxious urgency in *What Do You Say After You Say Hello*, which indicated some desperation for change and a more forceful, concrete approach whereby he needed people to sit up and listen to shed the shackles of script.

For many, this meant a reduction of the theory to a taxonomy of behaviors (Erskine, 1991, p. 68). In Erskine's view, this led to TA losing its strength in providing glimpses into the architecture of the person's psyche. Script cure that was mostly associated with Berne's earlier writings lost its popularity in the face of an approach that promised social control in a quicker, more hands-on manner. The latter occupied increasingly more space in Berne's later writings.

Over time, these contradictions resulted in polarized perspectives regarding the structural model of ego states versus the functional model of ego states, or in a use of the theory that would sadly not account for this lack of explanatory strength. Some authors began to make distinctions and to organize those contrasting elements which pervaded the theory and, in so doing, remained exclusively anchored in a TA framework (for example, Joines, who in a 1976 article in the *Transactional Analysis Journal* made significant differentiations between the structure and the function of ego states, or Cox, who continued to develop an understanding of structure and function in an article in 1999). There were also authors who, in their search for articulating consistent models, resorted to data and research outside transactional analysis. To illustrate this, we will refer in this chapter to the work of Pio Scilligo, whose ideas generated a self-standing approach, namely, social-cognitive transactional analysis, and to that of Richard Erskine, who laid the foundations of an Integrative approach to TA.

We may understand this movement toward other models and theories as both an aspiration toward developing knowledge, as well as a reaction to dynamics emerging within the TA community. The latter comes across in the writings of various authors. For instance, in 2008, the *Transactional Analysis Journal* published excerpts of a roundtable discussion about perspectives on the unconscious. Michele Novellino, one of the contributors, made some remarks about the atmosphere experienced in the community. In his view, strongly supported by Campos (2003), the TA world was scarred by two significant phenomena, namely, authoritarianism and competitiveness. The consequence of the first was an institutionalization of the theory, generating various protective and self-protective processes in relation to external contributions, thereby leaving little room for potential fertile influences from more recent scientific works. Additionally, competitiveness further led to "conflicting phenomena rather than critical confrontation" (p. 251). We may quite easily infer that this level of power dynamics would have stifled growth inside the community. Hence, for some, the possibility for maturation might have emerged at the intersection between transactional analysis and other psychotherapeutic systems.

Bridging the Gap Between Research and Clinical Practice

In various places throughout the book, we have emphasized the importance of reflecting on a particular model or theory in the context of the author's biography and various social as well as historical phenomena unfolding at the time. We propose adopting a similar lens as we explore the social-cognitive perspective on transactional analysis articulated by Pio Scilligo.

As a professional background, Scilligo was both a clinician, as well as a researcher. He trained with Bob and Mary Goulding, John McNeel, Peter Pearson, Ellyn Bader, and Jim Simkin, an early seminal figure in the history of Gestalt therapy. Scilligo (2002) wrote that, in working with them, he learned that it was possible to admire people and still disagree with their model.

His interest in research was reflected in sustained activities and complex projects: He collaborated with the Istituto di Ricerca sui Processi Intrapsichici e Relazionali (Institute for Research on the Intrapsychic and Relational Processes or IRPIR) and the Istituto di Formazione e Ricerca per Educatori e Psicoterapeuti (Institute for Training and Research for Educators and Psychotherapists or IFREP), together with the Universita' Pontificia Salesiana (Salesian Pontifical University or UPS) in Rome, to the creation of the Laboratorio di Ricerca sul Sè e l'Identità (Laboratory for Research on the Self and Identity or LARSI) (De Luca & Tosi, 2011).

In a personal conversation with Susanna Bianchini and Carla de Nitto, both involved in the scientific work of IFREP, we discovered that Scilligo used to be a Salesian priest and that for many years, he directed a Catholic school in China. His activity there started presenting particular challenges to him, in the sense that he could notice, yet not explain thoroughly, the fact that some students belonging to disadvantaged social classes had performed more poorly than students belonging to more advantaged social classes. To obtain a deeper understanding of this phenomenon, he moved to California to study psychology and, having completed his Ph.D. in Social Psychology, he studied more about the various ways in which the social context could be a significant influencing factor in academic performance. Therefore, the role played by the context in the individual's life began to gain more visibility and scientific interest in Scilligo's work.

Transactional analysts who became involved in further developing his thinking articulated the dilemma he was struggling with in terms of holding the tension between nomothetic (i.e., universal statements or laws) and idiographic (i.e., something concrete or individual) considerations, as they apply to psychological research and inquiry (De Luca & Tosi, 2011). In their view, Scilligo's aspiration was to bridge the gap between the observable interpersonal discourse and the phenomenological intrapsychic experience. The outcome of this endeavor materialized itself in the creation of a social-cognitive approach to transactional analysis (SCTA).

One of the pillars of this approach was Berne's model of ego states. Scilligo found value in the Bernean definition of ego states, especially in the fact that they were understood in their complexity as having phenomenological, operational, and pragmatic aspects. Moreover, he highlighted the fact that ego states were well described so as to point out the relational origins of psychic life. There were two elements, however, where Scilligo's view departed from Berne (De Luca & Tosi, 2011). The first one was that he considered it was based on an outdated theory of the mind, according to which psychological functions are direct expressions of neurological structures. The second one was that Berne did not sufficiently develop the affective and the power dimensions inherent in ego states. In Scilligo's view, this resulted in difficulties with concepts being properly operationalized and researched.

As a clinician, he appreciated the richness of a psychodynamic understanding of the mind which could offer insight into intrapsychic and developmental processes, thereby creating the opportunity for more robust change. Therefore, a further development of the theory and a movement beyond the limitations of Berne's model needed to be rooted in a psychodynamic, in-depth understanding of the psyche, while allowing concepts to be examined through a researcher's lens. Scilligo's response to this challenge was to turn to the notion of "schema," as understood by Lorna Benjamin (1974), a researcher and clinical psychologist with whom he collaborated on various LARSI projects. Benjamin's work rested on developmental theories and socio-cognitive sciences. Her understanding of psychological functioning became the second pillar of Scilligo's revised model of ego states.

The concept of (cognitive) "schema" offered Scilligo a way of addressing the limitation of Berne's understanding of the mind and providing an alternative perspective to the idea that psychological functions are direct expressions of neurological structures. Cognitive schemas are not considered to be static structures, but emergent processes evoked by the interaction of multiple neural elements. They are web-like potentials which become instantiated based on the strength of their neural connections, something which is in turn dependent on the person's interpretation of various internal or external inputs. Therefore, the mind rests on dynamic processes, neurological and psychological phenomena, as well as contextual factors, which develop complex interactions. Given that everything varies, the distinction between structure and function no longer has scientific validity. What initially seemed to be an irresolvable contradiction or a lack of theoretical consistency could now be revised and looked at from a different lens.

In this case how would ego states be defined? How would one apply the model to clinical practice? Would this new perspective facilitate an integration of other psychodynamic concepts, such as transference, into transactional analysis theory and practice?

From a SCTA framework, ego states are "active social-cognitive processes, or schemas, continually being re-created in the dynamic interaction between the individual and her or his environment" (De Luca & Tosi, 2011, p. 211). What becomes of paramount importance in this definition is that Scilligo drew on the relational nature of ego states, as conceptualized by Berne and that he considered ego states capable of evolving throughout life.

Therefore, Scilligo's view was that when operationalized, each ego state would be translated through three mental representations which he named surfaces. The first two surfaces were a direct reflection of the ego states being relational in origin; they were called the Initiator and the Responder surfaces. Using the vocabulary of transactional analysis, they were associated with the Parent ego state and the Child ego state, respectively. The third surface was named the Self and accounted for various intrapsychic processes, unlike the first two which referred to interpersonal dynamics. This latter surface was considered to be more encompassing than the Adult ego state.

In order to achieve more consistency for the model, Scilligo looked for ways of bridging the gap between the interpersonal and the intrapsychic, something which would provide the model with pragmatic depth. In doing so, he resorted to the notion of introject: This explained intrapsychic dynamics as being formed on the basis of significant relationships in the past and resulting in relational patterns available in the present. The outcome was the description of four manifestations (qualities) prototypical for each mental representation, termed as rebellious, free, protective, and critical. Therefore, the clinician would be able to notice, for example, a Rebellious Parent, as well as a Rebellious Child or Adult; a Critical Child, as well as a Critical Parent or Adult, and so on.

Scilligo also deepened the understanding of the phenomenological nature of ego states by emphasizing three significant dimensions which he considered insufficiently developed in Bernean theory, namely, the affective dimension, the power dimension, and the developmental dimension. Each of these dimensions was represented as continuums which described various nuances of the person's internal experience, placed between the polarities existent at the end of each continuum. In remaining loyal to the importance of these dynamic tensions that characterized psychological life, Scilligo captured something of Berne's writings about the agency of the self (Cornell, 2015), and its capacity to be active and generative.

To synthesize the above, from a SCTA perspective, the ego state model can only be understood and applied into practice if considered operationally, pragmatically, and phenomenologically at the same time. The result, supported by factor analysis research carried out by Scilligo (2009) and his colleagues, is a multitude of mental representations which have particular identifiable qualities and concrete manifestations. What transpires is the fact that the Parent, Adult, and Child ego states are not necessarily distinct ego states, but that they share various qualities and that they are intricately interrelated. Here is, for example, how the Adult ego state was understood.

What we call "Adult" is the predominance of psychological processes characterized by the capacity to observe, analyze, synthesize, and so on, where thoughts, feelings, and behaviors are more differentiated and structured. Moreover, the Adult is characterized by different nuances of affectivity and activity, as are the Parent and Child, which means that we have to look at the quality or feel of the Adult ego state process, not only the content, in order to define which prototypical aspect of the Adult ego state is activated at any given moment (De Luca & Tosi, 2011, p. 217).

However, this view of the Adult ego state remained distinct from the integrated Adult model (Cornell, 2015), as it accounted for the way in which the Parent and the Child continued to be relevant for the functioning of the mind in the here-and-now. In SCTA, the equivalent of the integrated Adult was the well-being system.

This system corresponds to a network of ego states, in particular, the activation of the Free Adult, Free Child, Protective Child, and Protective Adult, with a moderate presence of the Free Parent and Protective Parent. This is then a dynamic system characterized by loving affiliation and balanced interdependence (Tossi et al., 2015, p. 201).

Another contribution made by Scilligo's social-cognitive model was to highlight the importance played by transferential processes and to find ways, anchored both in research and clinical practice, to define and describe transferential dynamics.

First and foremost, Scilligo supported the idea that transference was a natural process which occurred in normal psychological life, not only in the therapeutic relationship, but also in interactions with supervisors, mentors, spouses, friends, and so on. A second premise was that transference was not only rooted in psychosexual drives, an idea highly valued in the classical Freudian tradition, but also in "fundamental human needs for tenderness, connectedness, self-expression, effectiveness, and security" (Scilligo, 2011, p. 197). Therefore, the attachment system throughout the person's historical development was incredibly relevant in understanding transference. Last but not least, like in the case of ego states, Scilligo considered that transference could be approached from an operational perspective, a phenomenological perspective, and a pragmatic one, being therefore a phenomenon that could be measured and researched.

When operationalized, transference was defined as the automatic, unconscious activation of a bundle of mental representations which included:

(1) representations of the significant other, including memories, expectations of, and inferences about that person; (2) representations of the self that one experienced with that earlier significant other, including any associated affective states and self-evaluative conclusions (e.g., perceptions of being lovable, irritating, repulsive, or engaging); and (3) prototypical behavioral sequences intended to manage interactions with that significant other.
(Scilligo, 2011, p. 198)

What comes across from this definition is the fact that, like Berne, Scilligo focused not only on the projective nature of transference, but also on the importance of introjective transference, as this is a process that not only influences the way in which we perceive others, but it is equally active in determining our inner sense of self and possibility (Cornell, 2015).

Phenomenologically, the experience of being immersed in a transferential process was described as intimately linked with memories from the past, expectations of the person from the significant other, as well as with the corresponding affect.

In terms of manifestations, the following aspects would be considered signals of transferential processes being played out: Inferences made about a person, the activation of specific goals or needs, the activation of a self-regulatory focus, or the emergence of a self-regulatory response.

When considered through this complex perspective, transference would become more accessible to research, thereby informing clinical practice, which was an important aspiration of all SCTA models throughout their development.

From our reading of SCTA theory what stands out is the articulation of a self-standing vocabulary as far as fundamental concepts are concerned. The outcome is a dimensional model of ego states which can inform the practitioner's clinical judgment and the methodological decisions made with regard to treatment. De Luca and Tosi (2011) support the idea that this view facilitates the emergence of more scientific clarity, whereas the traditional (Bernean) model remains valuable, as it offers the possibility for more immediate and intuitive understanding. Furthermore, the authors argue that the "SCTA model allows the clinician and researcher to move back and forth, to bridge between the two models as different needs arise" (p. 217). We consider that this claim is rather difficult to make, given that concepts of ego states have acquired quite different meanings within the two models. Although they might have some aspects in common, such as the relational origins of psychological life, for example, their conceptualization actually rests on rather different understandings of how the mind works. Using the two models alternatively could, in our view, result in unclear diagnosis and confusion regarding treatment interventions. We are more inclined to understand that the SCTA model has acquired a degree of consistency and coherence that enables it to have quite a distinct identity, this means that SCTA practitioners can entertain their own dialogue with other (traditional or more contemporary) models elaborated in transactional analysis.

This brings us perhaps closer to yet another aspect that Pio Scilligo emphasized in his work, namely, the importance of meaning and the interpretive nature of knowledge. His stance was one supporting the importance of contemporary hermeneutics, as an alternative to both objectivism and relativism, both tending to present polarized views about the process of acquiring knowledge. Scilligo (2010) wrote that

> ... hermeneutic is a meta-theory that gives a better explanation for the applications and discoveries of empirical sciences, fully aware that the interpretations reached are never definitive or certain. The interpretative vision sits well with methodological pluralism. In other words, we can say that a fundamental point of the theory and research of the psychological and social sciences is the clarification of meaning according to which we live and is not limited to the pure and simple precise prevision, but is a critical use of it.
>
> (p. 68)

This aspiration toward scientific clarification and a critical use of meaning can serve as a robust alternative to the use of theory as a measure of truth or falsehood, as described at the beginning of this chapter.

When Conflict Is About Going Back and Integration Is About Moving Forward

We have pointed out that several authors and members of the TA community drew attention to a particular problematic aspect of Berne's writing, namely, the fact that his use of metaphors resulted in them becoming a literal understanding of human functioning. This view was also supported by Richard Erskine (1991) when he wrote that the functions of ego states which were "first adjectives to describe intrapsychic dynamics later became nouns (adapted Child and Adapted Child)" (p. 68). Therefore, in his view, this approach resulted in a loss of theoretical consistency, leaving the concepts devoid of the depth provided by a psychodynamic understanding and reducing them to a set of behavioral descriptions. Moreover, it prevented the practitioner from understanding the notion of defense mechanisms and ego functioning (Erskine, 1988).

Erskine emphasized the idea that another reason why the Bernean model lacked robustness was the fact that it was anchored mostly in a theory of personality, without having sufficiently developed a theory of motivation. In Erskine's view, articulating appropriate links between theories of personality and theories of motivation would enhance the practice and would support the formulation of a consistent methodology (Erskine, 1998).

In his attempt to address these inconsistencies, Erskine drew upon various models outside transactional analysis, part of which was rooted in his background prior to training in TA, namely, client-centered therapy and Gestalt therapy. Additional influences came from neo-Freudian theories, the British object relations school, or self-psychology, along with an extensive clinical experience of working with children. The result was a form of psychotherapy entitled integrative psychotherapy which rested on specific principles, a self-standing theoretical understanding of the mind and a self-standing methodology.

The basic philosophical principles elaborated by Erskine and his colleagues highlighted the fact that people are relationship-seeking beings and interdependent throughout life (O'Reilly-Knapp & Erskine, 2003). Hence, it was considered that psychological suffering stemmed from relational disruptions, and not "psychopathology." In this context, it was meaningful to assume that the therapeutic process should be prioritized over the content of the therapy, in the sense that the way in which the therapist related to the client was of paramount importance (Erskine et al., 2023). Other principles which complemented this view supported the idea that human beings have intrinsic value and an innate thrust to grow, that focusing on internal and external contact was considered essential to human functioning and that experience needed to be understood as being organized at various levels (physiological, affective, cognitive, and behavioral) (Erskine et al., 2023).

Integrative psychotherapy was a welcomed extension to TA concepts for those who had become skeptical about the demand that was being placed on clients for adaptation and fast cure. For some, there was a huge relief that practitioners were giving validity to clients' phenomenology and a sense of reality to their childhood experiences. Erskine (2023, personal communication) wished to make it clear that his intention was not to create a new brand but to extend the theory to honor the importance of early relational needs. From his point of view, the name integrative psychotherapy served a necessity: It was coined because at the time, universities were becoming resistant to lectures on TA or Gestalt, as these approaches had been gathering criticism due to some questionable practices.

At this point, the term "integrative" might find echoes in the reader's mind or it might stir curiosity. What was being integrated? Was it a process that addressed the methodology of the therapeutic process or rather the internal structure of the client? In the absence of integration, was the alternative a process of fragmentation? What was the result of integration?

In their 1996 article, "Methods of an Integrative Psychotherapy," Erskine and Trautmann spoke directly to the multiple meanings of the notion, that of providing an alternative to personality fragmentation, of bringing together theoretical aspects of the theory in a coherent, consistent way and of making use of various approaches to treatment without remaining eclectic.

The authors' understanding of cure and the origin of psychological problems was intimately linked with Berne's original view of personality organization (1961). Consequently, within the theory of personality they fell back on, the Child ego state was conceptualized as a set of archaic fixations, or developmental arrests, and the Parent ego state as a repository for unassimilated, introjected aspects from the person's history. The healthy ego state, therefore, was the Adult ego state, since it was the one in charge of integrating (assimilating) content and experiences stored in the Child and the Parent, which would otherwise remain fragmented. Functioning from the Adult allowed the person to be aware of what happened inside and outside—in a way that was congruent with the developmental age and enabled the integration of information from the present with aspects of the past, as well as an awareness about how the past influenced the present moment. As long as this was possible, theory seemed to suggest that the person's psyche could be kept at bay from psychological problems. Those emerged when the introjected and/or archaic ideas, images, and emotions contaminated the here-and-now perceptions of the Adult ego state (Erskine, 1988), distorting the phenomenological experience of the person to the point where it resembled a here-and-now state of mind, although responses emerged from unintegrated, fixated ego states. The reader can perhaps gradually grasp this building tension between the past and the present, between what is fixated, archaic, and what belongs to the here-and-now. This tension was conceptualized as an intrapsychic conflict that determined the entire organization of the personality, a conflict that was relational and developmental in its origins and nature (Erskine, 1991) and that maintained the psyche in a fragmented fashion. Furthermore, the perpetuation of internal conflict was seen as fertile ground for projections and, potentially, for aspects of large-scale social violence, such as nuclear wars. In his acceptance speech for the Eric Berne Memorial Award in 1979, Erskine advocates for the importance of raising awareness with regard to a "hidden scare" that lies within us (in our reading, this refers to contents pertaining to archaic ego states), so that we can eventually use it and achieve peaceful conflict resolutions (Erskine, 1983).

The key toward alleviating suffering (both internal and external) was, therefore, resolving internal conflicts and integrating fixated ego states into the person's Adult ego state:

> An integrative intrapsychic approach to transactional analysis psychotherapy consists of deconfusing the archeopsychic ego states and relaxing fixated archaic defenses, emending and/or decommissioning the exteropsychic ego states to resolve internal conflicts between archeopsychic ego states and exteropsychic ego states, and facilitating the integration of one's life experiences into a neopsychic ego.
> (Erskine, 1988, p. 66)

The author continues to refer to this process as a way of "making whole" a self whose whole-ness was destroyed (i.e., fragmented as a result of trauma) and who needs to become once more a cohesive self:

> We aim to create an experience of unbroken feeling-connectedness. The client's sense of self and sense of relatedness that develop seem crucial to the process of integration and wholeness, particularly when there have been specific, ego-fragmenting traumas in the client's life ...
> (Erskine & Trautmann, 1996, p. 317)

As we make space for this perspective in our minds and reflect on it, we find ourselves tempted to hear it both as an aspiration to the relentless cries and groans of a severely traumatized self, as well as a plea for reparation, as a desire to correct the wrongdoing and restore a sense of tranquility in a place that was long troubled or in pain. We begin to wonder to what extent was this understanding of integration is making whole a collusion with parts of the person that might find it unimaginable to contemplate destruction and that cannot bear the sight of permanent scars left by tragedy and catastrophe. We may consider the possibility that this perspective might make the theory of integrative psychotherapy rather blind to various aspects related to aggression, ambivalence, and contradictory states of mind as elements which foster maturation and growth. Furthermore, we may highlight the fact that it rests on a vision of the healthy mind as something unitary, continuous, a vision that contrasts with more contemporary approaches. The latter ones articulate an understanding of the normal development of the self as something that is discontinuous, non-unitary (Stuthridge, 2006). Therefore, the lack of unity is not necessarily a defense against trauma, but a trait of ordinary human functioning. In this context, the psychotherapeutic task becomes that of creating meaning, which in our view is something different from "decommissioning the exteropsychic ego states" (Erskine, 1988, p. 66); rather, it is that of simultaneously holding multiple aspects into awareness, with as many phenomenological characteristics as possible (sensations, affects, thoughts, fantasies, impulses), thereby enhancing the vitality of a complex mental life.

As mentioned above, the integrative approach emphasized the importance of articulating a theory of motivation that could accompany a theory of personality, the two operating as tools used to further elaborate an appropriate methodology for clinical practice. Hence, Erskine revitalized and further developed Berne's theory of hungers (1961): the hunger for stimuli, the hunger for structure, and the hunger for relationship. He described them as drives being in dynamic balance, a disruption in any of them generating an overcompensation in at least one of the others (Erskine, 1998). However, from our reading of the integrative model, the hunger for relationship seems to have taken priority, occupying a lot of the authors' reflective space. In their view, the notion of strokes and script managed to address the hunger for stimuli and for structure, respectively. In contrast, the third type of psychological hunger lacked a more in-depth theoretical understanding. Erskine considered that it was precisely the premise that humans were relationship-seeking beings which gave meaning to a theory of motivation (O'Reilly-Knapp & Erskine, 2003). Therefore, it was paramount to design a framework that would enable the clinician to take this aspect into account in an appropriate way. This framework had at its core the notion of "relational needs": In the authors' view, these were the fundamental motivators of human behavior and they were met through contact with a significant other (O'Reilly-Knapp & Erskine, 2003). If contact was disrupted, then the needs would no longer be met and, in order to avoid discomfort, the person would make script decisions that became fixated (Erskine & Trautmann, 1996). The basic eight relational needs were the following: the need for security; the need for validation, affirmation and significance within a relationship; the need for acceptance by a stable, dependable, and protective other; the need for confirmation of personal experience; the need for self-definition; the need to have an impact on the other person; the need to have the other initiate; and the need to express love (Erskine & Trautmann, 1996).

Given that a lot of the literature in integrative psychotherapy is focused on this particular hunger, we may wonder how that may impact or bias the practitioner's understanding of the hunger for stimuli and the hunger for structure which operate within the client's mind. Does the relationship then become the main (or, indeed, exclusive) organizing principle of the psyche? What happens in cases where relationships represent threatening territory? In our view, this emphasis tends to skew the clinician's sight to the point where it may exclude significant aspects of how the mind processes information and creates meaning. In the remaining chapters, we will further elaborate this idea about how relationship may sometimes get in the way, or other times work in the service of the mind processing information.

Before doing so, however, we find it important to show how this theory of motivation was integrated within the theory of personality described above, thereby generating a methodology that integrative psychotherapy practitioners could rely on. Typical interventions, which were all contact-facilitating and relationship-oriented, included inquiry, attunement, involvement, and juxtaposition (O'Reilly-Knapp & Erskine, 2003).

Inquiry described a particular stance that the therapist needed to find within him-/herself, one that was open to discovering the client, so that the client could eventually discover his/her own sense of self.

Attunement refers to the sensitivity required from the therapist and the identification with the client's experience, an identification that needs to be communicated back to the person. These aspects were intimately related to the notion of empathy, something which was extensively developed by Erskine et al. (2023) in their book, *Beyond Empathy. A Therapy of Contact-in-Relationship*, first published in 1999.

Involvement comprised the acknowledgment, normalization, and validation of the client's experience. It was considered a type of presence that allows the client to soften his/her defenses and to use the therapeutic relationship as a space in which old patterns were relinquished and new ways of relating were being created.

The phenomenon of juxtaposition occurred when the client experienced a stark contrast between archaic needs or longings that were never met in childhood and what was provided in the therapeutic relationship.

The methodology also included a conceptualization of transference, which was understood as a description of the past, as well as an attempt to create meaning, as the expression of an intrapsychic conflict, as well as the desire for intimacy (O'Reilly-Knapp & Erskine, 2003). Transference, therefore, was viewed as referring both to the repeated relationship, and to the needed relationship. Again, the emphasis seems to be on the therapeutic relational experience as something that should be deeply nurturing, hence reparative and sustaining; in this context, it was the use of the therapist's self that was the key ingredient in satisfying relational needs and facilitating integration (Erskine & Trautmann, 1996).

As we become accustomed to the internal architecture of the integrative approach to transactional analysis, we may observe various similarities to other orientations, or thinking traditions that also belong to TA. This is the case, for example, of relational transactional analysis, which placed equal value on the role of the therapeutic relationship (for a detailed presentation of this approach, please consider reading Chapter 6). However, the emphasis there was not on obtaining reparation, the therapist would not provide the client with something that was lost, and it would not offer a corrective experience. Instead, the relationship was used to create a space for multiple subjectivities, both the client's and the therapist's, that could weave together a meaning that was neither entirely about the past, nor about the present, neither entirely about the client, nor about the therapist, but something different, that emerged anew.

Both the integrative approach to TA and co-creative TA (for a detailed presentation of this approach, please consider reading Chapter 5) rely on the same conceptualization of ego states. However, the first was adamant about the importance of working through past experiences, whereas the latter maintained a strong focus on working with what emerged in the here-and-now between the client and the practitioner. Additionally, within the integrative psychotherapy framework, (intrapsychic) conflict was viewed as a sign of fragmentation; practitioners working with a co-creative sensibility welcomed potential internal contradictions and understood them as a trait of normal psychological functioning.

Similarly to integrative psychotherapy, the social-cognitive approach described in the first part of this chapter acknowledged the role played by the need for contact and relatedness within the economy of human motivation. Yet, by using the notion of "schema" as part of the framework, the model provided by SCTA managed, in our view, to place equal emphasis on the individual's hunger for relationship, as well as the hunger for stimuli or structure, therefore offering a less skewed perspective on the interplay between the intrapsychic and the interpersonal dimension of human psychological life. Moreover, in the SCTA model, the Parent and the Child ego states continue to have a relevance for the person in the here-and-now, whereas the integrative psychotherapy approach takes the view that those two ego states are relics from the person's past, interfering with Adult functioning.

At the beginning of this chapter, we wrote that we would be discussing the ideas of authors who resorted to various models outside transactional analysis in order to resolve theoretical inconsistencies apparent in Berne's writings, therefore developing approaches which extended beyond the margins of TA, toward other orientations. Other authors addressed this lack of theoretical consistency in a different way, bringing input from alternative frameworks, yet remaining within the same perimeter of transactional analysis theory and practice. In the following chapter, we will be exploring their views, questions, and reflections, as contributions to the development of the already existing body of knowledge.

References

Benjamin, L. S. (1974). Structural analysis of social behavior (SASB). *Psychological Review.* 81, 392–425. https://doi.org/10.1037/h0037024

Berne, E. (1961). *TA in psychotherapy: A systematic individual and social psychiatry.* Grove Press & Evergreen Books.

Berne, E. (1972). *What do you say after you say hello? The psychology of human destiny.* Grove Press.

Campos, L. P. (2003). Care and maintenance of the tree of transactional analysis. *Transactional Analysis Journal.* 33:2, 115–125. https://doi.org/10.1177/036215370303300204

Cornell, W. F. (2010). Aspiration or adaptation?: An unresolved tension in Eric Berne's basic beliefs. *Transactional Analysis Journal*. 40:3–4, 243–253. https://doi.org/10.1177/036215371004000309

Cornell, W. F. (2015). Ego states in the social realm. *Transactional Analysis Journal*. 45:3, 191–199. https://doi.org/10.1177/0362153715597897

Cox, M. (1999). The relationship between ego state structure and function: A diagrammatic formulation. *Transactional Analysis Journal*. 29:1, 49–58. https://doi.org/10.1177/036215379902900109

De Luca, M. L., & Tosi, M. T. (2011). Social-cognitive transactional analysis: An introduction to Pio Scilligo's model of ego states. *Transactional Analysis Journal*. 41:3, 206–220. https://doi.org/10.1177/036215371104100303

Erskine, R. G. (1983). The ultimate psychological concern: Nuclear war. *Transactional Analysis Journal*. 13:1, 7–9. https://doi.org/10.1177/036215378301300103

Erskine, R. G. (1988). Ego structure, intrapsychic function, and defense mechanisms: A commentary on Eric Berne's original theoretical concepts. *Transactional Analysis Journal*. 18:1, 15–19. https://doi.org/10.1177/036215378801800104

Erskine, R. G. (1991). Transference and transactions: Critique from an intrapsychic and integrative perspective. *Transactional Analysis Journal*. 21:2, 63–76. https://doi.org/10.1177/036215379102100202

Erskine, R. G. (1998). The therapeutic relationship: Integrating motivation and personality theories. *Transactional Analysis Journal*. 28:2, 132–141. https://doi.org/10.1177/036215379802800206

Erskine, R. G., Moursund, J., & Trautmann, R. L. (2023). *Beyond empathy. A therapy of contact-in-relationship*. Routledge. (Original work published 1999)

Erskine, R. G., & Trautmann, R. L. (1996). Methods of an integrative psychotherapy. *Transactional Analysis Journal*. 26:4, 316–328. https://doi.org/10.1177/036215379602600410

Joines, V. S. (1976). Differentiating structural and functional. *Transactional Analysis Journal*. 6:4, 377–380. https://doi.org/10.1177/036215377600600404

Loria, B. R. (1990). Epistemology and reification of metaphor in transactional analysis. *Transactional Analysis Journal*. 20:3, 152–162. https://doi.org/10.1177/036215379002000303

O'Reilly-Knapp, M., & Erskine, R. G. (2003). Core concepts of an integrative transactional analysis. *Transactional Analysis Journal*. 33:2, 168–177. https://doi.org/10.1177/036215370303300208

Scilligo, P. (2002). 25 Anni di collaborazione che hanno visto nascere l'IRPIR e l'IFREP: Breve storia dai primi inizi fino ai nostri giorni. *Psicologia Psicoterapia e Salute*. 8:3, 211–236.

Scilligo, P. (2009). *Analisi transazionale socio-cognitiva* [Social-cognitive transactional analysis]. LAS.

Scilligo, P. (2010). The empirical basis of medicine in search of humanity and naturalistic psychotherapy in search of its hermeneutic roots. *International Journal of Transactional Analysis Research and Practice*. 1:1, 60–71. https://doi.org/10.29044/v1i1p60

Scilligo, P. (2011). Transference as a measurable social-cognitive process: An application of Scilligo's model of ego states. *Transactional Analysis Journal*. 41:3, 196–205. https://doi.org/10.1177/036215371104100302

Stuthridge, J. (2006). Inside out: A transactional analysis model of trauma. *Transactional Analysis Journal*. 36:4, 270–283. https://doi.org/10.1177/036215370603600403

Tossi, M. T., De Luca, M. L., & Messana, C. (2015). A response to Cornell's "Ego states in the social realm": Reflections on the theories of Pio Scilligo and Eric Berne, *Transactional Analysis Journal*. 45:3, 200–203. https://doi.org/10.1177/0362153715597723

Chapter 8

An Appreciation of a Dynamic, Sustainable Robust Theory and Those Who Ensure It

Up to this point in the book, we have observed the evolution of transactional analysis theory and application. We have observed twists and turns over seven decades and have placed this in the context and spirit of the times. We reflected on the emergence of various models and methodologies, as well as their meaning in relation to complex dynamics occurring within the transactional analysis (TA) community and in the wider social and political arena. As we accounted for the multiplicity of changes that TA theory underwent, we could also acknowledge the fact that this is a framework which seems to be resilient enough to accommodate significant shifts in perspective, thereby standing the test of time.

The book began with a description of the post-war era where access to affordable effective psychotherapy was sorely needed and expediency was of the essence. Berne's prolific writing with his emphasis on developing a theory of personality free from obscure terminology that could be easily shared, led to a burgeoning popularity and indeed a popularization of transactional analysis concepts.

The vigor with which concepts were debated in the San Francisco Seminars, fiercely competitive, in some ways, continues among transactional analysis today providing a dynamic, constantly growing theoretical base.

In January 1971, relatively soon after Berne's premature death, the president of the ITAA, Ken Everts, wrote in his editorial:

> Eric Berne has left us with a store of knowledge and an apparatus with which to implement it. I would hope that we will examine and study it for a year's time before we modify it too drastically. A canon has been bequeathed us and it behooves us to recognize it, acknowledge it as his before new approaches are mixed in and confused with it. May we document it as his and having done so build and profit by it.
>
> (1971, p. 4)

In the following year, Claude Steiner in his speech on receiving the Eric Berne Memorial Award for his "Script Matrix" (1972) article warned against the TA community stagnating. His view was that it was important to maintain a scientific approach, by this he appeared to mean observable reportable data. He guarded

DOI: 10.4324/9781003253013-8

against TA becoming a "revivalist religion" or a "highly attractive item in a marketing business" or an "orthodoxy where no-one dared to utter a creative word" or "a political quagmire dominated by a white male professional elite" (1972, p. 36).

Some may say that Steiner's warnings were prophetic, as at times accusations of religious verve or orthodoxy have been leveled at TA theory. Stagnation, however, is not one that could be applied. The *Transactional Analysis Journal*, now in its 53 years of publication, is a respected peer-reviewed journal published by a leading academic publisher and continues to grow.

The fundamental building blocks of TA theory, i.e., ego states, script, transactions, and games are still used by practitioners in varying ways to communicate and work with their clients, as well as in the professional community. Much like the early years, TA theory is alive and well in many areas, including, but not exclusively, in counseling and psychotherapy, organizational consultancy, education, social work, the criminal justice system, hospitals, churches, and more recently in political debate.

So far, we have examined and critiqued areas of TA that first became known as schools, that is, the classical, the cathexis, and the redecision schools, and latterly other approaches such as relational or a revisioning in co-creative transactional analysis. We have also reflected on four different fields of application and the potential hierarchical structure that ensued among the different approaches. In the previous chapter, we have examined and critiqued other theoretical approaches that rely heavily on transactional analysis, i.e., integrative psychotherapy and social-cognitive transactional analysis.

Alongside these new developments, there have been many practitioners who have made major contributions to the development of the theory, whose impact has not remained defined as a specific approach or a significant reworking of the theory as a whole. We now acknowledge some of them here for how they have substantially shaped the theory and application of TA across the decades.

An Acknowledgment of the Role of Unconscious Dynamics

Fanita English, one of Berne's contemporaries and sometimes a fierce critic of his behavior, maintained an active interest in TA until the end of her life aged 105 in 2022. In our view, English was the first in TA to openly challenge the misuse of transactional analysis theory. In her 1977 paper "Rackets and Racketeering as the Root of Games," she wrote

> ... it has become the fashion among some unsophisticated therapists to use the word (racket) in an accusatory manner to connote feelings they disapprove of, without addressing themselves to the facts that the patient who exhibits a racket or suffers from it internally is not "doing it on purpose"—i.e., within his present awareness and that the racket cannot be cured simply by naming it although identifying it is the first step to treatment.
>
> (English, 1977a, p. 4)

Like Berne, English trained as a psychoanalyst and became disillusioned and felt hurt by her own psychoanalysis (Röhl, 2021, p. 138). It is clear throughout her work that she maintained an abiding interest in the unconscious and refers to this aspect of Freud's work as groundbreaking (2021, p. 139). Her contributions to TA theory demonstrate a brilliant critical-thinking mind and a lively active, constantly evolving attitude to working with people. She was awarded the Eric Berne Scientific Memorial Award in 1979 for her work on "Rackets and Real Feelings" (1971, 1972) and the Eric Berne Memorial Award (EBMA) in 1997 for her work on "Hot-Potato Transmissions and Episcript" (1969).

All of her contributions she attributed to her work with people, in training and in therapy, and expressed that her updated views on script and unconscious motivators had evolved over the many years of her lifetime in practice.

Like ourselves, English believed TA theory to be continually unfolding and developing and that Berne himself would have continued to modify the theory had his life not been cut short.

English's contribution reliably offers more nuance than some of her contemporaries. She was adamant that script formation was a creative act that could not be summarized in one or two sentences (1977b, p. 290), and she preferred the idea of script conclusion to script decision.

> They [script decisions] can be recalled through verbal or visual memory and thus can be representative as part of the script. In contrast, conclusions are experienced viscerally, "in the gut," because they were arrived at non verbally during early childhood, that is between birth and about age four to five …
> (1977b, p. 291)

During her lifetime, English worked in many different areas including as an organizational consultant and her development of the idea of the "three-cornered contract" (English, 1975) has been invaluable to hosts of practitioners working with teams and in or with any kind of organization.

Always moving with the times, English argued that TA was bound "by an episcript of defensive arrogance that isolates us" (English, 2007b, p. 7), and even considered calling herself a "cognitive transactional analyst" (p. 7). This was in relation to cognitive therapies receiving good press in contrast to TA, which appeared to be moving into the background in mainstream attitudes to psychotherapy. This is indicative of her passion for finding the most useful and compassionate way to help her clients move on from limiting beliefs to living more expansive lives.

Alongside this pragmatic and effective approach to her work, English offered continual curiosity and depth to the development of theory. Her 2008 article "Unconscious Drives Re-Imagined" is a clear example of English reconceptualizing Freud's drive theory alongside Berne's theory of hungers producing a theory of three psychosomatic drives which she termed motivators, the word being suggested to her by James Allen, a contemporary of English and to whose work we now turn (English, 2008, p. 243).

Appreciating the Mind as a Constructor of Narratives

Allen, a psychiatrist in Oklahoma, was also a contributor to Berne's seminars in the later part of Berne's life and witnessed the brinkmanship and misogyny present in the seminars (personal communication, December 6, 2021). From his early writings in the *Bulletin*, we witness another lively curious mind bringing subtlety and reflection not only toward clients, but in practitioners. Early in his writings and contributions to TA and in response to English's (1969) theory of episcript and hot potato, we observe questioning of how a practitioner can avoid "gaining temporary freedom from their own script by passing it on like a hot potato to one of his clients" (Allen, 1970, p. 58). In the article, he suggests that as consultants become aware of this, they might aim to weaken the influence of the practitioners' script on the client with a subtle reframing of the process.

Often co-writing articles with his wife Barbara, Allen published numerous papers in the *Transactional Analysis Journal* since its first issue in 1971 plus many more in medical journals. These articles interweaved psychiatry, sociology, psychology, theology, biology, spirituality, and neurobiology within a TA framework. Allen is experienced by many TA colleagues as someone of modesty and humility who maintains a respectful dialogue with his colleagues. It was possibly something of a surprise to the community when in the 1980s the Allens presented ideas which challenged the status quo in TA. In a letter to the *Transactional Analysis Journal* editor in 1989, Allen wrote:

> During the past few months, my wife and I have received a number of letters and calls from people expressing excitement, confusion, and even horror over ideas they are beginning to discern in our work.
>
> (Allen, 1989, p. 118)

And goes on to say:

> First, our basic position is that evidence is accumulating to suggest that each of us actually creates the self he or she considers himself or herself to be, his or her script, and the world he or she inhabits. We do this constantly and "in the now," reviewing, creating, and recreating our pasts and our futures. Thus, in some cases, we may actually be creating in the present the injunctions we believe we received, and the experiences we believe we had.
>
> (Allen, 1989, p. 118)

The Allens were beginning to question the certitude that had prevailed in TA, bringing more questioning and exploration. They, with others (Cornell, 1988), also began the shift in TA theory from children being the passive recipients of script messages to a consideration of the creative part we all play in the formation of our script. In 1998, they were awarded the Eric Berne Memorial Award for their contributions to theory. The scholarly articles cited in the award nomination involved a critique of narrative and constructivist therapies and placed script analysis and redecision therapy in what they "might call rather grandly, perhaps, an emerging constructivist or constructionist school of transactional analysis" (Allen & Allen,

1998, p. 13). We noticed the tentativeness in the Allens' language about the emergence of such a *school* and, in our wonderings as to why this did not form, we reflected that a constructionist sensibility would indeed suggest that nothing is fixed and different meanings emerge. Indeed, it is part of the Allens' legacy that we have learned to appreciate that stories are reshaped and re-interpreted and we are "entitled to more than one story" (Allen & Allen, 1995, p. 329).

Different stories and the way we interpret them was the topic of a vigorous debate in 2005 between Claude Steiner and Michelle Novellino published in the *Transactional Analysis Journal* as "Theoretical Diversity: A Debate about Transactional Analysis and Psychoanalysis." This followed the EBMA being awarded to Michelle Novellino for his article "Unconscious Communication and Interpretation in Transactional Analysis." Steiner's argument was that there were colleagues who were attempting to reshape transactional analysis into a psychoanalytic framework reversing the very intention of Berne. "Berne created an alternative to psychoanalysis—not a branch, but a radical departure, developed because the practice of psychoanalysis, as Berne knew it, was to his way of thinking, fundamentally mistaken" (Steiner & Novellino, 2005, p. 111). Novellino responded that in his view "research at the psychodynamic level of the therapeutic relationship can lead to progress in Bernean theory and technique both within our own community as well as externally in relation to colleagues who are not transactional analysts."

Keeping TA Theory Alive

This leads us to recognition of the major contribution to TA theory and practice made by Bill Cornell who has built bridges between the disciplines of TA, body psychotherapy, and psychoanalysis. Each discipline and many scholars within them have benefited from Cornell's thoughtfulness and provocative challenge that he makes to theory, between different theories and between theorists from the different disciplines.

Cornell has not only made major contributions to the development of the theory; he has also made very active contributions to the national and international TA organizations. Cornell was editor of *The Script* newsletter for 13 years and encouraged lively debate between TA practitioners and writers. In his time as editor, he wrote provocative editorials and entered into dialogue with many different authors, facilitating much discussion between writers in the community. We think the excerpt below typifies the dialogue he encouraged between people. The lead article was one where Fanita English had suggested that she may call herself a "cognitive transactional analyst" to align with the recognition that was being given to cognitive behavioral therapy. Cornell's response entitled "No Fanita, I'm not a Cognitive Transactional Analyst," to us, shows Cornell's deep commitment to transactional analysis, and to dialogue. He wrote

> We have much in common with many contemporary disciplines. We have much to teach and much to learn with our colleagues in a broad range of disciplines. I think and deeply believe that we need to retain our identities as transactional

analysts without additional labels and to be willing to demonstrate what we know and examine what we do not know or do as well as others.

(2007, p. 2)

Cornell's writings show a rare combination of direct, honest, and often contentious opinions alongside his deep commitment to being open to question. As editor both of *The Script* from 1997 to 2010 and the *Transactional Analysis Journal* from 2003 to 2018, he has invited or one might say cajoled many TA practitioners and contributors from other disciplines to put forward their ideas, in the spirit of keeping the theory alive. Cornell's first article for the *Transactional Analysis Journal*, in 1975, was entitled "Wake Up Sleepy" and we quote him below from his speech as a recipient of the Eric Berne Memorial Award: "I guess we could say I've been writing to wake people up ever since" (2011, p. 12).

Cornell writes clearly of his strong opposition to the founding of schools in TA. He believes they shut down thinking and creativity. His commitment being always first and foremost to his clients, he wrote in his sometimes outspoken way of his concern that "Schools create structures that better serve the narcissistic needs of the leaders and members than the diverse and ever-challenging needs of their clients."

(2011, p. 15)

It is hard to do justice or even pick out the main aspects of Cornell's contributions to the development of TA theory as he is forever pushing the boundaries, questioning assumptions, and bringing new aspects of the theory to life. Like English, he writes that it is his clients who push him to learn more, to question more, and to push more. If he doesn't understand something, he will find a way of learning more and generously sharing it through his writing and teaching. The EBMA was presented to Cornell in 2010 on the basis of three main articles, "Life Script Theory: A Critical Review from a Developmental Perspective" (1988), "Babies, Brains, and Bodies: Somatic Foundations of the Child Ego State" (2003), and an article jointly written with Landaiche, "Impasse and Intimacy: Applying Berne's Concept of Script Protocol" (Cornell & Landaiche, 2006). These articles capture the contributions that Cornell is mainly recognized for, namely, script as an emergent and continuous process of living, second the vitality and wisdom to be found in the Child ego state, and third the expansion of Berne's concept of protocol leading to further work by Cornell on "Berne's shift away from the language of the unconscious" and the dilemma this has caused for transactional analysts.

Cornell is indeed a Berne scholar, throughout his work, he both honors the history and the scope of TA in all its applications, and he challenges the limitations of the theory and indeed of attitudes in our community. Cornell interviewed Berne's youngest son, Terry, on the 40th anniversary of the publication of *Games People Play* and the publication of a new edition. Cornell also presented alongside Terry

Berne (2004) at an event in Paris, arranged to discuss the impact of Berne's script on the development of transactional analysis.

> I was honored to offer a day of thoughts and reflections on Berne's complex and often difficult life and how it shaped transactional analysis. It was delightful and moving to do it with Terry Berne. It was challenging to look at TA theory and practice through that particular lens. The day was deeply enriched by Terry's open account of his father.
>
> (Hawkes, 2021, p. 6)

True to his desire to keep "waking people up" (2011, p. 12), Cornell often pays particular attention to those areas that Berne avoided, i.e., sexuality and politics. In a recent publication and special issue of *Psychotherapy and Politics International*, which was dedicated to transactional analysis and edited by Cornell and Tudor, Cornell wrote:

> Re-reading Berne's "Man as a Political Animal" is both moving and chilling; and it's a powerful, heart-felt piece of writing. We can see so vividly his distress after the war and his alarm at the human costs of Hitler's rise to power; and we witness the power of governments to silence opposition, or even moral reflection and accountability. I can look back on Berne's decision to remove this section from subsequent editions of this book and his subsequent public positioning of transactional analysis as a-political as an effort to protect his new model and his transactional analysis colleagues—and I can look back and see the consequences of the silence that follows trauma.
>
> (2020, p. 7)

Ending this chapter with a return to Berne's first book and the decision to remove that chapter allows us to appreciate the unfolding of this dynamic robust theory and those that are continuing to develop the theory while honoring the roots and foundations. The book series published by Routledge and edited by Cornell entitled "Innovations in Transactional Analysis" now boasts ten titles in a wide-ranging series encompassing three books on group work and others that contextualize transactional analysis in the current political and social climate. This climate in fact does appear to call for a return to Berne's original ideas of social justice, radical reform, and the importance of the group as well as the individual. Our national and international TA organizations are also taking up this mantle addressing social and world issues. We do indeed, like Terry Berne, think that Berne would look upon the current international TA community with pride.

References

Allen, J. R. (1970). Episcript intervention: A role for the mental health consultant. *Transactional Analysis Bulletin*. 9:34, 58.

Allen, J. R. (1989). Letter to the editor. *Transactional Analysis Journal*. 19:2, 118–119. https://doi.org/10.1177/036215378901900210

Allen, J. R., & Allen, B. A. (1995). Narrative theory, redecision therapy, and postmodernism. *Transactional Analysis Journal*. 25:4, 327–334. https://doi.org/10.1177/036215379502500408

Allen, J. R., & Allen, B. A. (1998). Redecision therapy: Through a narrative lens. In M. Hoyt(Ed.), *The handbook of constructive therapies: Innovative approaches from leading practitioners* (pp. 31–46). Jossey-Bass.

Berne, T., & Cornell, W. F. (2004). Remembering Eric Berne: A conversation with Terry Berne. *The Script*. 34:8, 6–7.

Cornell, W. F. (1988). Life script theory: A critical review from a developmental perspective. *Transactional Analysis Journal*. 18:4, 270–282. https://doi.org/10.1177/036215378801800402

Cornell, W. F. (2003). Babies, brains, and bodies: Somatic foundations of the Child ego state. In C. Sills, & H. Hargaden (Eds.), *Ego States* (pp. 28–54). Worth Publishing.

Cornell, W. F. (2007). Editorially yours. No Fanita, I'm not a cognitive transactional analyst. *The Script*. 37:5, 2.

Cornell, W. F. (2011). Keeping our work alive: Reflections on writing upon receiving the 2010 Eric Berne Memorial Award. *Transactional Analysis Journal*. 41:1, 11–15. https://doi.org/10.1177/036215371104100104

Cornell, W. F., & Landaiche, N. M. III (2006). Impasse and intimacy: Applying Berne's concept of script protocol. *Transactional Analysis Journal*. 36:3, 196–213. https://doi.org/10.1177/036215370603600304

Cornell, W. F., & Tudor, K. (2020). Reviewing the special issue "Transactional Analysis and Politics": A reflective dialogue. *Psychotherapy and Politics International*. 18:3, 1–12. https://doi.org/10.1002/ppi.1571

English, F. (1969). Episcript and the "hot potato" game. *Transactional Analysis Bulletin*. 8:32, 77–82.

English, F. (1971). The substitution factor: Rackets and real feelings. *Transactional Analysis Journal*. 1:4, 27–32. https://doi.org/10.1177/036215377100100408

English, F. (1972). Rackets and real feelings. *Transactional Analysis Journal*. 2:1, 23–25. https://doi.org/10.1177/036215377200200108

English, F. (1975). The three-cornered contract. *Transactional Analysis Journal*. 5:4, 383–384. https://doi.org/10.1177/036215377500500413

English, F. (1977a). Rackets and racketeering as the root of games. In R. N. Blakeney (Ed.), *Current issues in transactional analysis: The first ITAA European conference* (pp. 3–28). Brunner/Mazel.

English, F. (1977b). What shall I do tomorrow? In G. Barnes (Ed.), *Transactional analysis after Eric Berne* (pp. 287–352). Harper's College Press.

English, F. (2007). I'm now a cognitive transactional analyst, are you? *The Script*. 37:5, 1.

English, F. (2008). Unconscious drives re-imagined. *Transactional Analysis Journal*. 38:3, 238–246. https://doi.org/10.1177/036215370803800306

Everts, K. (1971). The president's page. *Transactional Analysis Journal*. 1:1, 4. https://doi.org/10.1177/036215377100100101

Hawkes, L. (2021). "Our roots and our wings": Berne's script and TA's script. *The Script*. 51:8, 6.

Röhl, S. (2021). *Fanita English, a psychotherapist's life and work from psychoanalysis to transactional analysis and Gestalt therapy*. Herstellung und Verlag: Books on Demand.

Steiner, C. (1972). 1971 Eric Berne memorial scientific award lecture. *Transactional Analysis Journal*. 2:1, 34–37. https://doi.org/10.1177/036215377200200113

Steiner, C., & Novellino, M. (2005). Theoretical diversity: A debate about transactional analysis and psychoanalysis. *Transactional Analysis Journal*. 35:2, 110–118. https://doi.org/10.1177/036215370503500202

Chapter 9

Evolution and Innovation: Some Ways Forward

Honoring the Legacy and Welcoming Mutative Change

Our final chapter brings reflections on those that precede it alongside our offerings of how we envision transactional analysis (TA) theory continuing to develop into the future.

Previous chapters have honored the evolution of the theory, the context in which the theory was formed, and the pitfalls of pioneers being wedded to the theory they have developed. We have also appreciated practitioners pushing boundaries and developing new thinking, especially those that respectfully acknowledge the roots of the ideas. We appreciate those who bring new thinking that accounts for new contexts and progress in areas such as neuroscience, gender fluidity, sexual orientation, and politics to name but a few.

We reflect on how Berne and his followers, in their desire to create something new, effective, and pragmatic, often brought an attitude of posturing, competitiveness, and superiority, something that we believe diluted rather than supported the significance of the new developments. We have seen how TA as a theory has been critiqued by others for its apparent simplicity, alongside the use of jargon and slogans, potentially creating an atmosphere of exclusivity. At the same time, we have equally acknowledged the value of this robust theory across a number of applications.

In our research into a more detailed and nuanced history of TA, we have been able to highlight tensions in the early stages of developing the theory. For example, we have acknowledged that even though Berne was intending to create a system where knowledge was shared, in the earlier days it was the practitioner who held the power to define reality and confront patients whose ideas differed. We have noted in his need to define a new effective system, one main tension of Berne's was that of wanting to be recognized by the community of psychoanalysis from where he came and yet disparaging its practice at the same time.

We noticed themes in the previous chapters that highlight what we believe is an insufficient and inconsistent conceptualization of loss. In the context of the theory being developed in the aftermath of the Second World War, we hypothesize that essential grief and mourning after so many years of war was overshadowed by relief, celebration, and positivism.

In fact, Berne's life was one of many unmourned losses (Heathcote, 2016), and as we consider this, we reflect on how TA theory itself became more of a search for certainty. In doing so, it became used more as an imposition of how things *should be*. Meaning-making was sacrificed in the face of technique; gaining social control was prioritized over exploring one's internal world with a sense of wonder. The practitioner's mind was not so much a curious mind, but an impatient one, eager to establish "the truth," or define "reality" from a rather authoritarian stance.

The dominant psychoanalytic trend in the United States was also a product of Second World War trauma, with many psychoanalysts fleeing Nazi Germany and Austria. As these exiled psychoanalysts brought their theory to the United States, ego psychology became the dominant mode. The main tenet of ego psychology at this time was to help people develop a "capacity to adapt to the prevailing social reality" (Cornell, personal communication, September 28, 2023). This approach involved a move away from the focus on Freud's drive theory and away from the unconscious. From these beginnings and from Berne's relationship with Paul Federn, we can see how reality-testing became so important in transactional analysis. Given the circumstances of the post-war era and the search for something tangible, it is also understandable that thinking became more closed and rigid, and that the ideas which brought relief from suffering became solidified into dogma. From here, we observe trends where the verve and enthusiasm for TA theory to bring about profound change was used as an imposition of one reality on another in the name of breaking down a defensive system. It is interesting to note the combative terminology in this post-war era that, although well intended, served in some, to invite over-adaptation and a reinforced defensive system. While psychoanalytic drive theory needed further exploration, the shift to working with that which could easily be brought into consciousness was in our view a step too far, such that important meaning-making through phenomenology and bodily experience was sacrificed in the search for expediency and certainty.

> As Eric's thinking imbued the ego states with increasing internal as well as social/transactional reality, the point of ascribing important issues like script to this theoretical black hole of the "unconscious" was becoming moot. TA became increasingly a decisional theory ... The EGO as a schmuck trapped in the orbit of the black hole of unconsciousness was ejected to the outer rim of the galaxy ... Also, by then he was isolated (by choice, in part) from all of his peers who could have validated and enriched his thinking. He had only us, his disciples, a limited, if intoxicating, source of sustenance.
>
> (Groder, in Cornell, 2008, p. 95)

Earlier modifications to classic transactional analysis theory had tended to swing from thesis to antithesis without evidence of any synthesis of ideas. For example, different approaches emphasized that psychotherapeutic intervention needed to be directed toward the Parent ego state (Schiffian reparenting), while others (redecision psychotherapists) highlighted the importance of work with the Child ego state. We notice a lack of space for reflection and a tendency toward polarization, the perpetuation of an "either this, or that" paradigm. The result of these movements between thesis and antithesis in the absence of synthesis was a deadening of the curious mind, a fragmentation of TA theory that did not leave room for dialogue. Ideas were turned into "something like cement" (Blackstone, 1993, p. 217), and they hardened to the point where it became difficult to change their shape, or transform them in order to accommodate a more complex clinical landscape.

> ... theory need not become confining or carved in stone. Rather, it can be played with and stirred up as theorists continue to learn and grow.
> (Blackstone, 1993, p. 218)

We understand this play with theory as a mindful play, one that involves discovery, curiosity, and imagination (Winnicott, 1971). It is not one that dilutes the link between the various layers that practitioners need to account for in their practice, namely, how they come to an understanding of methodology (the philosophy of method), epistemology (the theory of knowledge), ontology (the essence of human beings), and axiology (the nature of value) (Tudor, in press).

In the absence of reflective questioning and exploration, transactional analysis theory eventually came up against its own blind spots, some of which elicited tragic consequences, as was the case of the reparenting approach practiced within the Cathexis Institute and discussed at length in a previous chapter. Similarly, a lot of the theory about group work lacked the necessary interest and an appropriate framework to address more complex unconscious dynamics, such as conflict, aggression, mistrust, or anxiety (Cornell, 2016). Therefore, it remained inefficient (or even misleading) in the attempt to offer a more robust understanding of phenomena such as racism and the way in which this is passed down from one generation to another (Dalal, 2016).

As time progressed, however, the foundation of the theory itself stood the test of time and new thinking did begin to emerge bringing challenges. New generations of transactional analysts were starting to question the dogma and bring in their own questions about certainty. We reflect that as a third generation of transactional analysts emerge, there might be an atmosphere created where topics that used to be no-go areas for our ancestors might be available for processing, and that this might lead practitioners toward a richer, more integrated approach (Apprey, 2014).

For example, as thinking gradually began opening up, there was room for perspectives of writers like Rowland (2016) and Minikin (2024), who invited more pluralist perspectives, or Stuthridge (2012), who put forward theories on the role of context and about the mind as a complex architecture of self-states.

However, the meeting of minds between generations was sometimes accompanied by friction. In the early 2000s, there was vigorous debate between first- and second-generation transactional analysts, Steiner, Campos, English, Stewart, Joines, and in the first instance Hargaden, who was representing the relational approach. At that time Hargaden presented a proposal at a UK conference that the time had come for TA to acknowledge some of the things that had previously remained "in the shadow" (p. 7). That is, an honoring of vulnerability and an appreciation of "the feminine, the relational, the connectedness" (p. 7).

Hargaden had proposed that the name change that Berne made in 1943, prior to which he was called Bernstein, represented a turning away from his Jewishness and a turning away from vulnerability.

Much debate ensued and there appeared for quite some years a fierce competitive atmosphere, especially in the UK and between old and new theorists. Claude Steiner (2006) wrote:

> Berne was interested in contracts, not because he was afraid of the vulnerable or the uncontrollable, but because he was intensely interested in ensuring that transactional analysis, unlike psychoanalysis, be an effective psychotherapy with concrete results. And he believed, as do I, that the endless, repetitive "jazz" that invades psychotherapy journals and, alas, recently, our own *TAJ*, has no relation to the solving of people's problems.
>
> (p. 332)

Once more, in witnessing such debates, we might notice our own impulses of advocating for one idea or another, ferociously insisting on reclaiming the psychoanalytic background of TA, for instance, or vigorously opposing it and supporting an approach based on effective solutions and achievable goals instead. However, in our view, both options foreclose the opportunity of understanding the role that context plays when we, as practitioners, form an understanding with regard to what our job is. In addition, we run the risk of imposing our own meanings and frames of reference, instead of facilitating this process for the people who come to see us.

As early as 2002, Hargaden and Sills articulated the fact that therapists need to take into account the characteristics of the socio-historical context in order to be able to have a more appropriate understanding of clinical phenomena:

> ... when Berne first wrote, the common client was putatively an inhibited, rule-bound individual who needed the metaphorical "solvent" of therapy to loosen the confines of his or her script. As we move into the twenty-first century, the "typical" client is one who needs not solvent but "glue"—a way of integrating and building his or her sense of self in the world.
>
> (p. 3)

More recently, various TA authors wrote about the importance of acknowledging vulnerability, both in the client, and also the psychotherapist. In 2016, the *Transactional Analysis Journal* dedicated an entire issue to this theme. In that issue, Rowland published a paper where she offered a postmodernist critique on the way in which culture and society legitimate various discourses as ready-made meanings that people might use defensively in order to bypass a more elaborate process of meaning-making. Given its complexity, this process would elicit various degrees of instability, anxiety, lack of control, and other existential fears. Rowland articulated the fact that "we have a lacuna at the heart of psychotherapy theory where the individual meets society, where psychology meets sociology, and where the personal meets the political" (pp. 282–283) and that this lacuna needs addressing.

Her stance is one that describes how being in contact with our own vulnerabilities, as professionals and individuals, opens the possibility of having a felt sense of the client's struggles, or phenomenological realities, thereby metabolizing aspects of experience which might otherwise appear to be intolerable.

> ... I do not want to privilege feeling over thinking or process over structure ... I am learning to understand and value that there are many different forms of knowing, thinking, and meaning-making. When we try, as therapists, to "get it right," I believe we are more likely to close down on particular kinds of thinking and knowing as we cling to the theory of our modality as if it were a life raft ... Perhaps when we allow ourselves to think critically and conceptually about meaning-making, we can also allow ourselves the luxury of experimentation and creativity within the therapeutic relationship.
> (p. 284)

Gradually, the importance of having a metaperspective was emphasized. In a paper published in 2015, José Grégoire wrote about the process of thinking that is required in the making of theory. His view was that theory is the result of a form of specialized thinking which resorts to two modes: focused thinking, which involves a cognitive process (the work with concepts and referential language), and integrated thinking, which is more receptive to information coming from noncognitive dynamics (the processing of sensory, emotional, and relational signals). The two modes of thinking function alongside each other, in collaboration, rather than in competition. Paying attention to this way of developing theory eventually allows for a more flexible arrangement between scientific rigor and clinical experience.

Such reflections and approaches to theory encouraged authors to address some of the blind spots identified in TA theory. To go back to the examples mentioned above, the understanding of psychosis and schizophrenia was considerably deepened through the work of Mellacqua (2020). In his book, he critically reviewed the reparenting approach and developed a model that accounted for the archaic, nonverbal particularities that were part of the nature of such disturbances, as well as the severe forms of splitting in the psychotic mind which required different forms of intervention than those put forward and practiced within the Schiffian tradition. Mellacqua's views are also consistent with the views of other authors who offered a critical reflection on the reparenting approach (Cornell, 2022).

Also, the perspective regarding working with groups transformed and matured. For one thing, the focus of the practitioner gradually moved elsewhere: Instead of finding value in the urge to control the group dynamics and in remaining (objectively or analytically) removed from them, there was more space for conceptualizing the importance of using one's countertransference. Referring to the traditional Bernean view of group work, Petriglieri and Wood (2003) wrote:

> Group consultation is neither plumbing nor surgery, however, and no one—regardless of his or her level of knowledge and skills or formal role—can enter a group and be unaffected by its dynamics, maintain a detached self-control, identify

collective dysfunction, intervene with surgical precision, and establish control of the group. A surgeon makes contact with the physical body of an anesthetized patient through latex gloves and stainless steel blades. A consultant makes contact with the complexity of a group through a largely irrational matrix of conscious and unconscious individual and collective psychological factors—thoughts, feelings, and images. Consultants cannot avoid getting their hands dirty. To pretend they can restrict their potential effectiveness unnecessarily.

(p. 333)

More specifically, the authors wrote about the importance of being receptive to projective identifications when working with groups, which involves being in touch with potentially turbulent internal experiences, areas of discomfort, unpredictability, or uncertainty. They considered this to be part of the consultant's[1] job and function to process unconscious content that the group might be struggling with.

Similarly, in his papers, Landaiche (2009, 2012, 2013, 2014) gave voice to the fact that group work involves being sensitive to unconscious processes, something which is as much a function of the mind, as it is of the body. He acknowledged the role of the practitioner's vulnerability in this endeavor, the necessity to tolerate encounters with various degrees of disturbance and, yet, remain open to learning from it. Landaiche's view (2021) is one embedded in the theory of Berne, Bion, and Bowen and reflects the idea that groups are self-standing, complex organisms, which need to be understood as such by someone willing to engage as a participant–observer, curious about the phenomenological aspects of group life and ready to, at times, experience failure, shame, and loss.

We notice these collective efforts of revising transactional analysis theory and appreciate their value. To us, they demonstrate that TA can be practiced from a place of accounting for complexity, limitation, multiplicity, and paradox. This enables us to take a different road when reflecting on the ways in which we formulate our diagnostic assessments, or our intervention strategies, a road where the quest for "omnipotence" and "truth" is replaced with the experience of encountering the other:

> To say Hello rightly is to see the other person as a phenomenon, to happen to him and to be ready for him to happen to you.
>
> (Berne, 1972, pp. 4–5)

Inside–Out and Outside–In

Transactional analysis is an integrative therapy that has needed to open its doors to other modalities, contribute to them and as well as learn from them. It has been available to learn from both humanistic and psychoanalytical camps. It has been at risk of being considered as eclectic and so has experienced an ongoing struggle with identity. The three philosophical premises that came to be well known as "People are OK," "Everyone has the capacity to think," and "People decide their own destiny, and these decisions can be changed" (Stewart & Joines, 1987) are potentially meaningful and important. However, in this leaning toward clarity and universality, there arises the risk of becoming superficial. For these premises to stand up to the spirit in which they were formulated, they need to be thought and talked about with the complexity and depth to which this body of theory was born.

To summarize, we have charted the development of the theory from the beginning with Berne's psychoanalytic roots and work on intuition to a theory that was applied in a much more cognitive behavioral way. Each generation has found ways that this extraordinarily robust theory can be adapted to understand what goes inside of people, in between people, and potentially in relation to whatever is going on in various nations throughout the world and between nations.

There have been many reflections as to why, although TA is used far and wide in a variety of settings to good effect, it is still considered a theory and application that sits on the margins of more widely recognized modalities. TA is often used as the basis for new theories, for example, schema therapy (Young et al., 2003) which uses the ideas of Vulnerable Child, Punitive Parent, and Healthy Adult without any reference to TA.

As we reflect on the progression of the theory over nearly six decades, we recognize that radical new approaches often have to be rigid in the first instance in order to penetrate the field of application. As its proponents mature and develop in their thinking, so the approach appears to become more flexible, incorporating and synthesizing historical and new ideas.

For instance, we have recently witnessed a resurgence of interest in the radical psychiatry movement that was started in the 1970s by Claude Steiner and Hogie Wycroft, and how these radical roots are developing more relevance in our increasingly disturbed and disturbing world. These ideas point to the importance of accounting for the various power dynamics that permeate the systems we live in (our families, our professional communities, or even the wider forms of societal organization, such as our countries) (Sedgwick, 2021). It is important, however, to understand these forces from a place of relatedness, where there is a resilient interest in discovering the other's subjectivity and a commitment to plurality, rather than advocating for "the right way." In her book, *Radical-Relational Perspectives in Transactional Analysis*, Minikin manages to find this edge and invites the TA practitioner to maintain an active, reflective mind:

> ... I am saying that when the going gets tough, the capacity to hold on to our minds whilst moving between internal subjective states to relatedness, influence, and affectedness with others is ongoing work. The patient is not merely an innocent victim to an oppressive system but an active subject who has struggled with experiences of alienation alongside growing insight and wisdom. I believe the same is true for our experience of ourselves within our communities.
>
> (2024, p. 150)

In his own way, Tudor (in press) emphasized the importance of acknowledging that transactional analysis cannot be neutral, or "apolitical," and that it is ultimately a method of intervention that has significant social and political implications. Tudor analyzed and supported the idea that TA exists within a particular context, and that there are active exchanges between them that transactional analysts need to take into account, both in their theoretical reflections, as well as in their praxis:

> Those who view TA primarily as a professional practice (in whatever field of application) may attach great(er) importance to the neutrality of the professional and the apolitical nature of professional organisations. Those of us who come from a background of social service, and even social and political activism, will tend to take a more social and political view of professions and professionals (Shaw & Tudor, 2022)—and a more critical view of who is living and prospering in and as a result of TA.
>
> (Tudor, in press)

Acknowledging the weight that context carries facilitated communication between TA and other approaches. As we incorporate the importance of phenomenological experience, we can observe transactional analysts integrate the inside–out and outside–in modes of experience to continue to develop a powerful and pragmatic approach to human relations.

We have seen the identity of TA grow internationally from the roots where the founders appeared to fight for superiority to one where ideas are shared across modalities and TA is appreciated by practitioners for whom this theory is not their primary theoretical base.

In reflecting on ways to maintain this robustness and to facilitate further growth of our frameworks, we found ourselves passionately making a plea for the important role played by the self-examination of our theories. Holding a place in our minds for this kind of systematic "practice" supports us to have a mind of our own (Caper, 1998), one that is not over-invested in a particular model, or approach to the point where it risks becoming dogmatic, or even violently destructive. In their own attempt at de-idealizing theory, relational psychoanalysts also gave voice to the importance of engaging in critical thinking when it comes to the models clinicians adhere to. Their joint efforts resulted in a book, edited by Aron et al. (2018). In the introduction to this book, they wrote:

> Here's a paradox: Psychoanalysis is, above all, a process of self-reflection. We ask our patients to revisit their life narratives, to open them up to reflectivity, inquiry, dialogue, and new perspectives. Self-examination and self-critique: For our patients, this is the conduit to growth. Yet within the psychoanalytic field, we haven't used our own methodology. We haven't subjected our theories to self-examination. In fact, from its earliest beginnings, psychoanalysts have gathered protective circles around our—selves. Professional affiliation seems

to require theoretical loyalty, and that loyalty oath seems opposed to critical self-examination.

(p. 1)

We have found the questions they asked themselves about relational psychoanalytic theory a useful compass as we have been reflecting on the history and particularities of transactional analysis theory:

> Where are our problems and limitations? How might we think about the critiques that have been made of us by other theoretical orientations? Where and how might we want to integrate the thinking of others? How might we want to recall our theories of origin?
>
> (p. 3)

In dialogue, we have also formulated answers of our own. Some might bear echoes in the reader's mind, and others not so much. Regardless of such outcome, we have found it valuable to ask ourselves these questions, to consider them in relation to fellow minds, as well as to sometimes be destabilized enough by them so as to eventually form new understandings.

Telling the Tale

As we draw near the closing of our book, we find ourselves reflecting on developing theory as a process of making meaning, which bears similarities to how our clients might choose to make meaning of their own personal histories and life experiences:

> … language is not a neutral reflection of some objective reality. Rather, reality is an illusion created by language. Words represent actions such that narratives relationally enact powerful, subjective meanings. Our stories and storytelling thus construct our realities. We are, in a fundamental sense, the story we tell about ourselves, other people, and our world. Our reality represents experiences that we subject to our frame of reference. In this way, our frame of reference represents our book of tales. The client's meaning-making is a function of his or her book of tales. These are situated within wider cultural discourses and are (re)produced through language.
>
> (Kellet, 2004, p. 2)

Just as the client tells his or her story, with this book we have also set out to tell our own story about TA theory, in the way in which we have experienced it in our own body–minds. This is perhaps one of many tales that might have been told; yet, it is a tale that we hope to have written reflectively and responsibly. It is a tale that describes our journey through TA with colleagues both dead and alive, inspired by ongoing dialogue with fellow companions, TA authors themselves and members of the community, to whom we are grateful for accompanying us on the road. Our aspiration is that this story will be played with and continue to expand.

As we move toward publication, we reflect on the spirit and generosity of those who have dared to put forward new ideas and reshape what has gone before. As with every type of research, we found some surprises. Our hunches told us that each development of the theory was a shaking off of previously held assumptions, a "putting a new show on the road" (Berne, 1972, p. 403). In fact, we were pleasantly surprised at the consistency of new ideas that paid attention to and honored the theory that had preceded it. In the new era, we are now seeing a generation of writers expanding the application of TA and continuing to reflect on the roots. We hope this publication that looks at early innovations will serve well as a reference point for anyone who is interested in placing this robust and flexible theory within the context of when it first emerged and the context within which it continues to develop.

Note

1 "Consultant" is the term preferred by Petriglieri and Wood (2003, p. 332) when referring to the practitioner who works in a group setting.

References

Apprey, M. (2014). A pluperfect errand: A turbulent return to beginnings in the transgenerational transmission of destructive aggression. *Free Associations: Psychoanalysis and Culture, Media, Groups, Politics*. 66, 16–29.

Aron, L., Grand, S., & Slochower, J. (Eds.) (2018). *De-idealizing relational theory. A critique from within*. Routledge.

Berne, E. (1972). *What do you say after you say hello? The psychology of human destiny*. Corgi Books.

Blackstone, P. (1993). The dynamic child: Integration of second-order structure, object relations, and self psychology. *Transactional Analysis Journal*. 23:4, 216–234. https://doi.org/10.1177/036215379302300406

Caper, R. (1998). *A mind of one's own: A psychoanalytic view of self and object*. The New Library of Psychoanalysis.

Cornell, W. F. (2008). What do you say if you don't say "unconscious"?: Dilemmas created for transactional analysts by Berne's shift away from the language of unconscious experience. *Transactional Analysis Journal*. 38:2, 93–100. https://doi.org/10.1177/036215370803800202

Cornell, W. F. (2016). In conflict and community. A century of turbulence working and living in groups. *Transactional Analysis Journal*. 46:2, 136–148. https://doi.org/10.1177/0362153716632494

Cornell, W. F. (2022). Schiffian reparenting theory reexamined through contemporary lenses: Comprehending the meanings of psychotic experience. *Transactional Analysis Journal*. 52:1, 40–58. https://doi.org/10.1080/03621537.2021.2011035

Dalal, F. (2016). The individual and the group. The twin tyrannies of internalism and individualism. *Transactional Analysis Journal*. 46:2, 88–100. https://doi.org/10.1177/0362153716631517

Grégoire, J. (2015). Thinking, theory, and experience in the helping professions: A phenomenological description. *Transactional Analysis Journal*. 45:1, 59–71. https://doi.org/10.1177/0362153715571096

Hargaden, H., & Sills, C. (2002). *Transactional analysis. A relational perspective*. Routledge.

Heathcote, A. (2016). Eric Berne and loss. *Transactional Analysis Journal*. 46:3, 232–243. https://doi.org/10.1177/0362153716648979

Kellet, P. (2004). The truth is out there: Constructing contamination. *The Script*. 34:1, 1–2.

Landaiche, M. N. III (2021). *Groups in transactional analysis, object relations, and family systems*. Routledge.

Landaiche, N. M. (2009). Understanding social pain dynamics in human relations. *Transactional Analysis Journal*. 39:3, 229–238. https://doi.org/10.1177/036215370903900306

Landaiche, N. M. (2012). Learning and hating in groups. *Transactional Analysis Journal*. 42:3, 186–198. https://doi.org/10.1177/036215371204200305

Landaiche, N. M. (2013). Looking for trouble in groups developing the professional's capacity. *Transactional Analysis Journal*. 43:4, 296–310. https://doi.org/10.1177/0362153713516296

Landaiche, N. M. (2014). Failure and shame in professional practice: The role of social pain, the haunting of loss. *Transactional Analysis Journal*. 44:4, 268–278. https://doi.org/10.1177/0362153714561433

Mellacqua, Z. (2020). *Transactional analysis of schizophrenia. The naked self*. Routledge.

Minikin, K. S. (2024). *Radical-relational perspectives in transactional analysis. Oppression, alienation, reclamation*. Routledge.

Petriglieri, G., & Wood, J. D. (2003). The invisible revealed: Collusion as an entry to the group unconscious. *Transactional Analysis Journal*. 33:4, 332–343. https://doi.org/10.1177/036215370303300408

Rowland, H. (2016). On vulnerability. *Transactional Analysis Journal*. 46:4, 277–287. https://doi.org/10.1177/0362153716662874

Sedgwick, J. (2021). *Contextual transactional analysis: The inseparability of self and world*. Routledge.

Steiner, C. (2006). Transactional analysis and psychoanalysis: Writing styles. *Transactional Analysis Journal*. 36:4, 330–334. https://doi.org/10.1177/0362153716662874

Stewart, I., & Joines, V. (1987). *TA today: A new introduction to transactional analysis*. Lifespace Publishing.

Stuthridge, J. (2012). Traversing the fault lines: Trauma and enactment. *Transactional Analysis Journal*. 42:4, 238–251. https://doi.org/10.1177/036215371204200402

Tudor, K. (in press). *Transactional analysis proper—And improper: Selected and new papers*. Routledge.

Winnicott, D. W. (1971). *Playing and reality*. Tavistock Publications.

Young, J. E., Klosko, J. S., & Weishaar, M. E. (2003). *Schema therapy: A practitioner's guide*. Guilford Press.

Index

adult 7–8, 18, 35–37, 39–41, 52, 60, 64, 68, 69, 70, 80–86, 97, 104, 105, 112, 115–116, 119–120, 139
Allen, B. 77, 97, 106, 128–129, 132
Allen, J. 76–79, 87, 97, 108, 127–129, 131–132
Arbor, A. 90, 109
Aron, L. 94–95, 108–109, 140, 142
aspiration 8, 12, 14, 48, 51, 55–56, 58, 60, 62, 68, 72–73, 111–114, 117–118, 120, 124, 142

Bateson, G. 3, 78, 87
behavioral change 34, 37, 40, 49
Butler, J. 96

child 7–8, 11, 34–39, 41, 56, 60, 64–65, 66–70, 73, 80, 82–83, 85–86, 92–94, 97–98, 101–104, 109, 112, 115–116, 118–119, 123, 130, 134, 139
Cixous, H. 98
Clarkson, P. 81, 87, 91–92, 109
clinical failure 60–62, 101
co-creative vii, 76, 80, 81, 83–86, 88, 123, 126
communism 13
competition x. 35–36, 41, 51, 63, 83, 123
contracting 67, 71
Cornell, W. F. iv, viii, ix, xi, xii, xiii, 15, 26, 29, 33–34, 36, 39, 42, 44, 46, 50, 52–53, 65, 74, 77, 79, 83, 87, 91, 107, 109, 112, 116–117, 124, 128–132, 134–135, 137
corrective 37–39, 106, 123
counter transference 59, 72, 93, 95, 102–107, 137
Crossman, P. 32–34, 36, 44, 53, 62, 74

cure 10, 20, 23, 25–26, 33–34, 36, 39–40, 67, 71, 73–74, 89, 103, 107, 112, 119, 125, 128
Cyprian St Cyr 22, 31–32

dancing girls 33
deferral 6
dependency 49, 58–59, 67–69, 71, 72
diagnosis 4, 21, 28, 89, 117
Dr Horsley 22, 31–32
Drye, R. 70, 74

ego boundaries 7–8, 82, 87
Ego Image 6–7, 28
Ego States iv, 3, 6–13, 15, 18, 28, 34, 37–39, 41, 60, 63, 70, 72–74, 78, 80–82, 92–93, 97–98, 101–106, 108–110, 112, 114–121, 123–124, 126, 130, 132, 134
English 33–35, 37, 39–42, 56, 74, 91, 109, 126–130, 132, 135
Eric Berne xv, 2–6, 8–9, 11, 13, 16–17, 21–24, 27–31, 34, 36, 38, 42, 49–50, 53–57, 60, 65, 74–75, 82, 88, 101, 111, 120, 124–125, 127–128, 130, 132, 134, 143
Everts, K. 30, 125, 132

fascism 13
Federn, P. 2, 6–9, 29, 38–39, 42, 92, 109
Four Horsemen 34–35
frame of reference 62–65, 85, 96, 106, 141
Freud 8, 23, 29, 36, 36, 54–55, 57–58, 94, 116, 118, 127, 134

game analysis 8, 10–11, 14–16, 21
Games People Play 16–17, 23, 28–29, 38, 42, 44, 87, 130
Gestalt 20, 25, 42, 65, 67, 69, 72, 74, 80, 88, 113, 118–119, 132

Gilligan, C. 76, 87
Goulding, M. 38, 42, 58, 65, 66, 74, 81, 82, 87, 97, 113
Goulding, R. 38, 42, 58, 65, 66, 74, 81, 82, 87, 97, 113
group psychotherapy 1–2, 8–9, 11, 15, 19–20, 26, 29, 38, 50–52

Hargaden, H. xiv, 79, 84, 86, 88, 92–93, 96–105, 109, 132, 135–136, 142
holding 104
Hot Potato Game 39–40, 42, 127–128, 132
HUAC 4

idealizing transference 103
integrative 80, 82, 85, 113, 119, 120, 121–124, 126, 138
intersubjective 81, 96
intrapsychic xi, 16, 49, 51, 67, 69, 72, 83, 86, 94, 112–115, 118, 120, 122–124
intuition 3–7, 27, 28, 36, 57, 66, 74, 77, 139
invitation 34, 79, 104–105

Jacobs, A. 48, 54, 89–90, 109
Jorgensen, E. W. 30–33, 36, 42
Jorgensen, H. I. 30–33, 36, 42

Karpman, S. 26, 35, 37, 41
Klein, M. 94, 109
Kohlberg, L. 76
Kupfer, D. 30, 42

Landaiche, N. M. xiv, 51, 54, 60, 74, 130, 132, 138, 143

Martian 24
McNeel, J. 71–74, 113
melancholia 1
Minimal Basic Science Curriculum 41
mirror transference 103
Mitchell, S. A. 94–95, 109
Montreal Childhood 13, 28, 53

negative transference 68, 103
nonconscious 57, 85, 106

objectification 90, 93

palimpsest 14, 20
parent 35–36, 41, 60, 64, 68–69, 70, 72–73, 80, 82–83, 85, 101–102, 112, 115–116, 119, 123, 134, 139

passivity 63, 96
pathology 58, 61–64, 66, 67, 78, 80–81, 85–86
Penfield, W. 8–9, 29
permission 44–45, 52–54, 64, 66, 68, 104
phenomenological enquiry
phenomenology 81, 86, 92, 102, 119, 134
Piaget 8
postmodern 80, 83, 96, 100, 110
power x, 32, 41, 49, 51–53, 57, 59, 66–68, 70–72, 74, 83, 85, 90–91, 96, 113–115, 131, 133, 139
primal image 55
protocol 14, 20, 25, 57, 93, 105, 130, 132
psyche viii, xi, 3, 5, 12, 55–56, 62, 65–66, 70, 72, 85–86, 92, 95, 101, 107–108, 112, 114, 120, 122
psychoanalysis ix–xi, 2, 4–5, 9–10, 16, 18–21, 25, 28–29, 33, 36, 38, 40, 42–43, 49–50, 54–56, 58, 64, 79, 88, 94–95, 102, 106, 109–110, 127, 129, 132, 136, 140, 142–143
psychosis (functioning) 10, 73, 75, 91, 109, 137

redecision vii, 37–38, 41, 55, 58, 65–71, 73–74, 89, 102, 109, 111, 126, 128, 132, 134
reparenting 37, 39, 42, 58, 62, 64–65, 68, 73–75, 89–91, 97, 101–102, 109–110, 134–135, 137, 142
reality-testing 10, 134
regression 12, 36, 52, 59–62, 65
regressive 60–61, 90, 102
relational vii, xii, 37, 79, 83, 85–86, 88–89, 91–95, 97, 99–102, 104–109, 112–115, 117, 119–122, 126, 135, 137, 139–143
repressive 2, 18
resonance xi, 5, 85, 95
rivalry 33, 35–36, 41, 63
Rouzie, M. 90, 109

San Francisco Psychoanalytic Institute 6
San Francisco Social Psychiatry Seminars x, xv, 12, 15, 30–33, 35–36, 43, 64
Satir, V. 35, 78, 84, 88
Schiff 38–39, 58–65, 75, 101, 109
schizophrenia 38–39, 58–60, 62–65, 75, 137, 143
self-disclosure 104, 105, 108
Sills, C. xiv, 79, 84, 86, 88, 92–93, 96–109, 132, 136, 142

socio-cultural determinations 96
staff-patient staff conference 11, 43, 53, 74
Stark, M. 37
Steiner, C. 4, 26, 29, 34, 36–37, 42, 44–45, 50, 54, 80, 83, 125
Stern, Daniel 79–80, 85, 88, 94–95, 97–98, 110
Stern, Donnel 5, 29, 36, 42
subjectivity 11, 89, 90, 92, 95, 105–106, 108, 139
Summers, G. xiv, 79–81, 83–86, 88
superiority 133, 140

tensions x, xi, 43, 48, 69, 91, 105, 112, 115, 133
The Mind in Action ix, xii, 2–3, 27, 29
Transactional Analysis Bulletin 12, 15, 16, 17, 27, 31, 34, 35, 36, 37, 38, 40, 43, 62
Transactional Analysis Journal iii, 40, 45, 76, 89, 90, 91, 112, 113, 126, 128, 129, 130

transference 10, 26, 36, 38, 57, 59, 62, 65–68, 70, 72, 90, 93–95, 97, 102–107, 109, 115–117, 122, 124
transformational transferences 105
Tudor, K. xiv, 79–86, 88, 131–132, 135, 140, 143

unformulated Experience 5, 29, 36, 42

war ix–x, 1, 13, 18, 29, 49, 54, 58, 73, 124–125, 131, 133–134
we-ness 80
Weiss, E. 6, 9, 29
What do you say after you say Hello 23, 26–29, 32, 41–42, 112, 123, 142
Winnicott, D. W. 94, 110, 135, 143
Woods, K. 91–92, 110

For Product Safety Concerns and Information please contact our EU representative GPSR@taylorandfrancis.com
Taylor & Francis Verlag GmbH, Kaufingerstraße 24, 80331 München, Germany

www.ingramcontent.com/pod-product-compliance
Ingram Content Group UK Ltd.
Pitfield, Milton Keynes, MK11 3LW, UK
UKHW031437120325
456146UK00005B/109